WHAT CRITICS ARE SAYING

Eileen Tabios has an enormous tonal range in her poetry. A breathless intensity may be her most characteristic mode. — *kultureflash: Headlines From London*

[Eileen Tabios] is writing not only as if her life depended on it but also as if there were no tomorrow. Lines between the genres and forms blur with Tabios, who uses performance and the visual arts as spark plugs for her poetry. For her, poetry is the only way to live, and she intends to suck the marrow and everything else out of it. — *The Philippine Star*

On *MENAGE A TROIS WITH THE 21ST CENTURY* (Poems)
[A] scholarly affair..., a romp in the upside-down meadows of Dada, and a fantastic romance between the present, past and future....The result is a brilliant juggle.
— **Dave Johnson,** *Asian Reporter*

On *REPRODUCTIONS OF THE EMPTY FLAGPOLE* (Poems)
Eileen Tabios' first book of poetry to be published in the United States and this volume of art-inspired prose poems should bring to an American audience what the Philippine and Southeast Asian publishing world has already known for several years: Eileen Tabios is a world class poet with serious talent. In ancient Greece, philosophers defined ekphrasis as a vivid description intended to bring the subject before the mind's eye of the listener. [She] is ultimately successful in this artistic enterprise of bringing the subject before the mind's eye of the readers and these readers will not only be enlightened but informed.
— **Nick Carbo,** *2ndAvenuePoetry*

Tabios investigates sensual and personal histories, conjuring subtle games of domination and submission against a backdrop of physical dislocation and echoing the conundrums of a colonized land....[H]er central demands — to perceive freely, to investigate color, to be a fully responsive being. "Can you pay the price for risking perception and imperceptibility?" she asks,...and then answers, "I trust in radiance. Let: Us."
— *Publishers Weekly*

Reproductions of the Empty Flagpole is important both for purposes of study in creative rhetorics or poetics, and as a most satisfying, pleasurable read.
— **Chris Murray,** *Sentence: a Journal of Prose Poetics*

Tabios has a remarkable ability to move from the abstract and the intellectual to the sensual and the tangible. She's a poet of the streets, and she's above the streets, in her own head, exploring and mapping her own consciousness where ever it takes her, even into the realm of "psychological insecurity."
— **Jonah Raskin,** *The Press Democrat*

[Tabios] pledges allegiance to her art. And the act of writing is a political one, staking out territory word by word.... Her prose-poems are fiercely intelligent, though they're lush, musical, sensuous, mysterious. Yet it is in the erotic landscape of the flesh that she seeks refuge. But that geography, too, is not without its territorial disputes... This is not the world of fixed identities.... It's a different world, whose poets are forging a cultural identity that is post-colonial, revolutionary, universal, and peaceful. Theirs won't be a unifying flag under one god, but one that's as various as the hands that raise it.
— **Leza Lowitz,** *Pacific Time, KQED 88.5 FM*

Reproductions of the Empty Flagpole is able to narrate the political implications of place and identity without giving up the desirous, inquisitive or uncertain nature of human interactions. From Greece to Nepal, New York to the Mindanao Sea, the multiple paragraphs of these poems consistently demonstrate a devotion to the life of the pronouns which people them.
— **Noah Eli Gordon,** *St. Marks Poetry Project Newsletter*

Tabios' prolific meditations on writing, living and loving in modern times solidifies her role as one of the foremost Filipino American poets of the 21st century. A great read.
— **Neela A. Banerjee's "LitPicks,"** *Asian Week*

[O]ne of my favorite books of 2002. Rachel Barenblat says in "Prose and Microfiction," the "writer of a prose poem does away with the expectations of verse,...freed to borrow from other forms and create something new and surprising." [Tabios] has created something new...her work does borrow from a dizzying number of other forms of discourse, forms shaped lovingly into gardens that tempt the reader into exploring their verdant depths....[K]eep our ears alert for wild, hungry sounds in the shadows."
— **Clayton A. Couch,** *Sidereality*

[Tabios] not only welcomes, but encourages her reader's active participation in determining her poems' meanings. ...Hence, there is no one "wrong" or "right" reading. She is generous and democratic in leaving these poems open-ended, even going so far as to omit the periods that end prose sentences: Why should the limitations of a physical page end a poem? .... Similarly, the reader must imagine, even invent the poem continuing beyond the page. The reader, then, completes the experience of the poem begun by the poet. These poems become about us, the readers, what we have put into them, how we have chosen to experience them.
—**Barbara Jane Reyes,** *Tamafhyr Mountain Poetry* **and** *The International Examiner's Pacific Reader*

I find myself appreciating these poems as compositions with no sharply-framed "subject matter;" instead, I discover each one as a diamond-faceted free configuration of a singular and ever-shifting poetic mindset. The poems are made accessible to the reader through the use of clear, sensuous, and widely (and wildly) allusive diction. I can think of Ted Hughes writing these poems, were he to use a female persona with the sensibilities and multi-cultural experience of an Eileen Tabios. *Saludos!*
—**Luis Cabalquinto,** *OurOwnVoice*

Is it so rare to be completely changed by what you have read? To instantly want to hand the book to someone and say, "Please read this!" Well, it has happened to me. Eileen R. Tabios has written a book that will leave you flipping back to the first page in hopes that you have indeed forgotten to read a page, that one or hopefully two of the pages were stuck together somehow, and you have the chance to read more... The language seethes with a beauty that one usually would inherit through translation or through personal diaries. It's a personal story she tells with each new poem that exists to provide us with beauty...
—**Chris Mansel,** *The Muse Apprentice Guild*

...in Tabios' own inexhaustible experiments in the written word all schools and philosophies and deconstructivist axioms can go hang... // Some detractors may label Tabios' work pretentious but that may be just another way of saying it is way ahead of its time and so would understandably make many a new critic uncomfortable. // Or that she has a big ego which is true of many a controversial and ground-breaking artist. But only in the sense that Mallarme and Valery and the rest of those weird, turn of the last century French poets were ground-breaking and whose very poetry was a way of life.
—**Juaniyo Arcellana,** *The Philippine Star*

Her poetry exudes unabashed sensuality, artistry, intelligence. In Tabios, I have discovered a poet whose works are a cultural activist's. For the Little Brown Brother to re-write his colonizer's language into unexpected structure and exacting, stimulating prose that comes out as poetry excellence—it is an act of activism in itself. // The seeing [in her poetry...] is less about eyesight and more about insight. ... Her prose poetry [is] ample with abstract and disjointed thoughts that evoke smells, sensations, memories. The poetry is a play on our feelings from moment to moment, abstraction to abstraction and they should not be ignored. ... Every moment of our lives, our five senses and our inner feelings are working together, we are connecting our physical world with our metaphysical. How do we learn to be attune to this? We become aware. The poems are exercises in awareness of the moment: "I soothed my hands with the wet walls of a beer bottle..."
—**Perla Daley, October 2002 "Book of the Month,"** *BagongPinay*

A substantial collection....One might say that [Mei-mei] Berssenbrugge and Tabios's most important similarity is that both produce some of the most innovative work on the scene today....[*Reproductions of the Empty Flagpole* features] moments of extraordinary apolitical beauty."
—**Qian Xi Teng,** *Columbia University Daily Spectator*

On *BEHIND THE BLUE CANVAS* (Short Stories)
"I wish more writers would find a way to work within the nexus of sexuality/writing and art. It often seems to me to be a geography of concerns that 'serious' poets and fiction writers work around—that for all of the politics around sexuality there often seems to be little concern for the contexts and concerns of sexual people themselves. Eileen Tabios has made an impressive foray onto a contested terrain with these evocations of artists and their passionate entanglements."
—**Tom Beckett,** *Forum Asia Magazine*

On *MY ROMANCE* (Poems and Art Essays)
In *My Romance*, which juxtaposes poetry and visual art writings, Eileen Tabios carefully addresses political ramifications of art-making/reception and aesthetic issues.... Tabios concisely elucidates the history of Spanish and U.S. colonization of the Philippines, post-Marcos corruption, and the Filipino diaspora, and this strengthens her interpretations of symbolic aspects of color. In Carlos Villa's work, gray "references how Filipinos are often faced with the impossible task of choosing between . . . the Philippines or the U.S." ... Tabios writes compellingly, as well, on artists who explore perception, spirituality, and psychology. In "Teacher," *My Romance*'s cover painting, Max Gimblett achieves a fissure-spanning "wholeness" when "the circle on

the right panel of the diptych extends into the left panel so that it includes within its span the crack between the diptych's two panels" and imitates natural and psychic "fractures." "The circle allows for the break even as it doesn't break," and, by "crowd[ing] the edge of the canvas," it even points "beyond the edges of the painting" to incorporate "the world within the painting" ... Indeed, *My Romance*'s collaging of poetry, historical data, symbolic analysis of art, and formal evaluation itself embodies a critique of reductiveness and a championing of pluralism with a critical edge.
—**Thomas Fink**, *MELUS Journal (Multi-Ethnic Literatures of the U.S.)*

The idea of a book about Art written as a love poem surprised me. What is new here is Eileen's approach to Art ... as a way to engage the world. [It is] an engagement with the world...that includes history, politics, identity, and spirituality. Indeed all of life....She includes other poets to show how other poets' works act as triggers to memory, sensations, and perceptions, as well as koans to ponder....as if to say that the poet's world is inclusive and expansive.
—**Leny M. Strobel**, *PINOY POETICS: A Collection of Autobiographical and Critical Essays on Filipino and Filipino-American Poetics*

My Romance is a deceptively packaged jewel of a book. By its title alone, one expects a torrid recount of a love affair between a pirate and a kidnapped royal personate. Giraffe Books' pink soft cover packaging promises lighthearted reading of lighthearted prose. Beware of flipping open these pages because as sure as a magic wand, black lightning will strike and one finds oneself carried away to unheard of places: the mysterious universe of the artists' creative processes.
—**Reme Grefalda**, *OurOwnVoice*

On *BEYOND LIFE SENTENCES* (Poems)
Dialogic imagination and Bahktin. Postcolonial. Hybrid. Diasporic. Polyvocal. Multiply-located. Postmodern. I feel that [Eileen's poems] resist labels but somehow acquiesce to the reader's whim for labels even only to indulge my addiction to narrativizing the Filipino American experience. // ... A sentence in her poem "The Empty Flagpole" — "What does it say about me when I ask for asylum in places where people wish to leave?" — reminds me of the many times I despise the sacrifices required of me as an immigrant, making me wish for the other shore of the homeland. Yet over there throngs wish to seek asylum in the U.S., and everyday hundreds of people line the streets outside the U.S. Embassy before daybreak for a minute chance of being granted a visa. // What Eileen's poetry makes me consider is this: When the sorrow of our colonial past is released and we come to know our Philippine history as the history of the world, Eileen's poetry becomes an act of rounding up the fragments of our narrative. And as she integrates these fragments (those parts of our identities forged by migration and citizenship elsewhere) into her own sense of Filipinoness, I still come away with the sense that the homeland is still the source of that inspiration.
—**Leny M. Strobel**, *README*

On *THE ANCHORED ANGEL: SELECTED WRITINGS BY JOSE GARCIA VILLA*
(Poems, Essays, Fiction)
The Anchored Angel, excellently edited by Eileen Tabios (who also edited the seminal *Black Lightning*), is a study in how a relatively small contribution to two nations' literatures could serve to transform an entire discourse, once the discourse is forced open by the contradictions of poetry and a poet's life.
—**Brian Kim Stefans**, *ARRAS: New Media Poetry and Poetics*

The Anchored Angel is a moving tribute to an artist whose work deserves much more attention. Perhaps even more important, this edition begins to fill in the gaps of knowledge about this author, the impact of his work and critical thought...and its literary significance to modernist writing in the United States, as well as the Philippines.
—**Jean Gier**, *The International Examiner's Pacific Reader*

On *BLACK LIGHTNING* (Interviews/Essays on Poetry)
Here 14 Asian American poets display the process of their poems and discuss their sources of inspiration, which include paintings, readings, personal encounters, countries of origin, and the sight of "dog piss." Tabios ... presents drafts of poems from early stages through numerous alterations, deletions (sometimes entire pages), and additions, all with explanations. This makes for slow reading but engrossing revelations and ultimately rewarding insights into the birth of a poem. Tabios's skillful interviews help the poets reveal their modus operandi. That the writers are Asian American hardly matters; this is a valuable source for poets, aspiring poets, and poetry-lovers. Recommended for creative writing collections.
—**Kitty Chen Dean**, *Library Journal*

I TAKE THEE, ENGLISH, FOR MY BELOVED

Eileen R. Tabios

Marsh Hawk Press New York 2005

First Edition

Marsh Hawk Press books are published by Poetry Mailing List, a not-for-profit corporation under Internal Revenue Code.

Typography: Sandy McIntosh
Cover Photo: Fallen Angel's Sense of Humor

Agyamanac Unay (God Will Be The One To Return The Favor) to those who supported various aspects of this project, including but not limited to: Thomas Pollock, John Yau, Barry Schwabsky, Jose Ayala, Thomas Fink, Sandy McIntosh, Leny M. Strobel, Michelle Bautista, Summi Kaipa, Jukka-Pekka Kervinen, Nick Carbo, Jean Vengua, Kenneth Gurney, Barbara Jane Reyes, Kevin Killian, Alfred A. Yuson and Ron Silliman.

The hay(na)ku poems by Joseph Garver and Kirsten Kaschock, as well as the essay by Ron Silliman, are reprinted with permission of the authors.

Acknowledgements continue on P. 501.

Library of Congress Cataloging-in-Publication Data

Tabios, Eileen.
I take thee, English, for my beloved / Eileen R. Tabios.-- 1st ed.
        p. cm.
ISBN 0-9759197-3-3
1. Tabios, Eileen—Language. 2. English language. I. Title.
PS3570.A234I17 2005
818'.54—dc22

                    2004020678

Marsh Hawk Press
P.O. Box 206
East Rockaway, New York 11518
www.marshhawkpress.org

CONTENTS

I.   ENGLISH: THE COURTSHIP

LUCIFER'S ATTEMPTS AT NARRATIVE

YES, I DO

CRUCIAL BLISS

DEFINITIONS

Bay Area Poets Help Celebrate Eileen R. Tabios' marriage to "Mr/s Poetry" at the Pusod Center Gallery, Berkeley, CA on August 10, 2002. Bridal Party (left to right): Tony Robles, Oscar Peñaranda, Barbara Jane Reyes (in Eileen's original wedding dress), Eileen R. Tabios, Dori Caminong (in Pusod Founder Malou Babilonia's original wedding dress), Michelle Bautista, and Catalina Cariaga (who, with ukelele, provided wedding music). (Photo by Mike Price)

I. ENGLISH: THE COURTSHIP

I don't take English for granted. I have to fight for every word of it.
—Aleksandar Hemon

LUCIFER'S ATTEMPTS AT NARRATIVE

Why Lucifer? In Roman astronomy, Lucifer was the name given to the morning star (the star we now know by another Roman name, Venus). The morning star appears in the heavens just before dawn, heralding the rising sun. The name derives from the Latin term lucem ferre, *bringer, or bearer, of light. In the Hebrew text the expression used to describe the Babylonian king before his death is Helal, son of Shahar, which can best be translated as "Day star, son of the Dawn."…*

The scholars authorized by … King James I to translate the Bible into current English did not use the original Hebrew texts, but used versions translated … largely by St. Jerome in the fourth century. Jerome had mistranslated the Hebraic metaphor, "Day star, son of the Dawn," as "Lucifer," and over the centuries a metamorphosis took place. Lucifer the morning star became a disobedient angel, cast out of heaven to rule eternally in hell. Theologians, writers, and poets interwove the myth with the doctrine of the Fall, and in Christian tradition Lucifer is now the same as Satan, the Devil, and — ironically — the Prince of Darkness.
—*from* A Pilgrim's Path *by John J. Robinson*

"Falling Up"

1.

Indeed, this difficulty in dying. The world sees me as a humpback. Only air relishes these velvety feathers I bear. Well, once you did. But you paused before my black brassiere. On my deathbed I shall remember you as a pair of hands hovering. The "Jewish No," you informed me, is defined as "reluctant, awkward." *But still a No*, I whispered. I could not dam my leak. What I didn't know was the landscape your eyes foretold: a sunlit sky. A silk thread descending a golden glimmer. You recognized the one pulling open the blue trapdoor, the one who discovered seams against light. The face you tasted and at whom you now smile as you remind, "Honey, angels may fall but they never die."

2.

To be an angel is to be alone in a smudged gown, fingers poking through holes burnt by epistemology. I drink from ancient goblets whose cracked rims snag my lips into a burning bleeding: I know my skin as rust. (I know my skin as ruin.) I wonder what you tasted after I bit your lip, thus coaxing out your reluctant tongue. Did you see the garish orange evaporate from the quilted bedspread trapping us? Once, you said, we should only lie on beds of grass. Undoubtedly, this must be attributed to the scent of honeysuckle and how, beyond such meadow, the only sound heard from children is laughter.

3.

I told you of the baby rattlesnake whose skin was a pale green like the ink of this poem writing out what can never be articulated. No, not a poem but your name. Yes, a poem. If you would only tell me you allow me everything in your dreams. Oh, ignore my relapses — I know you define "daylight" as the meticulous watch against releasing signs I may interpret as *Hope*. The green infant was run over by a neighbor who, it is rumored, adores massive mahogany libraries jam-packed with tomes. Preferably with cracked leather covers. Preferably with yellowed pages brittle and brown at the edges. Preferably with gold-gilded letters. *Murder can remain mere story*, this big-bellied man once whispered over a cigar smoked down to the length of my rather enchanting thumb.

4.

And sound? That, I memorize as birds forming a toupee for trees, then ascending towards clouds — i.e., away from my stalking eyes. Yes, to explore the flesh above my right bicep is to see the permanent bruise from a riflestock's intimacy. I have done this before, have I not? Begin to write you spells as I prepare to leave for New York City? A landscape you, too, shall soon pace — this time, noticing the sky and knowing it as an "image"? The image of my gaze? Why must things change? It's not as if your fingers ever grazed the hollows formed when my knees bend.

5.

Ooooomph. Whose legs are dangling beneath the boiling sky? I would like to see a girl shrieking as her swing soars towards the sun, lace-edged skirt flaring. In such a scene, I even wouldn't mind you recyling an egregious golf shirt. Can yellow ever look good on a man? A man revealing socks striped purple, then green? Oh, let me pull you back into the adjacent movie's frame. Here, I am relishing the freedom of citing your authentic name. Here, initials compromise for words need never self-subvert. Here, meaning relishes existence. Here, you are and I am.

7.

I refuse these wings until I know your expression when the windows reveal a new morning behind my disheveled hair. Ignore how, nowadays, my feet walk two inches above ground. I refuse.

8.

My halo is okay. It holds up my jeans. But I am sorry it burnt your hands when you would have broken its circle. You can claim you simply wanted to restore it where it belongs. You can claim that all you want. (I do have lovely hair.) It may even be true. But my jeans, unshackled? I suppose even you might not have resisted the urge to tug them down. This explains the stigmata scarring the centers of your palms. An integrity I resent for, before it, I may as well have hiked up this skirt to climb atop marble, long-since cracked. I may as well be Galatea returned to the bloody pedestal.

9.

Admit it, though. You like the way I twirl my skirt when, occasionally, I accept the hold of these wings. You look up. I look down. *You look down. I look up.* We share the same laughter. Still, it's all so new. You know that. I suspect you only pretend to grumble when, yet again, I must come traipsing by with a ball of twine — begging you to hold the skein as I continue to practice navigating my way upward. You are the one I choose to tether me while I can still control these wings, while they are still strengthening for battling the sun. You are the one I am most reluctant to leave on ground.

10.

I shall also miss the roses. I have just learned to weed! The bush I once measured in inches now exceeds my pre-flight height. At least promise me, please, you shall only enter dim alleyways scented by roses. And please don't ever resent thorns. Before you ever stumbled across a lady with wounded eyes, she wore a crown of thorns. It was when she tossed away that legacy, you see, that her eyes broke into perpetually-damp wounds. Consider how you have always known her as The One Punished For Losing Her Virginity. Oh, my Love, I had lost it quite *raucously.*

Pre-

A gilded cage
offers advantages

The shimmer of gold
The gold

I hold the key
diamond-studded, of course

Beyond, the sky tempts
Yes, cobalt looks scented

Even the drop
from the opened door

beckons with enchantment
defined as "suffused light"

Let me weep longer then
for requisite tears

whose glue binds feathers
immoveable against the sun

If I must fly
this time

let me freeze
In unending flight

Subverting Flamenco

"At the flamenco"
overheard then trapped

from air shifting
thighs over next

table where restlessness
lies as three cell

phones. Does ever
-open mouth categorize

world into three numbers
or is he running

a game involving horses
or razor-bladed

roosters masquerading
as *Hope*? Which

area code would
he allocate to

The One Who Attempted
The Flamenco

But Compromised
into evanescent moments

of a martial arts
form of "no defense"

against this *Love*
I am painting

onto a sunbeam
departing from this city

we have mythologized
mutually but never

share? See the glimmer
from the damp kohl

the underside of ebony hair
the satin of red skirt

all heated by the rare
gem we can—and do—share

O Sun whose fire
barely approximates

the brewing contents
of a cauldron

I must cover with a lid
ironed by your discipline

"Desperate Trust"

I was so earnest
You are used to it

You comprehend melodrama
as my "angle of repose"

So many poetry books
disgorge broken feathers

"But Poetry never hurts me!"
you heard her speak…*earnestly!*

She saw mirrors in your eyes
She saw (motes in) your eyes

THIS POEM IS ABOUT YOU
is yesterday's fading headline

You confirmed everything
with a file for her "Archives"

Early in the 7th century B.C.
red roses forged a defensive weapon

By "hampering their movements
through the mountain pass"

Skeet Shooting

When air turns solid
to form a face of reticence

zero temperature plummets
to surface acrid perfume

similar to smoke wisping
from freshly-shot rifle

I always missed
targets rising before me

But, consistently, I cracked
clay pigeons attempting surprise

by rising from behind my shoulders
Purity specified by a lack

of intention is a sudden
set of eyes rising from memory

waters quivering to life
from pass of an indifferent rake

Still, never mind bullets
I offer fair warning:

I intend to penetrate sky
Watch to miss me

Untitled
(9/12/03)

Apparently, "unsurpassable
Song" is wrong

But how to limit
horizon

Ignore the blood
leaking from marble lips

Are not wings
expansively unfurled

I would compromise
for mere sainthood

But martyrs
cannot fly

Angels fly
ascend, descend, ascend, *soar*

"Witness in order
to miss me"

5NOV02 Letter to Andy Goldsworthy

Reworked the feathers
This time around a rock

I hoped this would focus
more on the rhythm of layers

Incoming tide prevented
the benefit of additional attention

The sea gently lifted
the feathers away from stone —

      ; "it was as if wings formed"

I found this so interesting
I decided to repeat my labor

      ; "laid feathers to form a circle"

But the sea became rough
pushing rather than lifting

The tension between sea and
stone frayed the curvatures

But it was a good experiment
I learnt something

about stone, sea, feathers…

Question

I am cognizant
my flight

relies on the ladder
of Babel

I speak
ergo, you love me

Why must my speech
be one with flight —

The paradox
of writing

You away from
me away from you

while you witness
all in silence

YES, I DO

O "Eerily Quiet Drive" Towards Baghdad
(3/15/03 news mixed with the words of 12th century Arab poets)

O monochrome of gray wool
       smoke cloaking landscape
            where snouts once berried juniper
O sky smooth as pelt proclaiming your distance

O cobalt pools once diaphanous as aloe fragrance

Here amidst the waning hours
a day of "real bullets"
penetrating storms of sand
the general promised, "We will make it painful"

O rain that nurtures by rupturing sky to wash away, *wash away*

O colts roaming pastures, O hoofs fleshed like pink lilacs

Over streams tree limbs did embrace, *did embrace*

O Americans not embraced with (80 varieties of) flowers

       Soldiers changing socks regularly
       cleaning feet with "baby wipes"

O fountains bombarding air with shooting stars

Once upon a time, a law of kisses on both cheeks

O lost legislation for embedding sapphires in eyes

O legions, O lost lost legions
O legions of loss
    O lost allegiance
      O lost lost allegiance

I DO

"I do not know English"
—from "I Do Not" by Michael Palmer

"Marunong akong Mag-Ingles" (I do know English)
— any 21ˢᵗ-century Filipino poet

I do know English.

I do know English for I have something to say about this latest peace stirring between a crack that's split a sidewalk traversing a dusty border melting at noon beneath an impassive sun.

I do know English and, therefore, when hungry, can ask for more than minimum wage, pointing repeatedly at my mouth and yours.

Such a gesture can only mean what it means: I do not want to remain hungry and I am looking at your mouth.

I do know English and still will not ask permission.

I shall call you "Master" with a lack of irony; lift my cotton blouse; cup my breasts to offer them to your eyes, your lips, your tongue; keen at the moon hiding at 11 a.m. to surface left tendon on my neck. For your teeth. And so on.

No need to decipher your response—and if you wish, go ahead: spank me.

I do know English. Therefore I can explain this painting of a fractured grid as the persistent flux of our "selves" as time unfolds.

There is a way to speak of our past or hopes for the future, the hot-air balloon woven from a rainbow's fragments now floating over St. Helena; your glasses I nearly broke when, afterwards, you flung me to the floor as violence is extreme and we demand the extreme from each other; your three moans in a San Francisco hallway after I fell to my knees; your silence in New York as I knocked on your door. There is a way to articulate your silence—a limousine running over a child on the streets of Manila and Shanghai.

There is a way to joke about full-haired actors running for President and the birth of a new American portrait: "Tight as a Florida election."

I do know English and so cannot comprehend why you write me no letters even as you unfailingly read mine.

Those where I write of the existence of a parallel universe to create a haven when your silence persists in this world I was forced to inherit.

Which does not mean I cannot differentiate between a reflection and a shadow, a threnody and a hiccup, the untrimmed bougainvillea bush mimicking a fire and the lawn lit by a burning cross.

I can prove Love exists by measuring increased blood flow to the brain's anterior cingulate cortex, the middle insula, the putamen and the caudate nucleus.

Nor is "putamen" a pasta unless I confirm to you that my weak eyesight misread "puttanesca" as the crimson moon began to rise, paling as it ascends for fate often exacts a price.

I can see an almond eye peer behind the fracture on a screen and know it is not you from the wafting scent of crushed encomiums.

I can remind you of the rose petals I mailed to you after releasing them from the padded cell between my thighs.

I slipped the petals inside a cream envelope embossed in gold with the seal of a midtown Manhattan hotel whose facade resembles a seven-layered wedding cake. Which we shall share only through the happiness of others. Which does not cancel *Hope*.

I can recite all of your poems as I memorized them through concept as well as sound.

I speak of a country disappearing and the impossibility of its replacement except within the tobacco-scented clench of your embrace.

I can tell you I am weary of games, though they continue. Manila's streets are suffused with protesters clamoring for an adulterer's impeachment. Their t-shirts are white to symbolize their demand for "purity." Space contains all forms, which means it lacks geometry. My lucid tongue has tasted the dust from monuments crumbling simply because seasons change.

Because I do know English, I have been variously called Miss Slanted Vagina, The Mail Order Bride, The One With The Shoe Fetish, The Squat Brunette Who Wears A Plaid Blazer Over A Polka-Dot Blouse, The Maid.

When I hear someone declare war while observing a yacht race in San Diego, I understand how "currency" becomes "debased."

They have named it The Tension Between The Popular Vote And The Electoral College.

I do know English.

Vulcan's Aftermath
— after Christian Vincent's "Cockfight (1999)"

Skyscrapers implode as streets buckle.
The city is torching its ancient violins.
If only I comprehend why we must meet in hotel rooms with monographed towels.
With stationery embossed silver by French lilies.
Why are you addicted to lobbies edged by blue marble wombs sprouting yellow
      grass?
Where all lucre is filthy.
Where hovering waitresses look underage except for their breasts or where skirts
      split.
Which Frenchman said the most erotic span is where a breach reveals female flesh?
The midriff between sweater and jeans?
The cleavage when a blue velvet blouse is unbuttoned?
(I can still feel the callused tips of your fingers clawing *there*.)

There must be another section of this city where even you would be at ease with
      revealing your face.
Where you would touch me from a motivation that excludes fear of mortality.
Where, as a poet has whispered, flowers need never be ferocious.
Where there is no such thing as invisible ink.
Where, as a poet has whispered, carnivores forget their nature.
There must be another neighborhood where cherry blossoms never miss their
      seasons.

Yet the flames continue rising and now the sky cringes from black smoke.
An angel sacrifices his wings only to be jailed by the Mayor and two Senators.
I raise my hand to beckon a waitress, my diamond ring beaming forth rapiers that
      slice at light.
I summon a girl with red hair who reeks of lilac perfume.
The split on her skirt reveals a ziggurat tattooed on her inner left thigh.
But I am most struck by her eyes—they lack color, and I am felled by this evidence of
      a life force dissipating.

If only the city has not spent a century squandering its water supply.
If only women were still expert at wearing their hair up.
If only blue velvet never slithered off my shoulders.
If only your hands were not chilled by the acts of former lovers.
If only my mother believed Rapunzel *wants* to be isolated in a turret.
If only Vulcan retained humility after he discovered fire.
If only, if only, men in dark suits paid pale boys to go to school instead of boxing
      with each other bare-fisted.

RAW MATERIAL

A door to open when you know she waits on his threshold
"I want to please you more than anyone ever has"
The hall for its walls to steady her as you fall into me
"You look good in a blindfold," he whispers before each bite
Each chair a planet to explore below our shifting thighs
"Not *that* tonight, so you can think about wanting it"
A window to block with a shade and protect a world
        more innocent than what you do to her body
You bare his teeth to announce: "I'd like to videotape you—
        when I'm an old man I want to watch and remember"
The bed to ignore for the depths of the floor
"Next time, some steel around your wrists"
A painting on the wall for one more witness

"Yes, I suppose I startled you"

Later he would say with a smile lurking within his eyes:

MY IMPOSSIBILITY OF LANGUOR

(i)
The impossibility of languor —

"where are you today?" —

Driftwood reveals complexion of moonshine —

Peach sundering around malignant pit —

Looking into the eyes of an ecstatic girl and seeing Antarctica throw emerald spears
that raise new continents in the Pacific —

Satori in the men's bathroom —

This very second, *where are you?* —

Reacting to the world with postal dead letters —

Four light bulbs stuffed with hair ("Hairitage," sculpture by Michael Arceaga) —

Sinigang soup from fish bones and tamarind —

The equivalent of an elegy —

Knowing life contains no "continuity girls" —

Here are lies, all well-intentioned —

(ii)
I am the poet yearning to meet the songs
I should have learned
Before writing the first word

Until then, my language relies on surface

The fate I choose is not to make
Linguistic surface synonymous with the non-transformative
And what is not Beauty
And what is never compassionate

Another mistake I hope to avoid
Is to believe my life is a cinema —

       Although I like to open her saxophone case
       To see its interior of cobalt velvet
       Of course, my finger also stretches
       Towards the shimmering surface

I am too old to live in my mind

The mirages I see are always heavier than space
But there is a reason
Why my flesh aches
For a stranger's stray touch

Rapunzel's Deaf Eyes

I live in a turret now
No stairs, no hair

*

Reading yourself
into a stranger's poem

for a "hidden track"
lying

beneath lemonade days
envied by all

except their owner
From looking elsewhere

bottles die
in the cellar

meat withers
in the freezer

children and spouses
lose innocence

Only the moon
remains to write

me of something
the rumors profess

is called "light"

Diary Leak

Bones for branches cracking beneath your feet Anger at furtive eyes that lost us
while air darkened and darkened More than one unsafe swerve into car horns blar-
ing Three meetings defined chronologically as

#1: kiss on both cheeks
#2: kiss on right cheek
#3: no kiss

LET ME FACE THE NARRATIVE THEN No match ever flared between us over
an even number of gold candles floating atop liqueur of melted jasmine pooled in
a crystal bowl spotlit by a moon's benediction *no match no match no match no match
no match no match no match no match no match no match no match no match no match no
match no match no match machete no match no match no match no match no match no match
no match no match no match no match no match no match no match no match no match no
match no match* My eyes presented twin dilations of the *aurora australis* but for an
absinthe beauty become irrelevant before a sigh you could not pretend into being
about, say, the economy rather than my increasingly thinning bones and furtive eyes
*thinning thinning thinning thinning thinning thinning thinning thinning thinning thin-
ning thinning thinning thinning thinning thinning thinning thinning thinning thinning
thinning thinning thinning thinning thinning thinning thinning thinning eyes thinning
thinning thinning thinning thinning thinning thinning thinning thinning thinning thinning
thinning thinning thinning thinning thinning thinning thinning thinning* Your body
shall never block my loyal sky *block block block block block block block block block block
block block block block block block plea block block block block block block block block block
block block block block block block block block block block* That I always wish to sight said
loyalty and said sky does not compensate for the impossibility of your body pressing
against mine behind a sand dune while children laugh from a reel outside our movie
discerned gratefully to bring joy within our frame as waves throw white lace bonnets
across the surface of a sea we would know only as a scent of salt familiar via musk on
our skin had we... *had we*

Letter to a Poet Discovering Second Wind
(or, *After Learning the Opposite of Algebra is Transcendence*)

(1)
You are drawing me
back to this "shivering" world

not of our own making

Between lines so thin
imagery actually mirrors *etched* identity

you shade in flesh, non-translucent

I had surpassed algebra's constraints
of finity. I was dry among waves

I was soaring. As a song I never wrote

proclaimed: *Baby, I was transcendent*
Darling, I was on my way

Then you picked up an old pencil
sharpened its point (then sharpened it again)

ennobling you now also to draw blood

As for this world not of our own
making, it comes with meadows hospitable enough

to host our furrowed eyes (those beds of grass!)

And the sky remains constant still
(like X, despite the adventures of X)

reliably all-embracing

even when white pages tear
and begin to bleed

So listen to an ancient whisper

stir to flow
within the duet of our veins

This is the now. This is the now

(2)
Of course the rose on the windowsill
shall open petals "like a beak"

to "scold." It is empowered

not by its admirably histrionic perfume
but for relaying the messages of gods

Persevere: keep listening to the whisper first articulated

by a silk-swaddled infant
who matured to choose against all wisdom

poetry developed by footprints on the sadhu's path

We are not "ballerinas who need not read"
We are not even critics despite our Ph.D.s

Nor are we journalists turning the present into past
This is the now. This is the now

This is the now and it is our *Preface*

(3)
As for gods angered by mortal ambition
now breaking granite lids lowered

over eyes confidently somnolent for years

to reveal pupils roiling with thunder
over stone lips similarly cracking

to hiss a baleful glare: *How dare you!*

raise the impoverished flannel of uneven lime stripes
warming your pale, thinned wrists

Wipe your face clean off their spit

No other world exists
but this one replete with the bombast of wind

the hand behind a brush dripping gray

But listen—allow—the whisper
of ancestors helpless against *Song*

and the sunlit colors of its notes

(which, when melted, conform into sapphires,
rubies, emeralds, cats' eyes....)

An overlong Preface does not
obviate a Chapter One

and the 10,000 chapters that shall follow

to become a body for a life's journey, muscles for
the **TITLE**, in capitals (bold and boldfaced)

of your freed tongue's choosing

(4)
Breathe. *This is the now*
You have drawn a hole

through the page—rupture, as it should be

(5)
Recall the image of every blank page
awaiting a poem

how the white field consistently lacks a map

complete with a smudged tattoo claiming
to *know* North from South, East from West

and the false grids pretending to measure distance

Inhale/Exhale. *This is the now*
Release your hand to erase the pedestals

of unchosen gods (white beards hiding teeth of black spears)

who would block your pencil's sharpened point
from penetrating the page—*Rapture*, as it should be

Fading *Profile II*

To wander the world beneath the riot
of stars: sweep dust

from a comet's tail
"singing" in egregious French

Not a single child remains
after obscure wars, however

Convulsing around a compulsion
I water the silent lock to your steel door

J'ai dénoué la chambre ou jedors
J'ai dénoué la chambre ou je rêve

I split figs in the middle of
this poem to cause a transition

blue monks swallowing pink raisins, pink
raisins swallowing old monks (giraffes!)

a postscript's intrusion
as subtle as a Swiss banker

Your toes leak mother-of-pearls
I dredged them up

from a tropical sea where corals defeat the dark

Season of Durian

"Durian defies categories"
—*Jose Ayala, 2001*

"Question: What do you mean by `idiomatic'?
"J.D.: A property that one cannot appropriate; it signs
you without belonging to you; ....about the invention of
a language or of a song... the musical signature of your
most unreadable history... the `old new language,' the
most archaic and the most novel, therefore unheard-of,
unreadable at present."
—*Jacques Derrida, Points... Interviews 1974-1994.*

I.
Somewhere, a crop
teases a wet opening
to soften bones

Nipples nail a man
into a silence
so loud the stars,
for once, are audible

To be human is to know
the body as "Hell" —
"Sweetness on the verge
of rot"

Inevitably (and sweetly)
limbs must panic
until you speak again with
the sampaguita's vocabulary
ignoring insomniac neighbors
and former lovers trying
to escape from shadows

Erase that line
between wanting and doing

When I say your name
inaugurate
the endless season of durian
with our inability to stop
burying our teeth into spicy crevices—
"nothing poetic about it"

All this, and I have yet to blossom

Would I go so far as to eat your body
(like Juana the Mad)
dicing your penis and testicles
while quaffing sweet jerez
as mating butterflies swarm
about our roaring heads?

Once, a man clenched a thorn
to steal a rose —
the price for smelling again
the ocean's spoor on her nape
as her skirt falls on a "bedroom floor
in the afternoon"

"Bite me again"

"Again"

And "as we undo more and more"
"will it have happened/ at all"
in that room whose windows
remain blocked by shades
to protect the world?

Fit in dominatus servitus
In mastery there is bondage
In servitude dominatus
In bondage there is mastery

I don't recall who among us
strapped on the harness

I do recall *Mojacar La Vieja* radiating
as a mountain glows
"when the moon is just right"

No fine frost shall desolate this darkness
where oral sex is never simulated
lest one suffers from writer's block
(for the poem must be authentic)

I feel nipples begin to thrum
listening to cicadas begin their gossip
(such as J. Lacaba's orgasm: is it truly,
at best, "middle class"?)

Another fodder for rumor-mongerers:
I volunteer to walk (barefoot)
a path strewn with glass slivers
for the remnants of your footsteps

I still sense the warm gaze
of your third eye

I have memorized the map
of moles
unfolding against your inner right thigh

II.
"The sun was setting" yet again
when you finally released me

Somewhere, a small dog was barking
at women disrobing by a river

Now I am singing paeans to new lives
quivering beneath dew
even if sweetness must mean
pain begins once more
for the mango tree waters its own shadow

Above all, a nude descends a staircase
to leave the painting
and earn its flesh
as "mercy comes handing you back to me"

You understand: despite my reputation
I am simply no good at one night stands
that turn body parts into a blurred chorus

I don't wish to lose the love
legends from my childhood
as when the lamp illuminated
a frenzy wetting sheets
while a hungry lizard peered
through a cloud of dusk
Or "the way / each digit of light" drops
in "an act
more utter than a deathbed confession"
(with "more kicks / than social relevance")
before concluding gloriously
like an opera through swollen lips

Forgetting unfolds
with stars falling like tin
fragments
floating in the fountains of the Alhambra

Another page turns in the book of whispers
unsuspecting

of a cathedral hidden
in the same space that might accept your seed

Tenderness, too, bucks loose
as if mercy is tangible—something we can grasp,
not like sunlight swamping a room
or a breast or cock floating across a mirror
(and their preceding and subsequent shadows)

I am trying to remember a poem
written on damp blue paper
and how, afterwards, raindrops
became blades
in that deep country I visited without masks

III.
So many things remain unsaid
despite the voluble speeches of tumbled hair

IV.
"The ant ascends the house with honey"

Sainthood requires the precedent of wickedness

It can be easy imitating a "master's manner" —
imagine a bird whose beak can pierce
bark to set a wilderness ablaze

Si tatyaw kung pumupog
When the rooster plunders
Mga inahi'y sumasabog
The hens simply scatter

There is a scar
otherwise known as "renewal"

While the taste of tears
is "chemical"
not like beads of crystal cascading
into the mound where wars are buried
whose durian scent means "all is well"

Like this long poem so unlike a virginal climax

Have I mentioned yet
the "flock of winged elephants"
moving in my belly at your touch?

Yes, the erotic can be "idiomatic" —
what howls
a dream language
roaring outside the frame

What howls
What roars

What howls

Tercets From The Book of Revelation
— *after Rupert Thomson's "The Book of Revelation"*

(i)
How does the air
come to pulse
like a muscle

As if your scent
lingers
before your arrival

How does the night
come to press
and smother

As if fresh wounds
must accompany
revelations

Church bells ring
over a dark street
to fracture glass

Or was it a childhood
memory evoking
how light becomes distant

A fine, silvery mist
descends
on a wall, a city

You reach me
by penetrating past
a train's smoke and whistle

Damp hair clings
to the nape
of your neck

How can the cause
for an absence
lose relevance

How many stories
do we deny
to obviate recitation

How do we pretend
no boats mutter
along the salted, wet dock

How did I give up
your child
for an imagined affair

A pine forest
breathes for me
behind an empty house

He looked happy
before meeting
a burglar's intimacy

You can reach me
by noticing how trees
shiver by the edge of a road

How a sun
flattens the water
of a grey canal

How does release
from what you love
become "unequivocal freedom"

Sunglasses hang
against her breastbone
from a silver chain

No limits surround
the purple sheen
to Montenegro lilies

Afterwards
why do you never
hold me

How do I find
the necessary vein
I must mine

To determine
the difference between
coincidence and grace

(ii)
How does one see
significance
in brackets studding a wall

Or be claimed
through a stranger's
tattoo

"I want to see you
again to know
I was not dreaming"

A church, a girl, a cloud,
a fragmented tune — of what
are they coordinates

Children cluster
within a tree's branches
like birds, fruit, pollen

A shirt cuff
so white
it forms an independent image

It has never been
my desire for men
to take second place

I always wake
before the alarm clock
begins to irradiate

A man weeps tonight
with the father
of a schizophrenic son

How does one offend
by innocently asking
"Are you happy?"

In Zanzibar
fruit bats
fragment a room's dimness

Upon meeting, you
knew to suggest
"Alchemy needs your silence"

Wildflowers override
the trenches
of a battlefield

There are days when
the world's kindness
forgives pastis imbibed at zinc bars

A man blows a saxophone
until the moon
turns to butter

To approximate immortality
through the art
of doing nothing

Burying stories
I cannot reveal
within those I can

Her hair offers
the scent of firecrackers
reaching for the Milky Way

"Put it in
me now,"
she whispers

When he wants
to protect me
he holds my wrist

The air pulses
like a muscle
attentive and fraught

Perhaps This Second Drift
—after "First Drift" by Andrew Joron

If we diminish, to be diminished—this recurring punch line so alien with its familiarity: cruelty is a flawed strategy and yet we discover our cheek against its torso—

If we cannot be more than our least lazy possibilities—the "older woman" weeps from a tongue offered to create a future memory of silk black hose rupturing over thighs of moonshine—

Beauty is reductive. Therefore, within a shadow box my palm perpetually caresses the 45-degree rise of your belly for I, the "older woman," heard how human history whispers: men with flat bellies should be trusted rarely. Which does not obviate my clinging to the piano's highest scale—

Toward a man with colorless eyes who transformed me into a virgin so he could roll cigars from tobacco leaves pressed against the tendons riveting my thighs.

"An excessive choral indwelling," as if perfumed, cushioned salons did not prevent Cellini from feeling the blissful difficulty of art—as if Claude and Cezanne did not obsess over one problem for all of their lives: the landscape's inarticulate rhythm through boulders in sienna, in sepia.

After the Jewish artist hammered three rows of nails against a white wall to evoke 17th century prisoners convicted of infanticide, the lamp and shadows conspired to weave a lace border I wanted to hem on my sleeves.

—In Athenian vase painting, the red-figure style allowed artists to describe gesture and expression for the first time; the technical advance destroyed the harmonious relation of all-black figures against light grounds. From this enforced binary, simultaneity was birthed through dimorphic vases through which the same scene was depicted in both red and black. To witness simultaneity, one must turn the vessel.

"We also (wanting elision)" would be dung on your fields, grow there the honeysuckle I would sip and lather on your lips as I tear the stitches from your coat to unearth pages you once wrote surreptitiously. (By the flicker of a flame from a quarter-inch candle stub.) All is my fodder: All is my father.

DEAR MR. SUNSHINE,

You scared the cat. Quivering now on windowsill. Occasional mewl. Tongues a paw you thought to skin. Rigid whiskers. Rainbow and pot ignored. To think she rubbed cheeks against your bony ankles. To think she raised plump belly for your scarred fingers. You scared Miss Kitty. Pissing on jacaranda. Nostrils flaring. A claw distending like penis losing foreskin. How to soften fur? Scared pussy longing to purrr. "Frenzy in the air." Nor can one confuse cat piss with the scent of jasmine wafting from etched amber glass labeled *The Garden of The Baby Worms*.

BANNED AND DETERMINED

*"In my poetry I do not try to find the words to express what I want to say.
In my poetry I try to find ways to express what the words have to say."*
— Carl Andre

A situation
that temporarily defeats
all training,
all previously articulated philosophies

Rosenquist fragments
explode in billboard sizes
even as focus narrows

A hallmark of criticism:
this "deeply felt response"

And so the day begins
with a wish
for color not to equal narrative
since the sky is shivering forth
gray

"Reticence"

Silence lengthens
scorpion's sting

nicked twice by
wordless "scare quotes"

the horizon
a mute(d) line

No fairy tale stallion
whipping a mane

into fringed
shawls

veiling
a sun's death

No sky torn
into strips

float-falling
as blue satin

ribbons
hemming a gown

never worn
dancing

in your arms
(music, for once,

not dissonant)
No wind

releasing cinnabar
or cinnamon

then rain
then sheen

of quicksilver
trapped in tubes

or "impassive gravel"
flickering amidst wet leaves

"Qui Vive?"

soot on wings

flesh as easily-marked as the white page

"immanence" a sheen on non-marble brow

thine eyes "playing things by ear"

*****

a clear bottle

within, a folded piece of paper

unfolded, graphite forms "No War, Please"

Please

*****

do you feel my palms

pressing

against the screen

redundant over impassive face

*****

an old story —

doing things that silence —

poems that fail

to make anything happen —

*****

Oh!

But.

New images released today reveal stars started shining 200 million years after the Big Bang, scientists said in announcing findings of the so-called WMAP mission which gazed on the universe when there were no stars, no galaxies, nothing except minute differences in temperature.

These temperature differences were as little as one-millionth of a degree, but that was enough to create vast hot and cold spots that signaled the beginning of the clumping that eventually became every known structure in the universe.

*****

The cross a tiny stigmata

intercepting the life line

wrinkling my palm

struggling now to open, *to open*

*****

struggling now to open

for what makes nothing happen

for silence become "Silence (2003)"

a monochromatic painting for reflections

*****

to imagine kissing is to feel her struggling

her resistance a proof of "how alive she is!"

a tight hold tightens further

"his tongue slipping between her lips"

The Spanish Story Between the Eyes
– *after Georges Bataille's* Story of the Eye

1.
A piece of the sky falling
A bluebird

Sir Edmond gave her his wrist to bite [55]

Vines leaking green pearls
July

raw-boned mare gallops across the arena,
lashing out …
dragging a huge, vile bundle of bowels
between her thighs
in the most dreadful wan colors,
a pearly white, pink and gray [56]

9 a.m. moon
pearly white, pink and gray

men instantly rushed over
to haul away Granero's body,
the right eye dangling from the head [64]

blue linen umbrella
still collapsed on patio

2.
Raw balls on Simone's plate
Bloodshot eyes

My vision descends inward
to leave mountains
stolid around my brick and limestone house
solid like your shoulder beneath your listening sight

the urinary liquefaction of the sky [65]

3.
no longer Kansas
no longer my landscape
no beloved hawk ever-circling the form of a halo

4.
I removed some candlesticks
with marble bases
from my room: I was afraid
she might kill me while I slept [95]

With the air of offering
a quivering delicacy centered on porcelain
he tells me:

over a bullfighting arena
the sky is always impure (torridly!)
as if tinged into yellow by urine

BREATHLESS

Dear Poem,

Where are you?

Love,
Eileen

DRAWN

She has tip-toed so many times
around her greatest virtue and flaw —

Once, she prevaricated by calling *it*
"I am in love with the world" —

Close but, like a poetics statement,
not quite enough to deserve a Cuban —

She is in love, most accurately,
with being in love, that pink wallow of *that* —

So, Dear One who happened to pass by
her window, looked through and witnessed —

a red velvet dress and thigh-high stocking tango
high heels flirting with dust motes and empty chairs —

"Should you take all this personally?"
What if I revealed one of her many dark secrets —

She is The One Who Slipped Off The Island
Of Long-Haired Women singing sailors to their deaths —

Of course you want to "pause" her damp flesh
between your palms, your eyes spotlights —

Will you see the quiver behind "Flame" lipstick as
your tongue plunges into Shakespearian heat —

Commitment costs, Dear One
Only the Poet can afford the price —

You could become addicted to counting the beats
of my pulse, a pale blue vein lashing —

against the inside of my skin as easily marked
as the pristine whiteness of a waiting page —

I am warning you because the world taught me
what my sisters never did: Love is bigger than falling —

so big I even shifted to the first person to say,
"Caution, my Dearest One. I am feeling Desire...." —

CAPRI

— for Thomas Pollock

And the day begins to be made

this discourse of light

so tantalizing one forgives the cloud

cheerfully straying through bends of alleyways

bougainvillea pleasingly consistent

uncracked gleam along cracked stones

this discourse of light

your shirt collar: Apollonian white

wet green the potential of olives, grapes

choir of birds unfurled against cobalt sky

these are not marks on a page

Ah Lunch! You await:

window presentation of trout on ice, seasalt lace over lemons

bottles of Gaja form Praetorian pi

waiter's napkin crisped by appropriate starch

wine, wine, you pouring a Tuscan son and sun

discourse of light *expanding veins*

O Capri: even austere Tiberius — that angry Tiberius — smiled

As Catherine Becomes "Kitty"

Brunette and allergic to black velvet, she adopted
brandy-laced tsuris from Mama who instructed
perfume must liberate memories searing
with Falstaffian grandiloquence and ruby lipstick—
e.g. foibles admired by Haile Selassie and Zasu Pitts.

From Mama's background of bridge and violin
she learned ekphrasis as a "discipline to furnish
her mind and enable grace anywhere on any occasion."
The goal? A gentleman to finance expeditions
to the Pyramids, Le Pavilion (New York), Villa d'Este,

Palm Springs (of course) and inevitable London.
She bowed her demeanor—despite stock market
acumen permeating the veins of ancestors,
despite "Switzerland until the braces come off,"
she is familiar with "life on the fringe."

she has worn dirndl and peered through lorgnettes
in "quick flop" movie scenes. She designed
her wedding outfit from props of a regional play: a straw
hat over a red-and-white print dress. She steeled
her backbone with "that terrible English strength

that makes you wonder why they lost India."

LUDIC + [...]
– for Jean Vengua

ridiculous absence
if only it were not
a life of baroque
sears bathingsuit
mermaid, just
that i am no
eyes under water
because of this
nonexistent guitar
plucking the strings
practice practice
less and pretend
of this absence
cheeks. because
pale remains
orchid and use
tisane drained
absence i have
(not yours)
yes my rib
shard needle
with thread
sew a dress
because of this
ridiculous absence

Ex-Faith

"a part time animal"

denim sky creasing folds for laundry

weight of a glance bereft of meaning

onset of carpal tunnel syndrome

umpteenth trial balloon an umpteenth burst

how now to alter twilight

the royal "we" yet another rug merchant

"Faith" delimited

O, longing for sapphires and legato!

drying lips engaged to open only with charity

as for starlight? once, unflappable (once)

now, how to lean on a reflection

mirror bearing insufficient breadth of chest

shall tonight's Monte D'Antico suffice?

The Piano Keys

Recall nuns
those pure white sleeves

a "tropical always"
squeezed mango piss

Hems of lace, but
never been girl

Ebony eyes
stunned sunlight, *stunned light*

Length-challenged fingers
stealing "First in Piano"

Black notes in veins
refuge from Catholici...

Needles in my eyes
impossible to deafen

                    *

Not possible to defend
against wings soot-blackened

but still rising, *rising*
unfamiliar with shame

or pure white sleeves
that seamless *white*

Atonal music
those eggs cracking

Ivory keys
a yellowing age

[R-FACTORS]
— for Jukka-Pekka Kervinen

"regret is an appalling waste of energy"
a retrospective that creates refugees
in hiding from a bribed ranger
's sunglasses seeking bandanaed reflections

Sunrays coating gray rocks
offer a sheen, pretty
but false as a repentance
also in hiding
for what is rational is not what serves the day:
right = negative X (wrong)

First-and-a-Half Principles
(or Rock Climbing's Ars Poetica)
— after "First Principles" by Lee Ballentine

tell only one
the most electric? the frayed arc
bring the close moment
spiral in
exhaust patterns
flawed mask
love uncertainty's fissures
a compass without directions
step up the count
betray taste
surge and conspire
sweetness
articulate blue-veined pulse
swallow, carnal
always cuddle afterwards
deconstipate throat
"I would by love's miracle"
accept dung
and all inheritances
will stand
will die open-eyed
living truthfully all lies
always uncoiling
Mars "pissing between breasts"
dandruff snowing the raised eyebrow
staring through ghosts
redundancy of scars
fold of marble
frozen sideway glance
dust revealing handprint
after slam of car trunk
sun weeping into cleavage
soon the scab shall fall
din of your silence
next method
shift in profile
the magnet of rust
bear news of our infidelities
strung with lyrics
nog egg
"ert" gas
against the breathless
holding
the illusion of rest
water to the well

slung rubber
digital impulse
eye gritted
questionable torque
it would halt at its lean
child of secretive men
swag gesture
laying scarlet on gaps
for optimism
lunge linger
no greed
lucid and
echo's shadow
Irkuts resonating
pastel doors, gray skies
as if "as if"
cobalt Arctic granite
which one of me
circle triangle square
gourd gored
accidental loser
conventional jailer
leaking good intentions
and between raindrops
doppelganger's wink
as if a tattoo immortalizes
your radiant tongue
penetrating
whilst I
smear granite
to no avail
beyond eyes swallowing the sky
fall in the laboratory
to climb 1800 feet high
(degree of difficulty: 5-14)
this Babel towards God

BRIX

The weeds speak —
        that the revelation surfaces without effecting surprise
        is a measure of progress —

        Cannot sense the boundaries, if any,
        defining the word "wonder"

The weeds speak
bending before the breeze
to rustle stiff leaves against each other

Bend closer to listen —
theirs is an incomprehensible language
translated to mean:
        it would be foolish to second-guess the sun

        soon, the harvest begins

MY APRIL

Had it lasted longer, would it have retained the integrity that shall incentivize us to look back?

Speaking as one experienced with a waiting long leached of anticipation…

Dusting now the ivory keys with my hair rather than tapping the highest note that consistently etches…

I return each weekend to the same black crow smashing itself against the library window, bloodying its beak from having fallen in love with its eyes reflecting cobalt sky…

The cat which does not exist on my window seat that does not exist licks itself where it does not exist before padding over to rub its fur that does not exist against my ankles that, sadly, do exist…

Rain leaving diamonds where they fall — soon, she shall weave a corset of rain for the poet veiled by hair…

Oh…

Chilled ankles…

Ankles of white marble as if you never leapt off the pedestal made by sad-eyed fathers…

As if his first kiss never unfolded without someone else from your future whispering in your ear: "He is just one of the many you must lovingly release."

As if his first kiss lacked the tang of a sea breeze from a childhood your poor memory keeps attempting to grasp…

The whisper leaking onto the white page: how many more approximations must one live through before reaching the peak of Lindos?

Searching for a horizon is a proven means for filling that eye with light until light spills, *light spills*…

Light spills like your finger that once traversed a descent across my cheek…

Yes, that, too….

Snow packed and rising against the beveled panes while our lips atop Alpine sweaters have never laughed by a blazing fire…

While we never watched us not blush in yet one more context unknown for "us."

Rise…

Stretch…

Walk to the window from which I shall not fling myself…

Blood on ledge obviates cliché from "unrequited love" —

Except you used the L-word. Except you were generous with the L-word…

How do certain things become ineffectual?

Some blueberries are most delicious when overripe, the purple staining the crevices of the oak table…

The color of pathos forever contained in crevices…

Java awaits.

Now, six million know this: here she can rehearse "Farewell" because he does not read me…

The ivory keys cracked and yellow — except the highest note still white like frozen light….

A virgin from music.

Untitled (Bookstore), 2000
— for John Yau

Where Mathematics Come From
The Stranger In The Mirror
The Twelve Wild Swans
In The Heart Of The Sea

Power, Money, Fame, Sex — A User's Guide
Beer And Circus
A Vast Conspiracy
Blood Of The Liberals

And Tiger Told The Shark — A
    Collection Of The Greatest True
    Golf Stories Of All Time
POTUS Speaks

The Case For Marriage
The Path Of Practice
Field Guide To The American Teenager
The Zen Of Listening

Immutable Laws Of Internet Branding
Darkness In El Dorado
A Brief History of Tomorrow
Brunelleschi's Rome

When Genius Failed
Spirit Matters
The Half-Jewish Book: A Celebration
Decoding Darkness

A Triangle of Secrets

I. ACCEPTANCE

There is conflict, conflictedness
but the drowning
is willed —

the willingness
of eyes stubbornly open
before onslaught of thorns

You want to know
"flowers"?
O, here is specificity of rose

II. "O, THERE WILL BE"

Yes, there will be
"despair"
Shivering

will never stop
But when a certain bird
leaves the pages of a legend

you will see amethyst
wings crack
for non-virtual flight

III. "SWALLOW HARD"

I am conflicted —
why would I wish
for you my inability

to swim?
Yes, the corals are lovely
and pink and alive and lovely

veins floating amidst the purple deep
But to "swallow hard" (my Love)
engenders aftermaths of gutting

ALICANTE

The smell of bread
rising for lunchtime rush

floods open windows
in hot waves

Ole, Lucentum
city of light

Swerving lane to lane
we power towards the sea

Her thin brown arms
twist the steering wheel

curving towards the harbor
blurring all colors

Ole, Lucentum
city of light

Gold bracelets draw
out the tan from her skin

I move my face closer
"Wait," she laughs, "First, lunch"

Ole, Lucentum
city of light

This is not my narrative
It does not matter

A book on flamenco
stamps roses on my cheeks

Ole, Lucentum
city of light

Algerians cluster on the quay
amidst suitcases stuffed

with carpets and breakfast cereals
waiting for the boat to Oran

CHAPTER NINE

I'd love to know fog's changed characteristics for wreathing itself about your lime-green scarf. Not these wet wisps of grey clinging to night air, then brushing me in order to dissolve. I suspect you would dissipate fog and my need for it. You still remember how to dance on beds without robbing feathers of their bounce. The end of winter is already in the air. "I wonder where I will be in the spring. And in the summer, dragging the suitcase swollen with bras and garters, stockings and panties down the loathsome road."

7:49 A.M., ST. HELENA

I know those in the valley look up to see grey sky. From the mountain, I witness the other side of the fog seen by those below. Above the fog, the sky is sunlit beryl. A clump of treetops spear through the mist to form an island in the distance. Loneliness is knowing you are the only one seeing blue shimmer at you. I shall bind my wings, descend today. Already, I feel my car lights blinking red to cut through grey haze. The color wheel is wrong. Red, mixed with grey, births blue.

ARS PICTURA

No one witnessed
the process

that collapsed a web
into a fraying thread

of white gossamer
once spun generously

by spiders seeking—
as we all do—

a source of nourishment.
The four-inch silk twine—

the sole aftermath
from a creature's ambition and need—

sticks on both ends to a window
baring the night's vast

darkness.
When a moth

appears, flitting wings
of white diaphanous gauze,

I am astonished
out of myself

by the sudden painting
set against a field

defined by the window pane—
my toes curl

from the same incandescence
I last saw in Albert Durer's

"Study of an Old Man's Head (1521)"
surrendered through brush

in ink and opaque white.
But as you once taught me,

*Once the image is perfect
it is no longer there.*

The same vision enraptured
by delight also sees

how the white string is helpless
against a sudden breeze—

one end loosens its grasp
against the unmoved glass.

The same gust buffets
the moth

now forced to fly away
to leave an image

suddenly flawed
by an imbalance

in composition.
Sometimes, it is *so* difficult

to learn the nuances
of black-and-white—

that the dangling fiber
of white must drop,

must drop,
to enable the merger of

bleached frame and dark glass
into an abstraction

depicting harmony.
Durer etched parallel curves

on an old man's brow
to effect a pattern flowing

seamlessly
toward a beard's

curled tresses.
I imagine the process

of a web unraveling
shares much in common

with what an artist must do—
must be brave enough to do—

to draw a horizon
which separates earth from sky.

If an image is compelling
it will not be forgotten,

you also bequeathed.
I know not to avert my eyes

as the picture shifts
and the white line

loosens its hold
to fall as it must,

as it must.
The spider's web

before it sundered
and the dance

between a moth
and a silken strand

are for the audience
to invest significance,

not the picture
to narrate.

For my memory
to become encaustic

over your smile
I will let you go

as I must,
as I must.

LIGHT SLIVER
– after "The Dog Eater" by Luis Cabalquinto

Along the edge
of a road

whose name
you have never known

glacier
lilies bloom

as yellow as
the piss on New York snow

Luis captured
in a poem

for evoking the moon
hovering on a childhood

street. Where dusk
dissolved

before a window
lit by a lantern beaming.

Where nothing existed
but an orange light

coaxing echoes
from the sparkle of fireflies

mating among the fronds
of ancient coconut trees.

A shutter in the mind
opens unexpectedly

and *that* suffices—
this knowing

something fertile
exists and grows

even where you think
you are lost

such as on this curving road

you did not mean to take
but find yourself
facing,

forward and backward
synonymous

with their lack of
guarantees.

PERSPECTIVES BEFORE EARTH FALLS

Suddenly, brown
conquered the landscape

still verdant
in my memory

except for hyacinths
blooming

crimson, silver and violet
in my memory.

There had been no premonition
for this heat

scalding the air,
making my nose twitch—

turkey vultures
hover and circle

not "in anticipation"
(as tourists say in passing).

The mud-winged birds
acknowledge

what humans fear:
merely anticipating death

already marks the end
of a certain existence.

Feel a vulture's spine
crack as it eagerly swoops

to drop behind
the ever-shifting horizon

for a felled creature
whose last gasp

split air
with a succinct plea:

"WATER."
How many have bled

from my blindness
to a power

we all share—
all of us

can
provide succor.

We are all capable
of becoming hummingbirds.

"Paradise"
can be

a version of truth,
not spawned

by a flaw
of memory.

I am seeing
a valley's delicacies

evaporate from a sun's
lack of mercy,

a sun without the pity
of an uneasy horizon

sparing my sight
from the aftermath

of a vulture's appetite.
When hyacinths bloom

they begin to die
as their fragile stems cannot

hold their ripe weight.
All this is not

what I meant to say.
What I mean to say is

have I truthfully
truthfully loved you?

Manila Rains

The rains arrived,
as they always do,

as calamities inevitably rise
where the poor live.

Consequently,
"the light pouring through Manila,"

my friend "M" says,
"has become dirty."

It was my first time
with these particular thoughts:

There is no cleansing
in the rain's aftermath?

Only more grime
to cling against light?

I marveled at nature's failure—
How can this be?

In Manila, the rains
wash away the tin

and cardboard shacks
leaning against

concrete walls topped
by jagged bits of glass

protecting lush lawns
trimmed by maids in mansions

whose owners import pure-
bred Siamese cats.

The felines are fed
white meat from boiled chickens

whose bones
many from the other side

of cement fences
would kill to lick

then boil again
for the pretense of soup.

Far from Manila,
I can write of these things

while my young friend "M"
writes poems on Copernicus and Dickinson.

We are not so different:
we are moved, we are troubled…

we understand how — dammit! —
one takes the weakness

of the sun
as a personal affront

by wasting the energy
to curse a mountain

for diminishing, or not.
How can this be?

If I write a poem
about you, Manila,

will your politicians respond
with more civility

than a man who never learned
post-coital manners?

Manila, I am asking,
for open eyes. I am pleading

like a woman in your bed,
Your songs need not always break

like green soda bottles
emptied then resurrected as

boundaries
of thorns frozen

atop unyielding fences. Manila,
your poets are writing to escape.

What You Don't Know About Me

— after "A Sketch For A Modern Love Poem"
by Tadeusz Rozewich, trans. by Czeslaw Milosz

He found me through the Internet—
so many things surface
in cyberspace we forget
to consider whether certain
matters are best left denied.

My former lover assumed
his wife would be equally
delighted to meet me.
Lunch was declared.
A trumpet could have blared.

I arrived with unwashed
hair and unmade face
except for (deliberately) blotchy
lipstick in a garish shade of red.

When I saw pity
smoothen the lines
from the wife's pimpled brow
I hoped for a high return
on my investment
of compassion

as I, too, am shadowed
by a brow-crunching
crisis I cannot attribute
to a "mid-life" scrutiny.

After a salad of crisp
Romaine leaves embellished
by polenta croutons, garlic,
and bits of smoked chicken
which I allowed to drop
(twice) on my denim lap
he shook my hand.
She hugged me. She
hugged me *exuberantly*.

I returned to the computer.
I logged on hoping
you are the one today
who has sent an e-mail.

You might recall

I have expressed the wish
to lick your eyelashes
and, wisely, you confirmed
"You are offering me
your mouth, your mouth."

A COAGULATION OF PIXELS

I never had this conversation with you I never told you of dampness of sheets ripping of a pillow falling onto the floor of right hand circling wrists while left urged thighs farther apart of tendons straining of veins pulsing to a primordial beat I never told you of two bodies wanting nothing less than osmosis and agonizing over the compromise

I never had this conversation with you You never felt me bite your lower lip then quickly back away *(oh, fear!)* only to have your mouth follow my fearful tongue slipping back into an interior you mapped until its scent became yours You never cupped my face between your palms while you sheathed frustration to demand "Where do you want these kisses to lead"

I never had this conversation with you I never told you something I'd only articulated to shadows at night I never told you something I foretold in poems I wrote as a child I never told you I was the one who ruptured the fragile sieve of my memory so that I will forget what I never told you "I am so alone"

I never had this conversation with you You never heard my latest dream where we entered an apartment that seemed to be mine A wide loft We could feel its warmth The room blossomed into blinding light so that we witnessed no perimeter We saw this limitless space from in front of a door that shut behind you In the dream I never revealed to you we remained within a narrow hallway though there was a huge expanse a few feet away In that hallway I began to whisper an untranslatable language of confusion I started to shake my head But you in an equally untranslatable language refused to give confusion the last word Gently but firmly you pushed me back against the wall so that I remained bound within your embrace So that I couldn't leave which is what I initially felt I should do In this dream whose narrative you never heard from me we came to leave that hallway to enter a room you never promised me in another dream and where after the sun left to attend to other aborted conversations bruises would come to surface to our mutual delight Even the pain of painting lavender against flesh would be better than all the many things that we never shared

I never had this conversation with you I never told you that your poems made me pause linger by your side (stray finger occasionally rising to trace your earlobes) then stay (once I even sat on your lap) I never told you that I was helpless against making one exception after another to rules I so meticulously structured so that I wouldn't fall through the grid You don't hear me now pleading with you to see me now as I drop as I plummet for you

I never had this conversation with you I never told you that someday I will pause at a city street corner Looking at admiring a greengrocer's display of fresh flowers Winter day but not too cold Coat unbuttoned A hand that will reach for red roses from a thought a hope that caressing waxy petals might release their perfume might un-freeze their fragrance Hear a sound Look up to see you I never told you that I predicted you will not be smiling Your brow in fact will be deeply furrowed For there is so much already that never was between us

I never had this conversation with you I never said hello I never said goodbye This was but a poem you wrote which I memorized to return to you I never had this conversation with you You never heard me You are not clenching your hands now as you don't hear me as you don't wish desperately for your palms to replace an erstwhile breeze for trapping my hair You are not licking your lips now as you remember how in a conversation that never occurred you half-growled half-purred before concluding "You taste delicious You rampant you"

I never spoke You never did not hear I never You never did not I never had this conversation with you where you repeated never repeated "Avidly rampant you"

Adjectives From The Last Time They Met

How do bellboys learn
to accept the most impoverished suitcase
as if it cossets a woman's auriferous secret

A mahogany table gleams
with the glimmer of unshed tears
but some postlude always dissipates

the vespertine effect of opulence:
in this case, deodorizing perfume—
cloying despite wide corridors of Persian carpets

She sits for a moment
in her wet, hors de combat raincoat,
eyes closed, wishing

she had talent for deep breathing,
for integral yoga. Beyond the Grand Guignol window
twin skyscrapers frame a gray lake

In a different year, she had witnessed a wall
melt behind Max Gimblett's "Hibiscus Coast (2001)"
She is haunted by this Roman a clef

painting of four golden circles
whose intersections transform
a flower into an archetype—a heart's caparison

How to convince desk clerks
confusion is a matter of philippic physics:
"too little time for too much to think"

A gilded mirror takes in
with much complacency (a lack of taphaphobia)
the All-ness of the damask-covered, King-sized bed

From the street, 32 floors below
a husband and wife enact a postmodern hastilude
despite their shared feeling of chthonic deja vu

How to make impresario earrings
of pink, dangling lucite
erase chagrin from her shoulders

when next she approaches
an adamantine podium embossed
with an insurance company's logo

Dusk shall offer hors d'ouevres
of a "conventional nature" (their colors scumbled on brass trays)
she anticipates without acrimony

A woman with emerald eyes
shall display feral teeth
between collagen-injected lips in sternutation

A man with a huge belly
billowing a shirt so white it blinds
shall monopolize the guacamole amidst argy-bargy

She shall try to butter a cracker
with eldritch, blue-veined cheese
But the sesame-dotted wafer shall break

disintegrating between her fingers
like a lost score with a furtive history
whose notes she is anguishing to recall, then obviate

She shall hover over a bowl
of fruit with nictitating skins, only to
balk at sensing grapes browning

along their edges. As she shudders
from hearing cream curdle
within its xanthic, porcelain pitcher

she shall see a former lover
for the first time in two decades—
his hands shall be pale and cyanic

like winter, soft like
his cartographer's tones as he addressed
her during the first year

of a sweet, awkward courtship
when her belly was still telegenic
and nipples demure

"Middle age," he shall say
"is lovely on you."
She shall lower already circumspect eyelids

from a panic on the brink
of becoming more than mild
She shall hear invisible bees caught in a trammel

Later, they shall share salmon
with black grill marks

made affable by cucumber salad

He shall query hesitantly, sensitively,
about children she has never birthed
Her breath shall sear her chest

"Did you ever keep our letters?"
he shall ask while scrambling for a nugatory subject
In response, she shall feel utterly *spilled*

A loud diner at the next table
shall catalogue a rebus of atrocities
witnessed by the sky over Rwanda

Once, for no obvious reason, she shall
yen for gold-rimmed china
and thick crystal she has never accepted

wrapped in gilded paper, bound by silver ribbons,
during an affair involving a taffeta gown, veil
and rented majordomo. Certain objects

are diminished when not received as gifts
They shall utter things (perhaps bipartisan;
perhaps none even shall be banal)

Still, one of them shall proclaim ex cathedra
"Farewell" through an abrupt concession:
Time does not help

How next shall an ineffable conversation unfold
when dessert must yet be served
then a speech heard from an honored guest

Another couple in the room
shall persist in a derring do quarrel, both knowing
silence is too liminal to beget victory

Before the night shall end everyone's gravamens
with centerfold lilies barely
holding on to lavender complexions,

a woman shall hiss in capitulation
at a man she has just met,
"Don't fuck with me"

and feel good for the first time
that year. As if she survived
the unsolved murder of her only child

After an honored guest's speech
that they shall hear as
the pellucid sound of mating fireflies

they once shared together
in a time involving air scented
with frangipani, now relegated to their dreams

they shall discover themselves acquiescent
in the woman's hotel room
The bed shall be encased in cashmere

One shall become Magdalene
who shall wash feet
before drying it with hair

They shall remember
another day with a fulgent sky
when her slip was damp with the sea

and he described the zoomorphic hour
"as salt, as salt"
while she curled her palms into fists

However it shall end
its pachydermic legacy shall be the sense
of a miracle that occurred

but so swiftly and tenderly
compassion shall always be a required
precedent to its auriferous memory

FUG

Didn't turn out the way I thought. You in lorgnettes now. "Fugacious" roots itself in the notion of fleeing. Low-waisted silk johdpurs. Fingers twitch from stumbling on kinship between "refuge" and "subterfuge." Couture ala David Beckham. From a botanist's persective, our conclusion is as plant parts that wither before typical dead-line. And what's this about you preferring cities speared by palm trees—what's this with such gauzed up relation to evanescence?

SHIFT

Somewhere, an artist spills crimson dye on a river to photograph the planet as if it's menstruating

While tribal women fling a bloodstained sheet over a balcony to prove the bride was a virgin

While a field of camellias unfurl against the side of a mountain whose descent penetrates a salty sea

*****

While a 1987 Nissan 300Z turbo screeches to a halt before a lady's legs molded by carmine trousers

While a Brazilian dances naked beneath a cape of scarlet feathers tied with gold tassels

While the diver breathlessly avoids touching the seaweed threading through fuchsia coral

*****

While their fingers touch as they reach for the same muffin laden with cranberries

While she dips a cherry in chocolate sauce before feeding it to a college sophomore because, once, Allan Manalo told her, "all sophomores are erotic"

While a young poet's verses keep slicing her flesh with oddly-juxtaposed paper cuts

*****

Another element outside the frame is the puddle of carmine silk that skimmed my breasts as it fell before your palms proceeded into the frame to cover them with a deceptive modesty in a painting entitled "Minimalism"

In The Empty Throne Room
– after Day of the Bees *by Thomas Sanchez*

The bee keeper cannot speak
"but he is not crippled"

He bears the nose of a "lucky boxer"
who deflected major blows
so the nose is imprinted
but not broken
by the brief, devastating lives
of swung fists

My thighs open to unleash
the honey of the sea —
salty froth before the heated sky of your gaze

Don't break me, please

The bee keeper cannot speak
but knows to bring the Queen home
Scraps of paper bear his scrawl:
Honey of Lavender, Honey of the Roses
of Abbe Senanque, Honey
of Mont Ventoux, Honey
of Wild Rosemary

We are always surrounded
by the centuries-old musk
of misspent passion from fervent pilgrims

Another man's gold loops around
my neck whose terrain you have memorized
with bared teeth
You ripped off another man's gold
to etch your brand around my wrists,
blue veins distended,   *throbbing*

"People cry at weddings
because they are jealous"

Christ wept when he washed the feet
of Mary Magdalene
for he knew the only parts of her body
he could touch, he could hold,
were Mary's two feet
already like fishes swimming away,
borne in the river rushing from him
towards a fate of more salt —

"Always, there is the heaven before the hell"

My Love, be a bee keeper
and I shall be your most fertile Queen
At the end of the rain-slick streets of Paris
awaits a honeycomb exuding
a dusty scent of pollen, the sweet
smell of lavender, the pungent
crush of wild thyme   rising
towards the dawning sky over Cathedral Sainte-Chapelle

THE HERMIT'S BIRTH
— after "Owl's Song" by Ted Hughes

Song
is staring back

In a bride's gown
you are frozen
smiling at a mirror
smiling back

Mirror silent
on what's smudging
your heel
shadows
leering
if they could be revealed
peeking back

Song
stares back

Velvet
silk, lace, et al
tied up in bows
unanimously trumpet
"Gifts!"
raucousness disguised
as up-tempo
when the truth is Song
looking over its perfumed shoulder
hoarse from relief
the past exists
forgets how looking back

notices a rip in the fabric
opening a wound
around the peephole
into a virgin's skin

then recovers into present
into future
what was seen as history
so that a finger pushes
the button for "Delete"
to create the only image
possible now to be seen
when Song ever looks back

ink
black

notes perpetual
-ly breaking over
what will become
immortalized
as a painting
on cracked canvas
of a fragmented grid

THE LIVING CANVAS
– for Marc Gaba

-1-

Sometimes the sunshine lies unbroken against sky so blue a girl would choose it as
the color for a bridesmaid's gown. Sometimes the sunshine lies. And what does it
signify that the sky convinces as a color? For instance: blue? Does light discriminate
like a girl choosing among the rainbow's complexion for a dress to commemorate a
formality? Sometimes a color is chosen for a certain consolation. Or, perhaps com-
pensation. I think of other motivations, e.g. to escape, to heal.

Am I listening to no one talking?

-2-

Sometimes the vultures are civil enough to hide and one forgets what one wishes
to recede from memory—as when I never listened to your silence so that the halo I
placed over you would retain the perfection of a circle. Am I choosing to believe a
vulture can change character—even become "civil"—to mollify myself over the role
you insist I play if I am to retain your attention? This attempt fails and, once more, I
am bereft: is not character an underlying grid, rather than the flux that may or may
not surface around its slats—through its formations of the cross?

What is the sound of active mouths hidden
among shadows ringing a campfire?

Have I become like a painting-sculpture by Alison de la Cruz? After painting a can-
vas a lapis lazuli blue, Alison broke its frames so that the painting will never mag-
netize a wall. It can only huddle on the floor—is this what I have become because I
recognize you find utter Beauty in Subjection? Then Abjection? In this manner do I
speculate—a snake gnawing its tail—for I have discerned through a difficult pilgrim-
age that what is glorious must contain elements of astonishment. Much like a curve
ending in a broken tip whose dangle draws a void. I say: the perfect circle exists
only in mathematical realms—perhaps this is my fashion of agreeing that Beauty
becomes visible through flaws which compel the viewer to imagine their reparations.
I suspect I may yet reconcile with the poses in which I allowed you to mold my flesh.
After all, I barely bled.

Is someone listening to me?

-3-

I have experienced purity like this seamless atmosphere of light only once before—it
was the night you mustered pity and whispered, "Goodbye"—a night unbroken by
stars to camouflage vultures swallowing. I imagine the concept of purity—and am
unable to prevent myself from questioning whether imagination is a synonym for
enlightenment. Sometimes? What I speculate with an utmost fortitude—thereby
transforming reverie into physical experience?—is that pity as a revelation scars the
observer in a manner that moves a sun to hide behind a cloud, a mountain, a sky-

scraper, a raised palm. Eyes close, but to a faltering dimness where each layer shed reveals another method for fattening vultures.

Once more, am I attempting redemption
through the failed strategy of conversation?

-4-
Thus, have I learned to treasure the limbs of leafless trees rising to mar the sky's canvas of seamless blue light — oh, that statement is a lie! A momentary rebellion before I lapse back to acknowledging: you and I have chosen a different way: winter is rarely the season for transcendence and, once more, the "sky" is mere theory until the assignment of the color blue casts flesh upon its illusion. Have we not heard the "sky" referred to as "ceiling," "brow," "plate" and "canvas"? Still — oh still! — when the weak muster their attempts, do not eyes dampen, whether in admiration or grief?

Do you share my obsession with redemption?

-5-
In the etchings of dark lines fracturing space I see the battles drawn by hope, by desire — though sometimes illusions, these are contingencies which should never be chastened: does not winter bring rains to succor growth? With a sigh, I note that characterizing a line as "dark" may be another delusion. Perhaps fractures are the true manifestations of pretty colors (like blue) — do not fractures compel the compassionate to offer their hands? What redeems without lucidity becoming a goat with a slit throat on an altar to a nonexistent god? Perhaps compassion? Perhaps compassion, the necessary predicate to all art, possesses the power to delete the words "chasten" and "chastened" from our shared vocabularies.

Why?

-6-
Do not stars obviate the dark? With utmost but fragile fortitude, I assert: stars attain radiance from their capacity for forgiveness. I posit (?): compassion illuminates. Reader, have you entered my field? Are you walking among my tall, restless grass; disturbing tiny creatures with the scuff of your boots; inhaling sugarcane; shivering slightly from the onset of night air? Are you overcome by solstice? Have you sacrificed the circle's perfection to become an ellipsis on a picture plane because the bulge of a curve evokes "something about to happen"? Then place your ear meticulously against my whisper: *Bow. Bend. Pick something up from the ground.*

For

"The Birth of Venus" by Boticelli
– for Christopher and James Dickey

I peeked through the doorway
to ensure no guard
sniffed the chilly air
of the cavernous hall
where my footsteps stalled.

I whispered to my boy,
"Go ahead. Touch it."
He placed his palm
against the paint. I covered
my son's hand with mine

To feel the painting exists,
To know my son lives,
To feel me there for the all of it.

HYPERTEXT, *DAW*

Ngani karon gihandom ko si Grasya
Even now I remember Grace
as a sepia stain collapsing my ancestors' photos
to reflect faces honestly
without uncertainty of environment, thus, context

Sampagita nga mosalingsing sa kinatas-an
And the jasmine climbs the trellis
while Marta raises her rayon skirt
to stamp out the flamenco before she dies

Winter liwan rugya   *Ginpapa ko ang luy-a*
It's winter again   I crushed the ginger
for the soup of carrots and orange rinds
I shall spoon for you between smooches
after your limp up Madison Avenue

Daytoy iti lubong nga mangar-aracop
This is the earth that holds us
where you grabbed for "rough sex" the intersection
I share with Courbet's "…Origin of the World" —
I nodded for I wanted more sugar torched
after you taught me "moonshine" is not liquid but light

Mangegco ti tak-tarak-tak ti sangaribo a cabalyo
I hear the thunder of a hundred hooves
as pictures fade to compromise the sounds of text—
there is no <ars poetica> but <arse poetica>

Never mind   *pabay-e lang*
with good health   *mayad lawas*
you can eventually go home to Antique

PRELUDE

You shall not complain over chains —
they shall be golden

You shall not mind broken eggs —
servuga scent heightened

You shall not object to the tattoo —
the ziggurat is my brand

You shall not refuse the burn of chocolate —
ice cubes wait on my palms

You shall not mind masked sculptures —
they are imitations but they imitate me

*We share the same sky unleashing blue
for dawn's color between my thighs*

You shall presume to bite my tongue
to prevent my words, "I am afraid"

You shall not flinch before the whip —
Welcome, welcome, *welcome*

KARMA'S SHARDS

A pattern continues
Though the bluff transcends
The end of the game

All because
Once, we shared
A chair become planet

A pattern extends
Though the game collapsed
Losses marked by emptied poker stakes

All because
Once, you branded my
Flesh with your mind

A pattern insists
Though the table is empty
Gambling eyes long since evaporated

All because
Once, you taught
Lessons you earned with false currency

A pattern laughs
Though walls have fallen
Dust colonizing all, especially laughter

All because
Once, erroneous definitions
Were applied to "Compassion"

A pattern unfolds
Though there is no game
There was never any game

MUDRA

— after "Tantric Suite" by Rod Paras-Perez

To kiss the moon
Suspended
Between the soles of her feet

She must become
The essence
Of flexibility

By sitting cross-legged
On the floor
And lowering her back

To form a circle
By dropping her brow
Between her knees

Not like a snake
Swallowing
Its tail

Like compassion
Flexing its muscles
To accept everything, everything, *everything*

CRUCIAL BLISS

I wrestled with my bed sheets   What I was looking for was this,
Innocent and tremulous like a vineyard
Deep and unscarred like the sky's other face,
A drop of soul amidst the clay
—from "THE GENESIS" by Odysseus Elytis

Pleasantly Plump

Suddenly I have no debts.

Suddenly the facade loses vagrancy. Shake that boot free of irritating grit.

No, dear, the sky is not an onion. Watching blue layers peel will not make you cry. You may even clap your hands, round your eyes and whisper, "I just realized, my Love: you have always been here. For me!"

With joy, I forego the vocabulary found in margins.

Tonight the pantry is pregnant with soups based on heavy cream and portobellos thicker than buffalo steaks.

I am as pliant as Sri Lankan grass. Kiss me.

Procedure is the Eden where we need not cover our bodies with leaves.

A "torn skirt" is a torn skirt, not a camellia ruptured by the wind before its blooming can be immortalized in, say, a tourist's photograph…that becomes a painting within a gilded frame.

Jessamine wafts over paddock.

Impending denouement of yellow diamonds smuggled between buxom breasts.

Soon, I shall stop holding press conferences.

Depart, all ye with cruel eyes!

Aum Mani Padme Hum, Aum Mani Padme Hum, Aum Mani Padme Hum…

The thought of helping you makes me smile—shall we spill vermouth on the sky?

Let us lose the language of scars—let us shake those lanterns to bestow myrrh and frankincense.

My Decision

I suppose I, too, am sympathetic to that "tender hour."

It could be dusk wafting down Park Avenue, thus, beginning the blinking of a red neon sign shaped as "666."

In the beginning was the Word?

Ah, but come now, no one tapped my shoulder with a sword to assign me the Tagalog "*ma-drama*" — the "dramatic privilege" — of whining over a midget's je ne sais quoi.

Yesterday, I saw your profile in a cafe gnawing a Madeleine for consolation.

Aikido would have proffered a better way.

As for that virgin moon, it is pretty, yes, in pink.

Which is not to say, one can avoid gutting one's innards if one is to hear gospel directly from God.

No, Sweetheart, I have stopped choosing words for their shock value: God, not "God."

There, a bee fleeing from a thin warden pauses to pollinate the trillium with its *ma-drama* leaves.

Like the neighbor hiding behind a curtain as he wrote a haiku about a thief pausing to tango with his shadow when the moon appeared, she sees things she wishes to articulate.

"Ideal Violet"

Asato Ma Sat Gamayo. Lead me from the unreal to the Real, chants the yogi.

How easy it can be to capitalize a letter when one is not concerned with poetry.

I, for one, rely on ancient manners—thank you, Dear, for my dropped handkerchief.

Once, a friend of my son flung his leather jacket over a puddle intersecting my path in crossing Bluemner Street.

Yes: all college sophomores are sophomoric, thus, erotic.

You, however, flung down the steel grate to divide us.

I, too, thought I'd lurk forever in the red phone booth looking up at your window.

Yellow light, yellow light—how many stars have you mugged?

How many stars sought to emulate dark angels by grabbing the tail of a comet dropping into a blind alley?

Don't let me change the subject again.

As I have insisted numerous times, the wind bouncing from the lake-trampoline need not be sub-zero.

I am grateful to anyone who holds open the door.

That I cannot capitalize "real" is not synonymous with polite applause.

Someone has been smart enough to identify "Ideal Violet" as a perennial hybrid with bright green leaves that bear clusters of fringed, 5-petalled blooms whose petals redden during the lemonade days of summer.

Rinzai Poem

Dew lingers on corsage left on bench in empty ferry.

Worst sightings are possible.

Day looks to be wet and gray — evoking window panes perpetually weeping in London.

But we all possess a memory of crucial bliss, though the majority may write otherwise.

Similarly, each war someday will end (ignore the rants of lazy philosophers).

In a dark theater, spilt popcorn recall nuggets of gold.

Or island vacations in Greece.

Sunlit.

Smile by considering this: the face of laughter is different each time.

Like a poem which cannot be rehearsed.

"What would you like to talk about today?"

Fly Luminously, Please

C'mon.

Don't lapse into "one tiptoe at a time."

That hunchback might be an angel hiding wings beneath trench coat.

Sometimes the world should be veiled.

How else would you realize the exquisite craft that enabled an anonymous seam-stress to stitch silver lilies on tissue-thin silk without rupturing the bolt of material that arrived through a needle's eye?

Sometimes the world *should* be veiled.

One can camouflage without conceding any diminishment of light from someone's halo.

Have I told you of the Arab boy who wove a rug now hanging above the Spanish Queen's bed?

At age six, he could see his future grid-locked within a grid formed by a factory room replete with looms and the harshness of raw wool.

The boy has never chewed gum while folding silver foil into an eagle.

Ars Poetica #10,002: Namaste

I heard myself all through these years, as a century changed its name, so that I bow now before what lurks behind the sky as I realize: I have started to say things I have not said before.

Dear Antique Mirror,

Perhaps you shouldn't use the dust of your ancestors as a solder in the aftermath.

An omen can be ascribed instead to a benign bit of amber.

May I offer tea from these leaves I brought back from a tiny stall in Kathmandu?

I am searching for a charm bracelet that requires only one charm (perhaps a silver sea horse, perhaps a silver horseshoe).

Notice that no one here is turning into a salt statue.

Those oversized safety-pins fail to mask commendable years of Ashtanga (linear hollow sculpted along a thigh bared by the rip of a leather skirt).

But the practice is supposed to be spiritual, not physical.

TANNIN
— for Bino A. Realuyo

Scabs immigrate from fingers that peeled them off scars: imitating shriveled rose petals, scabs caress the bottom of emptied cabernet bottles.

After turning useless things into metaphors and still finding them useless, I lapse into a post-midnight visitation.

Abject in my transparency.

Unlatch buttons on my scarlet (& stained) silk blouse.

"Prevarication" becomes a Martian word.

Damp eyes are mine.

Until, I recall a kind neighbor who built a corral for an old, bowlegged horse.

Equine eyes as kind as yours.

Pink Lemonade

I predicted your indifference, and I say it now as if articulation provides comfort.

Call an island "Isla Mujeres" and half of the population will always be sad, and half of that sad half will always be bitter.

Still, light finds a dance floor against this field of abandoned stones.

Some pillow still shields a stray tooth because a mother's fairy tale was believed.

We say, there's no need to limit your search for comfort among the footnotes.

On Isla Mujeres, 25% of the population may be sad but no acid scrawls graffiti against the walls of their bellies.

Women may be like fireflies—they constellate and then, for a moment, they all go dark at once.

But, inevitably, one will go shopping for a pink clochard.

A pink coyote with an extra cherry.

Circlet of pink sapphires to dangle (insouciantly) from a wrist.

More than one will proclaim, "Hell, it'll take more than that for me to stop wearing red high heels!"

Helen

Part of mortality's significance is that wars end.

Yesterday, I determined to stop watering down my perfumes.

Insomnia consistently leads me to a window overlooking silvery green foliage—*tanacetum argenteum*—whose species include the tansy which Ganymede drank to achieve immortality.

Once, I could have been tempted.

But to be human is to be forgiven.

The man in my bed shifts, flings an arm across the empty sheet—gladly, I witness him avoid an encounter with desolation.

Soon, summer shall bring a snowfall of daisies across these leaves whose mottles under a brightening moonlight begin to twinkle like a saddhu's eyes.

I can feel my hand reaching to stroke the white blooms as gently as I long to touch a newborn's brow.

By then, I swear my hand shall lack trembling.

I am nearly done with homesickness for Year Zero.

This is my second-to-last pledge: insomniac thoughts understate my capacity for milk.

This is my last pledge: I will not drink until all—all of you—have quenched your thirst.

Litotes

Like the path of a poem, she turns her face away from yours but you notice her eyes peek at your lips.

I describe the rapture of facing July 4 firecrackers just inches from glass smoked by my breath, and realize Twin Towers still hold up the stars in the New York City of my memory.

Another way to describe the taste of your mouth is "song of licorice."

Once, a soldier laughed as he swiped a sponge of vinegar against the cracked tongue of a crucified God.

I have always longed for the ability to lick the sensual syllables of the Gallic.

You conclude: "Do you want to kiss me?"

I turn my face away while my eyes furtively peek at your lips.

Many alternatives exist, but what occurs is the song of licorice.

It has been repeated through the ages: to be dead to one's self is to maximize delight in the tiniest of enchantments.

Let me release breath for the purpose of describing your scent.

DEFINITIONS

RESTIVE

— after "On God (En Garde)" by Archie Rand

The farmers are monitoring the sky. Rain dilutes sweetness in the grapes. Knuckles knot into themselves, mimic the knees of hundred-year-old grapevines. The cabernet hang like purple testicles. I am always fingering a bunch. Sometimes I pinch off a globe, split its skin before my lips and suck at its membrane. The farmers measure brix mathematically. I want my body to determine truth like Cezanne painted rocks instead of images. When I see the winged shadow glide over the fruit-laden fields of September's wine country, I know better than to question how my body doubles over. How my mouth gasps. I feel blood flowing out of a creature, somewhere, felled on its path. Its last vision will be a vulture's open beak. Sweetness, let the harvest begin under the most livid sun. "Sweetness" — perhaps I mean You, dear "God." Lord, I am praying for life and living — *I am making poems.*

CONTRETEMPS

Tables with flattened moons for the rest of impolite elbows. Or babysitting elbows. Burgundy veins ripple through marble surfaces. Smoke evaporates into hazelnut scent. Your porcelain cup surrounds the interrupted spiral of lemon skin. Hotel in a city across a bridge, on the other side of an area code, past some presumed boundary. But we were seen. I knew my arms stretching from sleeveless silk still flushed from your fingerprints in an earlier scene (where bruises were hunted). I was reaching to lay a palm against the edge of your smile. Which faded before my touch as we were seen.

122

EX CATHEDRA

Clash of brakes and gears. Finger beckons from semi's window. Driver has no load. Truck looks aborted. Or exhausted like a pencil stub. Gasoline-scented sparks light up midnight with orange fireflies. A.R. says, "God must give the artist equal voice." Bearded face approaches. I wait for the torrent of words that shall begin with "Asshole!" He has yet to see my sex. When I last saw fireflies as Platonic, not metaphor, they were mating in my grandmother's garden. Enthralled, I watched while my fingers trailed the curves on *capiz* windowpanes. White jasmine overflowed from clay pots and coupled with the scent of newly-blooming mint. You could see my breasts — brown aureoles — through diaphanous nightgown. Its short skirt revealed damp thighs below a narrow hem embroidered with pink and yellow roses. A.R. says, "Fear can only be countered with an unwarranted enthusiasm." The latest statistics reveal the smog in Houston has exceeded L.A.'s. I roll down my greasy window to begin reciting my version of fireflies. I have never been so ready to tweak the nose of Anger.

UNTOWARD

She has not looked back for three years. For three years, she lived her life by skimming the thinnest surfaces of an ice-covered body of water — what she did for ecstasy billowed the sails pulling her iceboat. She could twitch the rudder so easily to return to thicker ice or solid ground. But bliss is addictive, even as she feels her bones thinning from a lack of rest. She sensed that looking behind herself would present the painful image of white shards fragmenting black water. So she continues to knife towards the horizon as if the horizon could be a destination. Perhaps a point exists ahead where the ice gives way to warm water thickened by salt — it doesn't make her less or more eager. "Our deepest sense of what is fair and generous gets tossed aside so quickly in favor of a powerfully racing heart." Untoward, she has grown accustomed to breathing through her drowning.

KIBITZER

She purses her lips and tilts her head towards a dead beetle on the dirt road. *Three little pairs of legs carefully folded on his belly./ Instead of death's choices — neatness and order.** I hadn't realized death could be chaotic. I had been focused on the chaos of living. At times, I obviated chaos by emptying myself through meditation: the floor of a quiet room, one leg folded over the other, palms open towards the sky, eyes closed. At times, I obviated chaos — particularly when the floor became the ceiling of a deceptively-dark sky — for the sky loosened its blueness onto the oceans to create a canvas for the Milky Way — whose white stars shifted in a slow spiral to depict a harmony so difficult for the living to attain. I have always felt the sight of azure water as silk lingerie sheathing my veins.

BESMIRCH
— after "Images" by Valery Larbaud

Oh — dear Andalusian beggar! With your black feet and filthy face, yet you smile as you dance on the platform. You dance with such agitation it seems the holes in your "ash-gray skirt" are widening before our eyes. The men in the train see your twig-like thighs. Which doesn't prevent the rise of obscenities when your "little yellow belly" displays a roll. I want to scream Walt Whitman through the cigar smoke misting the dining car: "…the world is not joke,/ Nor any part of it a sham." Would you be the one to mock me then, dear Andalusian beggar? After all, you might whisper to me, "Sister, I am dancing only for pennies."

ZOOMORPHIC

—after Napa Valley's September 3, 2000 earthquake)

Again, the vulture sits on the tip of a cracked pine trunk. The bird often ruins the view from my yard…:*oh, lawn slipping off a mountain*. Eighteen miles away the town of Napa sweeps up the remnants of houses and stores after last night's 5.2 earthquake. Its upheaval jolted me out of a dreamless sleep in my mountain cabin where I bow from the starvation in Sierra Leone and other "news of the world." A five-year-old boy is in critical condition after he was hit by a brick. A forty-one-year-old man slashed his toe against broken glass—"none of the fish survived." No other casualties. One could call the aftermath to be a set of "acceptable losses." I do not: for the vulture's beady eyes, before they close to hide a knowledge I do not possess, have darkened—are dark. Sterling Vineyard gleams in the backdrop—I never thought I could feel relief by seeing buildings painted so white, so innocent and pure, so white.

GRAVAMEN

Rain etching down my stick-like legs. I was a girl—rain still possessed the ability to invade. "Open market"—stalls sheeted by blue plastic. Behind one film flapping insouciantly, dolls waited for me. Blonde curls, rayon dresses in aghast patterns combining red polka-dots and green military ships, stiff lace that will make me itch—I wanted them all. This morning, I sprinkled an entire can of fish food into a birdbath doomed for decimation by next week's tractors. I wanted the goldfish replete if my offering was to be their last meal. Tom noted, "But they eat until they burst." Aghast, I looked down at the roiling water ablaze with orange manna and orange fish. "At least they'll die ecstatic," I thought. The thought remained a thought instead of offering consolation. B.G. has written, "The poet slowly dies in his or her poem[,] making sure there are fragments remaining of the empire which created the poem, the empire of the poet's soul."

CAPITULATE

After making her first drawing, the young artist realized, "At the beginning every-thing is three times life-size." To draw is to fall in love. Drawing and Love share the same aftermath: Diminishment. Thus, we turn to Art and Love again and again to fall into lives much bigger than inheritance. She begins a line in the middle of the page. By ending invisibly off the page, the line thickens the gesture resonating the paper. When I fell in love with you—despite the constancy of my failures with love—I made the decision: *I Will Love You Forever*

INGENIOUS
—*after "Extracts From the Life of A Beetle" by Frank Andre Jamme; translated by Michael Tweed*

She did not doubt. he knew she lacked. the thinnest membrane as a shroud. to protect against rain. capsizing. as if a section of the pin-pricked sky. ruptured. so that water fell. as if from a giant bucket. capsized. "I'm trying to be responsible. now. I am 50 years old." he said. She ducked. her permed head. beneath his chin. He let his chin. become an umbrella. For. other things hold the potential to cap-size through. the rip in the sky. like peacocks lacking tails to strut. like "overly red masks." like a stranger waking behind my skin. like a stranger waking behind your skin. They fuck each other. with open eyes.

126

DERRING-DO

Because he considers her a woman who has been cherished by every man she's met, he forced her on her knees, trained her to crawl, and chained a dog collar around her Prussian-veined neck. Because "subjugation would be good for you." She swallowed his orders because she wanted to test her body differently from the artist who squatted to shit paint on a canvas flattened on a pristine floor, differently from the artist who rolled out a ticker-tape of love poems from her dry vagina, differently from the artist who "screwed" canvases by breaking their frames so that they huddled askew on the concrete. Because she also knew that when she whispered "Whatever you want" past the pink gem studding his manly ear, he realized he has wanted to be a "Master" for a long, long time. She gave this experienced sophisticate "a first!" So that she is secretly tickled pink whenever he tells her with fingers twisting her nipples, "I'm only giving you want you want." She is tickled pink even as he elicits her tears.

STRINGENT

Tanned arms. Tennis. Net play. Bad knees. Stubborn net play. "Trading long lines are for wusses" — as in poetic collaborations. Keep 'em short to facilitate writing "on the nerve" (as O'Hara said). Breath hurts. Ball explodes between two racquets. Then again. Again. Strings tightened to maximize recoil. Tightly leashed like attentive nerves. Stringent to enhance *jouissance* and *jouir* (as Barthes said). And bounce. Like sunlight opened by the impeccable knives of tennis whites rejecting the darkening impetus of sweat. All must be effortless, you see. Let painless pain skim nerve endings. Play and write stringently — want that. *Want.*

BIPARTISAN

Rows of old mahogany chairs. Rows of dark pin-stripes. Rows of wrinkled brows. Not a single smile. I wonder if your mouths enclose teeth. Or, simply, maws. And your policies—every city contains doorways populated by mothers with shopping carts. Ripe pears are being sliced somewhere, Congressmen, while the crystal bowls of your offices maintain still lives of fruit thrown away at the slightest mottle. Rows of aging men who have forgotten to be bipartisan. The blackbird musters "Collusion!" before frying itself on a utility line it thought offered the respite of a stable footing.

YEN

Your nipples surprised me with their two-inch circumference. I recalled the sun over Istanbul. And stopped bemoaning my failure to feel the pea beneath a thousand mattresses. Your nipples delighted me with their two-inch circumference. I recalled the moonshine you taught me to drink after we revved up the Harley to rupture night's diplomacy. And stopped bemoaning my thighs' inability to define the word "sleek." This day lacks room for doubt as you have proven your yen for me, me, me. Otherwise, Pumpkin, how would I know the measurement of your nipples' circumference. And how three strands of black hair mischievously wave beside your left nipple. On your otherwise bald chest. Atop your belly as smooth as a dune on Fire Island before the wind whips up a storm. Before the wind blows porcelain off the shelves to distribute fragments on the floor that will cut into my skin. So that when I breach Oriental rules of civility to turn my soles towards my face I will see the Pollock masterpiece I will have painted gleefully with blood. Pumpkin, I want even to bleed for you—my body is just the beginning of my stake at the poker table. Whose game I will win to help you finance your dental bill. To help you buy a new suit. Pinstriped and custom-made to mold the air over your nipples. With a circumference as wide, exponentially, as the vision we cast upon each other. The net we cast because we desire. Because we want so much we have stopped seeing the asshole on the moon. Because we want to wet each other past the limits of "forever." Which requires old-fashioned Romanticism—and still we don't balk. Because we desire to know the aftermath of infinity. To calculate pi to exactness. To fly toward the sun with wax wings if it means mutual osmosis between us in order to know all of the world. And what exists beyond explosion and implosion. What exists in-between and outside. Because after my tongue measured the circumference of your nipples, my teeth clung. Pumpkin, you reared into the dying caused only by witnessing Beauty when my teeth bit then clung.

CLYFFORD STILL STUDIES

I made up rhymes in dark and scary places,
And like a lyre I plucked the tired laces
Of my worn-out shoes, one foot beneath my heart.
—from "Wandering" by Arthur Rimbaud
(trans. by Paul Schmidt)

On The Limits of Context

—after PH-233, Oil on canvas (1945)

You know what I mean, that feeling of the very air pressing against you, the leaves whispering snidely overhead, the bees conspiring on what should be only a random-ly-executed attack

when you are not even in the country but in the Lower East Side of New York City, say—this same point being able to be made if you are in Berlin, Chicago, London, Manila, Albuquerque—and you feel nature at its most elemental disdaining your very existence

for, once more, you have been impatient with the husband, say—or wife, partner, parent, child, the one who loves you most—for no reason other than you have just considered a certain choice

you made, say, yesterday—about dinner, breakfast, lunch, afternoon tea or perhaps something not even involving food—and are disappointed—oh so disap-pointed! —in yourself for failing, yet again

to transcend your context

—yet again—

(although I will never consider Chicago to be a cold city since it birthed Nel-son Algren whose ring Simone De Beauvoir wore to her grave)

so that perhaps you could have achieved a situation about which, someday, someone you don't know could conclude about you:

you manifested *Grace*

On The Redemption Within Light
—*after PH-336, Oil on canvas (1950)*

Surely a refrigerator should be consistent in containing at least four eggs, a pint of milk, a quarter-circle of brie, caffeinated coffee, a bottle of *agua con gas*, a modest-sized dish of "leftovers" which always tastes better the second time around

so that you can assess comfortably whether a house, say—the same point being able to be made if you live in an apartment, shack, palace, houseboat, penthouse floor of a posh hotel—is also a home

even though the best definition of home that you have ever read is "not your street address" which nevertheless makes you fling up your hands to concede some tastes are doomed to be bourgeois, especially

those things that carry the most potential for waking you up in the middle of the night, ooozzzing sweat, bedcovers flung off because you thought you heard a sound that didn't belong in the same space where you sleep,

a space, say, like that which you have labeled "home" even though you consider home to be one of those words—or concepts—that inherently are in flux—for instance a poet's eye—

—or Love—

and now you must leave the warm bed—the bed from which one departs prematurely is always warm, isn't it?—to plant your soles against the chill of the floorboards

—the floor one walks reluctantly is always cold against bare feet, isn't it?—

and as you proverbially begin to make your way down the proverbial steps you begin thinking to yourself, "It better not be the damn cat!" for if Miss Lily—again this point could be made if the cat was named Mr. Rogers, Bup-kiss, Pusa, Bordeaux or Professor William Gass—was being naughty then you would consider again whether it's time to put the old cat to sleep, having lived for 24 human years now

(by the way William Gass wrote an absolutely terrific book, *Reading Rilke*, on the difficulties of translating this histrionically German—or Germanically histrionic—poet into English)

but then you stop to think halfway down the stairs, if it's not Miss Lily then the outcome could be more dire than bringing the cat to Bide-A-Wee the next day

for night is still here, you are still standing amidst shadows afraid to continue descending and this is not a poem where you welcome the uncertainty of the outcome

and now you know why the wildest and most fierce animal with the biggest teeth ever begot by history would freeze against a spotlight

but for you there is not even the light

which matters

for light always contains some sort of *Redemption*

On The Irresponsibility of Burnt-Out
—after PH-19, Oil on canvas (1950)

So many things occur to me when I think I am emptying my mind and they are often
clingy thoughts like the last bits of spaghetti sauce I always try to scrape from the
bottom of Paul Newman's jars, a saucepan impatiently waiting nearby,
     so that I should have known better than to lapse into a situation where a
white-haired artist is chastising me, say, for differentiating between "space" and
"landscape" — this same point being able to be made if I didn't concede the horizon to
be a line on a grid — because, though I am not old, I am not young
     or young enough to be allowed gentleness as a reply to thoughts which
should be "empty" but instead roll out of my mouth as super-realistic images so that
their stupidity — so dumb they are like animals in the sense that many have tried
to concoct a synonym for "visible" by proposing "animal-like" — is obvious for the
whole world to see
     — the gods being quite mischievous at times —
     so that I end up wishing I had never left my cozy bedroom, my cozy living
room, my cozy bathroom, my cozy kitchen — you get the drift in my pretending that
I live in flannel pajamas — that morning so that I would now not be the featured pre-
sentation here in how much of an idiot one can be
     — particularly when there was not even anything significant at stake
in the subject discussion which I despairingly recognize will precede wherever I go,
tarnishing my reputation —
(by the way it always seemed to me that if the difference between a human and an
animal is that the former exercises a higher intelligence, then human — not animal —
should be a more appropriate metaphor for visibility)
which is so unfortunate
     because I truly, truly want to be good
and if I could clearly articulate
     — which means, let me say it to get out of the way, it is not a given that a
human is more intelligent than an animal —
     then I wouldn't lapse so often into an embrace consisting only of my arms
and my chest as I whisper to myself, "You meant well"
     forlornly
     so that someone more helpless — more forlorn — than I
     would not suffer from my *Burnt-Out*

On My Knees in the Aftermath
—*after PH-49, Oil on canvas (1954)*

And—though I know this to be a Modernist, thus old-fashioned to some though
not to me, beginning—I am concerned over a dozen red roses, a bouquet encased
in translucent green plastic, gifted by one of my husband's business associates for
missing last night's dinner over which I didn't exactly put myself out—such is the job
of the caterer, particularly one financed as a business expense—but, yes, his absence
was a horrible lapse in manners

     so that it didn't matter that he's the "client"—this same point being able to be
made had he been my husband's boss, mentor, backer of some sorts, teacher or even
daughter so that he would have been both child and unable to further my husband's
huge ambitions—as much as he was rude

     and now he has sent me my favorite flowers—about which my husband's
secretary will later inform me that he had quizzed my husband after he finished
apologizing to him profusely—which pleases me but also worries me for I worry

     about anything which so freely exposes the fragility of existence, such as
flowers, roses, say—but which could have been packed salmon, white chocolate
truffles—yum, another favorite!—concert tickets for the coming weekend, a gift cer-
tificate from Saks or any other department store owned by a corporation concerned
by taxes so that income and liabilities are set to occur within a certain period for
facilitating "clean accounting"—

     such that I know I will forego water and sugar

     —sometimes an aspirin instead of sugar—

     in a crystal vase—I have at least 20 different types from cut crystal as wed-
ding presents from long ago—for a lengthy ribbon—perhaps cobalt in color, or
silver—

     a histrionic violet, too, would be acceptable as a dissonant but pleasing
contrast—

     that I can tie around their stems, shorn of thorns, of course, since they arrived
with the heavy embossed card of Madison Avenue's most expensive florist
before hanging them upside down from a kitchen rod I would have emptied of its
French-made copper pot

     in order to dry

     —to freeze a moment of glory in time—

     because I envy Juliet for she had Romeo, which also explains why I couldn't
commit adultery without telling him "I love you" though he never reciprocated with
the same words but redeemed himself by kissing me rather than making that cynical
moue with his lips

     —which once bit me; I'm still stunned by it—

     whose gesture I have memorized because it was *his* gesture

     (incidentally, packed salmon, when frozen, can last indefinitely but become
like senior citizens who have outlived their children)

     —which is why I am concerned about the red roses because, once again, I
must give to another what I would like to have for myself, in this case a pitch so per-
fect it should be fossilized in amber in order to last forever

     or, if petals, dried to maintain the full head of bloom—though the man I
love is sufficiently bald to have his remaining hair feel like scars when I fondled his
scalp—

or, if a woman like me, buried in volcanic ash with you in my arms and I in
yours in the same bed that we would call ours
  to bely the impossibility of transcendence lasting forever
  exacerbated by this concession that brings me now to my knees:
  we all live in an *Aftermath*

On Something Like Forgiveness
—*after PH-858, Oil on canvas (1972), and PH-48, Oil on canvas (1957)*

Some dreams you don't want to end, like my only one from last week where I found
myself crossing the street to be missed barely by a colossal truck crashing into a
lamppost, its back bursting open to unload white roses—flung up high like the first
gush of a Roman fountain—before dispersing into slowly floating petals—
taking their time—descending as if gravity had decided to be like a benign father and
loosened its hold—

    which, being nearby and having just been scared witless only to see a paint-
ing bloom against the dirty canvas of air that could be titled "Ecstasy No. 1"—this
same point being able to be made had I just opened a door to be stunned by a
grinning crowd yelling "Surprise!" before showering me with a cake lit by candles,
balloons and boxed presents in fine layers of pastel paper—made me put down my
briefcase

    to begin dancing, twirling round and round on the street, my hair falling
from its bun and blouse lifting itself out of my tight waistband as I twirled with my
face toward the sun and palms lifted toward the sky to feel the soft

    —oh, so soft they made me recall the blue-veined flesh just beneath your
tired, tired eyes!—

    petals raining down, down, down—so marvelous I probably would not have
cared if they'd been radioactive—

    as I twirled round, round, round

    except that surprises are rarely totally benign

    (is there not always someone in a party full of envy over the recipient of
many gifts)

    so that I preferred the dizziness—perhaps I even began to pray I would faint
for the blessed relief of unconsciousness—over the end of a dance—this same point
being able to be made about the end of a kiss, a wedding, an opera, a first date, the
painting of a painting—

    for I am not unusual, perhaps, in living only in moments rather than through
the seamless progression of time

    and I have come to wonder whether I should end my desires to try so
hard—to, as my precocious nephew once counseled me, "Just go Zen, Baby!"—

    so that I also will know joy as unsolicited
which would enable me to conclude that to breathe is to exercise faith—

    something like Glenn Gould turning his back on the world so that his music
would participate in evolution, something like the fragile violet feeling a chill but still
slipping its way out between a crack in ice stubbornly sheething the ground,

    something like you and I managing to keep our secret, *secret*

    something like *Forgiveness*

On Conceiving Silent Pleas(e)
—*after PH-635, Oil on canvas (1967)*

I believe I am reminding you that no one owns space, though you can cup it within a folded palm and feel the same power that ignites a short, fat man looking at his thin, tall wife—diamonds studding the platinum manacles around her scented neck and wrists—

"surely, there is a world somewhere that is more than endurable"—this same point being able to be made with a slight twist to—though not meaning the same as—"surely, there is a world somewhere that one can endure"—for everything has an opposite including, surely, grief

and so it comes again, this familiar and familiarly-dreaded feeling that a windowpane away breathes the face of a force that will leave you standing, yes, but as a gnarled tree bowed over buds that have broken promises to bloom

—if only for a moment as brief as a virgin's nervous peek—

which might explain why, my dear, I lash out sometimes when I have gone so far as to memorize the slope of your belly, the pucker of your knees—and other things that remains best unarticulated for strangers, too, are listening—for we learn our gods in childhood and mine taught me that ghosts resent ecstasy

if ecstasy is not something one prayed for with a dry throat, flushed cheeks, damp palms, and knees pressing against worn, velvet pews

in dim and damp cathedrals with crumbling walls and replete with bowls of dirty "holy water"

and I have been sufficiently histrionic to gather these flower buds after a storm, take them home, and place them carefully in a wide flat bowl—setting them down as gingerly as if they were the babies I would like to birth someday—amidst cerulean ribbon cuttings, crimson glass stones, carmine crayola nubs and garnet bottletops—refugees from other contexts which continue to evoke the living wherever they land simply by retaining the color red,

as if—or is it, because I believe—the vibrancy of a color proposes its own value

even as graveclothes for those whose deaths are premature for it occurs to me that I might live as long as a century but if I live by merely enduring then my death, too, will be premature and if circumstances make abhorrent the notion and act of prayer, let me not be silly enough to assume this means no one is listening

when I have thought silently behind an impassive face, *There are fragile creatures swimming innocently—a bit carelessly—between jagged blades of coral,*

when you have thought silently behind an impassive face, *Parents can be minor characters,*

when I have silently thought behind a mask, *Is futility a necessary precedent to a plea?*

when you have silently thought behind a mask, *Please*

On Obviating The Mundane
— *after PH-851, Oil on canvas (1972), and PH-998, Oil on canvas (1975)*

Is it the fragility of the highly-exposed spine — do you think? — ridge rising helplessly to draw attention to itself, that makes a woman's bare back — its exposure perhaps heightened by a stray tendril of hair, the discreet velvet straps of a silk bronze gown, or a tattooed dragonfly — so poignant it dislodges a long-rusty hook deep in your suddenly dry throat

when you have never in your life donned a tuxedo but are perched now in frayed running shorts and torn t-shirt on a stool in a kitchen with cracked linoleum floors wolfing down an English muffin — this same point being able to be made if you were clad in linen eating breakfast with *faux* silver fork and knife in the lobby of Singapore's Mandarin Hotel — and gazing inward to your deliberately overheated imagination for an image that bears the potential for affecting you — a bit of suffering even

— make you feel so sentimental you even recapture the nervous thrill of gearing yourself up to ask Susie Stanford to the high school senior prom decades ago —

she wore a white orchid with a center that blushed like a sunset — once you could compare anything to a sunset without feeling embarrassed —

because you woke this morning thinking, yes, so many years had to elapse before you realized there was never a kingdom awaiting your discovery — presumably after you first discovered yourself a King, a discovery whose probability, too, may be specious — but didn't feel this conclusion warranted the shift you felt the earth make on its axis so that your footsteps now are always a half-beat behind

except you also do not know what rhythm exactly is it that your steps are failing to catch as you move slowly between early sunrays slipping through the blinds

and, already, you anticipate you can become quite tedious with your friends whose patience you have tried over too many other things — such matters are for a different story except that they, too, are painful —

so that you considered exposing your mind to an image both erotic and innocent — something that would turn your fingers into claws from desire while feeling your knees melt from the very *palpability* of this lyrical vision ceasing to be mere picture but something so tangible you can smell the jasmine wreathing her hair, count the beat of the pulse flexing a vein along her pale wrists and see the tiny black mole just above her right buttock as your eyes sweep the expanse of her naked back

(the significance of a woman's bare back might also be heightened by the mysterious placement of a tiny tattoo of an initial, say, Q, which you will discover is not part of the alphabets in her name)

which is also an attempt to soften the armor that your beleaguered flesh has become — I suggest "armor" as I am reminded of Wilhelm Reich's theory that psychological traumas imprint themselves on the body in the form of muscular tension that, if unrelieved, hardens into armor —

for only a child has the ability to stare full-frontal at the sun without shading its eyes

— not as a challenge to, attack on, or dumbness over the gods but —

because the child wishes to see the subsequent dance by dime-sized, black circles slipping in and out of air

and the child believes the dizziness that occurs with the reward of this sight-
ing is a normal manifestation of having been moved by anything that bequeaths
rapture, say, for a child the dance of oversized dust motes slipping in and out of vis-
ibility like the proverbial Cheshire cat's grin

    rather than dizziness being something to fear

    now like the tremor you feel rippling through your veins

    as you fear — without or despite intention — you have lost your innocence

    without knowing how to define either the price or reward you garnered from
this loss

    and you are wishing your body to follow your mind's ability to be moved
by — even become sentimental from — a mere image of something you have never
physically experienced: a woman trustingly offering you the sight of her bare back —
and the ridge of her very critical spine that holds her up, props up her chin, against,
say, even a lover's betrayal

    — even a mother's betrayal —

    with such surprising, but nevertheless hoped-for, ability by your poor, old
body coming to obviate your pessimism,

    so that if everything is Mundane, so also nothing is *Mundane*

On Being Not Merely
—*after PH-118, Oil on canvas (1947)*

Oh no: It's not at all like that scene where he concluded he should try to learn the "language of love" — such an atypical twist of a phrase for him — so that it didn't matter that the epiphany occurred in a gas station's bathroom — which, being smelly, was bad enough but also — where the only toilet was stopped so that he had to back up and stand on tiptoes, his ass over the sink

when you are trying to determine whether to interrupt another scene you are witnessing now, whether, say, the adult is really the child's parent or a pederast kidnapper as you watch them on the sidewalk from the false security of your car, all windows raised — this same point being able to be made if you were there with me at the Waldorf the evening a benefit was held for Kosovo's refugees and you were wondering whether to give, or save it for, say, the Cancer Society, because someone spent real money dressing up the token refugee there in a glittering evening gown — and you were offended

— though her eyes remained as widely-stunned as, you imagine, when she left the smoking ruins of a beloved city to board the plane to New York — whose mayor is Giuliani, now trying to prevent Young British Artists from entering Brooklyn for one desecrated a Virgin Mary with elephant dung and the mayor is always courting the Catholic vote —

that something else underlines your minor role on this stage that is the world — once more, once more — through the rim of your vision — another spectre, too, of the illusion of lines, walls, grids, contexts, and so on except the alternative is not exactly better — certainly more depressing
— might even lapse into nihilism —

and you scoff at everyone, but mostly yourself — as usual, mostly yourself — as you have never been able — though you have tried just for the sheer relief of it — to stop believing that "it's the little things one can do that count" even in the face of Kosovo and, now, East Timor,

this feeling of utter helplessness — no, that's not quite it — this feeling of wonder, aghast wonder, at the *utter* helplessness

that turns all your actions sluggish

such as depositing a folded bill into a Methodist offering bowl when you visit your parents and must pretend you still attend church every Sunday

(and still no cure for cancer)

because what he felt the urge to explore, you see, is the "language of love"

— let's proclaim that again: "language of love" —

that anyone wishing to write such poetry as this century becomes a dog swallowing its tail is always cause for ecstasy —

and, moreover, he is the emperor of cynicism

or has been —

the significance of this being that he knows or has known the stance on which a confident cynic has stood or stands —

and still he wishes to speak this "language of love"

— a goal he pursues in a search truly wrenching to watch —

but not heart-rending, like, say, the discomfort of an epiphany in a gas station's filthy bathroom

for this new target of his attention stemmed from his engagement with a

mere stranger
    who happens to be me
    who happens to be a whore but not *Merely*

On The Inescapability of Fragility
—*after PH-235, Oil on canvas (1944)*

If you would only consider the effects of humiliation from the existence of teeth—
once, I did and one of the many costs of that adulterous affair was replacing the
silver with white to avoid drawing attention to my spoiled childhood's practice of
bribing maids to buy me lollipops without Mama's knowledge—would you also
consider, please, the promiscuity of my tongue

    but why would you consider this matter when men and women are also
different in this respect: in love, only one group upgrades their underwear—this
same point being able to be made with the observation that men in love might shave
but not with appearances in mind—which compels me to wonder how one's first
glimpse of one's self is always fraught-ly terrible, isn't it

    —though occasionally terrible in a terrific way, as when you catch yourself
making that phone call just to hear the thrill of how he pronounces "here" on the
message he left on his answering machine—

    and it's not from being part of a race whose pronunciation of "r" is persis-
tently uncertain and incurable by, say, even a new certificate of citizenship

    —but I shouldn't be going on and on when I truly do not care about the hol-
low where a tooth should exist in the left bottom quadrant of your grin—perhaps this
is why you rarely grin—

    for I admit to dissembling to defer saying something else, as if I was still the
girl I once was, so shy and yet longing so for that balloon of pink cotton candy except
I was with an uncle I had just met—who was so tall—and I was—oh! —so shy

    —yet I have experienced worse things since I wore pinafores and that inci-
dent's only aftermath is a wince whenever someone mentions the word "circus"—

    so that I believe what I am trying to say, my dear

    —my dear "You" who I now will reveal to be a different "You" from the
adult I seemed to have been addressing earlier in this poem—

    is, my dear, awkward, adolescent son of a business acquaintance and you
and I have found ourselves facing each other in an otherwise deserted garden after
we both left the holiday party back at the mansion of someone probably despicable—
left this party sponsored by a corporation but bringing together strangers as if we
were all one happy family

    —perhaps you're like me in that I became happy with my family only after I
left them for a city so far away that postcards can approximate affection—

    (it is true, by the way, that I once fell in love with a man missing a front tooth
and I share this moment of significance because I rarely write confessional poems)

    and what I must to say to you, dear awkward teenager, as I feel tears ready
to spring at how I must now offer you a "terrible glimpse of self" is not, *Honey, you
have spinach between your teeth*

    —particularly since you have just mustered up for me the most tentative
smile, the most sweet smile, I have ever witnessed—

    what I must say is, *Honey, your fly is open*

    —please, please, please don't come to mutilate kittens, shoot up post offices,
or live in ramshackle cabins you leave only for hacking up strangers for food—
and—ah yes!—I have always been moved to weep

    —and, all of us, let us now weep together in one cathartic gesture, yes, let us
all weep together—

over the utter lack of grace through which one departs from childhood
as if—as if! —what comes next never birthed that saying: Ignorance is Bliss—
as if we are not all *Fragile*

On Being Worthy of a Smile
—after PH-3845, Oil on canvas (1946)

I don't know: I'm dissatisfied—certainly disheartened—by the notion of death as "completion"—particularly suicide which seems a bit of a snivel—tell me, can one not feel just the tiniest bit silly with the head in the oven and, presumably, it could use a good cleaning for if you were that desperate it's likely you hadn't cleaned the oven for a while—and, say, there in the corner is the butt of the turkey from Thanksgiving last year—though, yes, I have been there—*there*—where suicide didn't seem so unhealthy

which is why I left New York for it's a city so open-minded—except for its mayor—it's become its own enemy with the takeover by barbarians—where, say, courting becomes just a synonym for exploration so that transplanted Midwesterners consistently get hurt because they were there to *love*, not conduct research—this same point being able to be made if I said that in New York even the most talented poet needs to and will fuck to get ahead—although I hasten to add, my point here is actually not one of cynicism

but an acknowledgment that we should try to treat children gently

for you and I, as children, were not treated gently and look at us now dressed in 100% polyester in yellow and brown

—and those shoes—what is that? vinyl?—

and in puce? If I were the type to emit, "Good Lord!" I would emit "Good Lord!"—

—though you say one can't be choosy in a Salvation Army store, we should never sacrifice our sense of aesthetics! —

—by the way, I would have learned to emit "Good Lord!" if I'd ever been a contemporary of Anne Sexton—

oh really, I am saying nothing, nothing, nothing here—a poetry teacher once advised, "repeating is fine, thrice is histrionic," and so make of that what you will—

I'm just being a horse

forgotten by its owner

stamping my feet for I long for the air flowing over my rippling muscles as if I were soaring over the rolling green hills of Ireland just a few feet from my window

—though I am in New Mexico, actually, and it's over 100 degrees today—

but the point being I am in my stall stamping my feet

to get away

(and another thing, take my word for it: the pain of unrequited love is not worth the poem it elicits—that is, if you're a poet who's got what it takes, and I'm not referring to vocabulary)

and that the day outside is cruelly ablaze while it is refreshingly cool inside the stables is no consolation

for it is dim here

and even celebrities commit suicide

so that, in conclusion, treat children gently

—mostly so that you can look in the mirror and feel

there—*there*!—is someone worthy of a *Smile*

On Becoming Lucid When It is Too Late
—after PH-348, Oil on canvas (1946-1947)

He was being inexplicable in his inimitable manner—the subject at hand being one of *confronting the atmosphere, naked* where a cliff gave way, where the lapis lazuli sky beckoned him to approach until his toes snagged air—and he felt his *blood darken*

    which is perfectly reasonable, I suppose, as clarity might be the least consideration one has in mind when psychically repeating that near miss down toward the surf rising so high where they slammed against boulders that the slapped water formed wraiths trying to ascend from some boiling, murky inferno—this same point being able to be made had I likened the waves to mists shape-shifting its way across a Wordsworth landscape—no wonder he stands now limp before me

    and I am wondering why I feel no pity

    —perhaps I've never liked him, only tolerated him because he is the oldest friend of another man I met recently with whom I would like to develop the kind of friendship that will persuade even me to offer him money—"take it, take it: don't worry about paying it back!"—if he ever encountered bad luck

    —which, nevertheless, begs the question of why I am wishing this new acquaintance bad luck when I believe I genuinely like him—unlike his buddy from elementary school who won't stop talking about his obsession for *a seamless cerulean sky* for succeeding where a Frankenthaler painting only approximates—the taking you all in to *a color's expanse where vision loses its rim*—is this what is meant by a "Jesus complex"

    —where one wishes someone to flounder so that one can be a savior—

    every time I reach bottom I surprise myself again by how much more I can plumb through to provide new grotesque meanings for a meagerness in spirit

    so that sometimes I wonder if the real test is turning 50: would one want to father a child or build a new house

    or let the picket fence out back continue to rot

    from *the stink of butterflies*—something just loosened by this creature in front of me trying his best to mimic a damp rag and I pause for a moment to wonder how butterflies shit and the nature of the stench associated with this implication—

    (in addition, he sniffles and before he actually does it my mind's eye already has seen this would-be sky traveler turn his nose to the left shoulder of his grubby t-shirt and rub it there—rub it there—disgusting, really and yet I am the one watching closely as if he is a rare blue rose rising from bird excrement)

    and until I can figure something out I am doomed to keep Mr. Runny Nose company, that is,

    figure out exactly what pact with the Devil I made

    for I know only one thing as I stand before you and that is I dine each evening on an antique mahogany table festooned with heavy silver, silk damask, cut crystal goblets, old Bordeaux, mounds of orchids, dripping candles, hills of grey caviar, and cuts from animals who died to give me the smallest—but choice!—parts of their huge bodies

    —surrounded by portraits of strangers from a different century whose presence court me from ornate gold frames despite my merciless dining habits—

    and I must discover the price I am supposed to pay

    for, most assuredly, there is something to be paid

    and something more to be known about that price

other than it makes my *blood darken*

so

that I suddenly pull this limp, miserable creature to me, suddenly pull him against my breast and rock him in a tight embrace—my left cheek pressed unprotestingly against his oily hair

—rock him, rock him—

so that from the depths of foreboding

I will have mustered comfort for someone

though I know, I know, I know

the storms have come and gone and it is all so very Late

—and yet, still this hint surfacing unexpectedly now, perhaps as a reward for soothing this destitute organism—barely human, now—without minding his drool on my expensive silk suit—this Faustian pact seems to have something to do with *vision losing its rim*

because, once, I valued lucidity—

which only makes me rear as I realize the lateness of the hour and that whatever will come

is quite inevitable and it is very *Late*

On The Dangers of the Metaphor
—*after PH-151, Oil on canvas (1950)*

"My face is a nut!" she proclaimed and I thought she meant herself crazy when, actually, she was referring to the sun over the Gobi—*ah, it's a tan!*, I thought about the grey-brown cast from hairline to jaws which was a discovery for me since we just met and, thus, I did not know her when her mask was like "mother-of-pearl"

    as her mother put it, before adding "like me" then pointing to her own face—which, however, I considered memorable mostly for its wrinkles—particularly along the fine skin beneath the eyes—so that I felt pity concurrent with uncertainty over whether "pity" was appropriate for—as Rilke has asked, do we really know anyone? —this same point being able to be made had I recalled the time you drank from a bottle of lemon juice instead of pouring just a little bit over the Greek appetizers of spiced ground beef being served by the mother of your college roommate who had invited you to their house one weekend—and I am spewing cocktail party chatter here for life is not always benign

    and I feel the need not to brood

    today—this day that greeted me with weak tea which was perfectly-pitched to match my mood—this desire not to be nervous—to walk through the day with my eyes wide open instead of peering

    furtively

    —and I, too, am finally done with surrealism—

    and ill-fitting shoes

    —I want my next complaint to be over a lousy bonnet—

    I don't wear hats but Easter is always impending

    —which is all a long, long way of saying I deliberately failed to ask this evening's featured guest—at Mr. and Mrs. Stanley Williams' penthouse apartment on Fifth Avenue directly across the Metropolitan Museum—how she felt surrounded by children with distended bellies and adults with bleeding gums

    —you see, I wasn't censoring myself by the presence of "polite company" so much as my latest epiphany: solace is good but a preemptive strike is more efficient

    to forestall this feeling of not belonging even among those who love generously

    —to love generously is a gift one gives and retains, prevents one from lingering along windowsills with a nearly empty glass of warm wine

    —oh, so much unease in this world,

    so often without a cause that one can identify, thus, resolve—or at least the honest effort to resolve—

    —do all colors become brittle—

    (even the waiters were happy but they're all emerging artists, according to the caterer who noted, too—and this is obviously significant—Mr. and Mrs. Stanley Williams encouraged them to feed themselves as well as the guests)

    and I no longer wish to be a character I am fictionalizing

    —my face is not a nut—

    I am only here

    trying my best not to be bereft—and I mean to succeed

    until I might as well be who just flew in from Africa

    darkened by the sun

    but not *Metaphorically*

On The False Redemption of Scale
—*after PH-424, Oil on canvas (1950)*

Then, this morning, that moment of discombobulation—a spider was crawling along the edge of the bathtub as I began to turn on the shower and my first inclination was to wash Daddy Long Legs down the drain but I paused because—you know, that Buddhist thing—but still I am not used to insects and do not know the difference between a tick that causes Lime disease versus a spider which I once read is benign—so I didn't *proactively* wash the spider down the drain but didn't turn off the water either so that, inevitably, the tide—become soapy, which couldn't have helped it—got to it and its demise became a black-and-white movie that I furtively watched from eyes peering between streams of diluted shampoo

    —a movie, I suppose, because I just wanted to distance myself from the whole thing—my inability to make a simple decision like, say, stop the water and gently pluck the spider—for whom I had begun inexplicably to feel love!—out of the tub and leave it on the windowsill—but, no, I just let the water run, congratulating myself that I didn't actually cup a palm, fill it with water and then *proactively* wash the spider down the drain—this same point being able to be made by shamefacedly admitting that, once, I alerted a financially-struggling shopkeeper to the thief *after*, rather than *before*, he ran out of the store with a package of screwdrivers—and I am so tired

    but it seems to me exhaustion is a cheap price to pay vis a vis the punishment I deserve—say, me strung up in chains, back naked to be flayed by the steel-tipped whip of a strong man whose face is encased in black leather—for being such a fence straddler

    —the spider is still clinging to the bathtub, its corpse now drying with my spent towel—

    which will also answer your question over my refusal to leave a marriage whose time is done because, still, my husband is a good man—

    there is no one better

    —and sex? Ah, sex—we all know the limitations of using sex as a paradigm for decisions—witness the history of aftermaths from men thinking with their, well, you know—

    surely, there is a new model just lurking around the corner

    —my marriage might not even be over, simply hibernating—

    (and, let me add—mea culpa, mea culpa—I like my showers scaldingly hot)

    for how one might spend a day without a wince

    —is it because my nature tends toward the fraught or is life really all this difficult—

    John A. observes so many flowerpots are empty, but, as usual the "nation's greatest bard" won't offer a conclusion—just that observation—unlike me who will not observe but ask plaintively, why are so many flowerpots empty

    —why won't I dislodge your memory when your type has spawned an entire branch of popular literature called "Why Men Cannot Help It"—

    so that maybe S___ is no better than me for compromising the scale of her paintings by sizing them for the tiny spaces of apartments in New York City where her gallery is located

    —I can still see the chrysanthemum she painted on the bottom right corner of a square painting, how the flower simply sat there instead of blooming so vividly it

would make a nose twitch with its imagined smell — it could have bloomed into itself
if the artist had enlarged the canvas by another three square feet —
    until I saw that forlorn chrysanthemum I never understood how mere space,
too, offers its own constraints
        —another lesson I should have learned long ago—
        and now I pick on spiders and things much smaller than I
        and there is no consolation
        in realizing I deliberately become cruel so that I, too, can become smaller
        so that someday there will be no tinier creature I can pick on
        —oh, how difficult, how difficult, this attempt to chain my nature—
        redemption clearly entails so much more than judgments on *Scale*

On The Delusion Called "Relief"
—*after PH-385, Oil on canvas (1949)*

The fullness of relief as I discovered the spider I thought I killed this morning still lives! —I thought I left its corpse drying by the damp towel but since the dead do not move and it's now clinging to a different spot on the tub I conclude: it lives!—and I shall name it Kumquat

and the deer has ceased to frighten—this same point being able to be made had I written, "*Nzuri sana, na wewe je*"—Kiswahili for "I am fine. And you?" which one might reply to the standard greeting of "Hello, how are you?"—why offer non sequiturs when one can muster Kiswahili

—despite the joy of relief I pause now to consider whether this poem should be sealed in a bottle and tossed into the ocean—or should I pity the fish—

bounce a ball, darling, not the kitten—

it is impossible to get over Rimbaud—

yes, it is a truism: if she's buying new panties she really is having an affair—

I am incapable of cooking cous-cous which is a shame as it's a word I would like to permeate my poems—it takes no more than five minutes to achieve its perfect consistency, which reveals what cooking and poetry share in common: I am incapable of the deft touch—

a recipe might call for two buds of garlic and I shall put in the whole head—

a recipe might call for a half-cup of wine and I shall empty half the bottle—

I boil chickens until flesh melts off the bones—

(of course—who called me mean? —I shall reveal the Kiswahili for "Hello, how are you?" is "*Hujambo, habari gani*")

sometimes the dead do move from the build-up of gases within the body's cavities

—sometimes the dead move, as they do for me, by evolving into ghosts obsessed with startling me with revelations like, Deep down I'm really amoral

—Deep down, I am an incubating disease

—Deep down, deep down I really just got lucky

—Not *that* Deep down I realize Kumquat must hate me

—yet again, a mote disturbing the surface—an error that will surface inevitably through the most multi-layered babble:

for certain creatures that wander throughout this vast universe

illusions are limited—there is no *Relief*

On Looking Back at the Unborn

—*after PH-950, Oil on canvas (1950), and Harry Matthews' "Rue de Rochechouart" in celebration of the centenary of the brassiere, invented by M. Hardt in Dresden in 1889*

I don't think you got it right about that prostitute shedding everything but her brassiere—you thought she wanted to keep her breasts levitated yet ascribed her decision to "modesty"

    when let me assure you to be totally nude is not as naked as being nude except for a brassiere—especially if the contraption distended those pears, as you said—this same point being able to be made if I reminded you that light always seems brighter when part of a chiaroscuro (positioned against the wet blanket of a shadow)—and, as you know—oh, you must know! —good exists for there is evil

    though I concede Fraulein Hardt undoubtedly cared about the sagging—here both sexes might actually speak the same planet's language as my lover has often consoled me: At least, they will never sag—actually I believe he used the word "droop"

    which evokes for me an old lady's throat, crepe paper flesh blurring the jaw-line

    —or how I feel whenever you leave after our monthly hour, doves cooing to me from the windowsill—to no avail—

    an old story: uneasy alignments

    —positions etched from looking back—diasporics say: Don't ever look back as you'll only see something no longer there

    —translation: regret—desire—or the intersection between regret and desire—

    and it's not that I'm deaf, but when I face forward I also see regret's droopy face—the sore-encrusted beggar I'll ignore, the stewardess who asks if I can understand English, the toddler whose thigh I'll pinch for the flesh is unmarred, the poet who tries to make me feel guilty because I pay my rent on time

    —I have never observed a banker express regret—perhaps an occupational hazard for money, not philosophy, is at stake—

    for money, not Beauty, was put at risk—as when a mortal made a decision and forgot to count: by choosing one out of three goddesses, he pleased one but offended two—I must shake my head over his lunacy

    —but perhaps he's just being a man speaking a language I do not understand, or perhaps, because he's a man he had no choice but to make a choice—

    (Mr. Matthews, Fraulein Hardt's decision was one of immodest display—yes, you were the one in Paris watching her strip but I am the one today who is a quickly-aging woman)

    this is all a rather long-winded way of suggesting women should never become bankers for to unmask with an exception is a position of maximizing exposure—nor can Beauty be quantified as its significance is as exponential as the wrath of two goddesses

    —thunder consistently re-establishes

    it is winter and, still, I long to kiss you with an open mouth

    —when I pin up my hair it is only to offer you the monopoly on releasing me from bondage—

    your fingers tangled in my promiscuous locks

    begin my faithful Immodesty

—a flamenco dancer stamps her feet and red velvet skirt whirls—
muscled thighs glistening
begin my faithful Immodesty
—I can get away with all of this
because
all of my children are Unborn

On The Excluded Word
—*after PH-369, Oil on canvas (1951)*

Oh, to think I once thought it romantic to be perpetually pursued by a memory — as if the origin is immune from time — the most mute of boulders erode, the coldest of ice thaws, the cruelest of parents die, and the most beloved of brothers made me cry — such are my thoughts *du jour* despite greeting the day as a new country, waking with a very specific resolution: today I shall comprehend the radiance of violet without once considering solstice

which arrived in the years of my childhood as a siren but whose sound I recall as chimes for it was a cacophony assured of its welcome by all the citizens of the war-crumpled city — this same point being able to be made had I conceded I remember you as a hand against my back urging me closer rather than the non-furtive glance at the clock, then non-whispered words, "It is late" —

perhaps because I have forgotten the identity of the author of these painful — or pained — words, even were I to identify with assurance the lips that formed them to be yours (full) or mine (bitten)

— I never refreshed my lipstick when it came time to leave as I wished you to see me as I always end with you: damp and moaning flesh

— a pearl loosened from its knot, the better to be swallowed —

an unseasonal storm in another country forms a dark path pelted by the fallen bodies of hyacinths, and its memory halts me in the middle of the street for, yet again, another "near miss" —

a hyacinth has never invaded my space but the concept of its fall — a fall, any fall — is so familiar that I am bound to an infinite number of phenomena in the vast, vast universe long after the erosion of physics —

so that I have learned to be discreet

(you know I ached to be devoured, which does not cancel this knowledge: you wished to devour me, so you did)

— yet even dust can become more fine — I grieve quite openly

for my grief has aligned itself with quantum physics to allow me a conclusion that approximates what I desire and yet earns my gratitude:

no concession ever existed

— I have never traveled through a decade trying to return to Ithaca —

there was never a concession to be made

— I eat red meat raw —

though a test often eliminates limits through the appearance of mottled flesh, I have made no concession

— nor do my wounds and/or my insouciance over them make me any different from anyone else —

I have made no concession

— nor should one image be privileged over another because the edges of one, poor thing, are blurred —

no concession, certainly not the concept of gusto

— what should never exist in the same room is a toddler, a wrench and someone else — it is almost unimaginable now that, once, you conscientiously called each morning after an encounter

— I might concede this: my vocabulary excludes *Chastening*

On Incurable Infidelities
— after PH-185, Oil on canvas (1945)

You are concerned about the palpability of the quiver, and I recognize—for I do not ride horses for the motion between my thighs but for moments of ascension as when heels dig firmly into air and face lifts to form ship's prow over rabid equine eyes

which allows me now to concede with nary a flinch: I have betrayed my inheritance by refusing to pin my hair up each morning—this same point being able to be made had I admitted I wear silk against intimate parts of my body for your fingers, *there*, will explore—but I *am* tired of obfuscations

though the glint in your eye, yes, defines the stab that would pin down a monarch butterfly—its fragile dust of cinnamon pollen—

oh: these days that harpoon my heart with longing for a child's unstinting laughter—as in this moment when I am beset by a strange woman's "How 'bout those Mets!" as I straddle a stool in a Chelsea bar,

or other moments more direct to the point: that is whenever light must break—as it consistently must—to penetrate water or wash against implacable walls

—you are often implacable—

I am often obtuse, even when self-defense is not called for—was it "an arrow or a song"?

—if I could offer you the world I would, though perhaps my generosity stems, too, from your reliable wisdom in rejecting all my offers as we both know I do not earn what money I spend with a profligacy unmatched throughout the history of cruel-eyed courtesans—

you shortcut my blather to note, you, on the other hand, would never offer me something each person can only learn on their own:

shadows are tangible, wrath resonates across the borders of centuries, fate might not contain redemption, loneliness always meets its vessel, shadows are tangible

(a lost mote of pollen dilutes the day as well as, someday, empty a lake whose existence you know only from a rumor in a lost ancient tome)

—and, though no longer aggrieved,

I am constrained by my unerring ability to empathize

with broken light—

this incurable addiction to grief—the whole clawing at the breast and prostrating atop a cold, stone floor in front of a crucifix—

riven, then "whip me, Mama, so I can feel"

—a boy mutilates himself to generate scabs for the collection he keeps in a forgotten father's cigar box

—this incurable addiction to that mocking twist to your lips, this incurable addiction to infidelities—oh: to *Infidelity*

On What You Justifiably Label "Deviance"
—*after PH-1072, Oil on canvas (1952)*

I have hungered for so long I'd forgotten my hunger existed until you evoked the memory of its persistence with yet another cancellation

of something you promised would happen at a distant point in the future for, once, I told you when you were still listening I often relish anticipation more than actual occurrence—this same point being able to be made had I shared how my dreams flourish whenever I leave my birthland to travel the world from a position of exile—though relief was unexpected

at seeing myself reflected as a stranger in people's open eyes—though relief is joy only in the manner of the color yellow approximating light, suddenly magnificent—or the wince evoking things which might be characterized by even poets as "unspeakable"

such as our mutual but unacknowledged realization we should have said "No" long ago instead of enacting your tongue's penetration into the moist space between my promiscuous lips

to make my entire body writhe—and it hasn't stopped writing yet—you know that, don't you?—at playing a vessel's role for containing my constant betrayals so that today I translate something like "la luna" into something like "the sun"

—and "versa vice"—

oh, my love: how did we ever come to this warp in space!

where I consider light as the mere easing of darkness—as when you admired how a black satin slip fell to reveal my thighs—

(but what does it say about me that despite my protests I continue to be addicted to the concept underlying this synonym for "cloud": "adrift"?)

still, I do not wish to repeat—for the thousandth time—the error of believing I am someone unique as I cannot believe no man before Edgar Allan Poe ever believed "the death of a beautiful young woman was the best choice for a great poem's appropriately poetic subject"

—except I am not truly beautiful for character is more than an accessory like a green feather and my spine was a thread long before it broke—

I only am reaching

as water springs from a fountain toward a scrumptiously sunlit sky

except I am found only in dim shadows that greet those who would look back

—my people say, "Don't ever look back"—

to see what is unspeakable, that which others have called "regret"

but which I articulate as "lost"

so that until amnesia or senility generously provide relief I will have to wear a suffocating wool cape seen only by others like me: angels who fell for the ecstasy of the fall

ignorant of ecstasy's twin—

this heavy cape that prevents wings from unfolding—

which you, Dear Collaborator, have also taught me

are the fork's sculpture on my brow, the olive stains beneath my eyes,

the furtive curve to my back that grows increasingly less furtive—which all combine to twist the shape of my flesh

to hint at the concept of what I have become—and, yes, I would wish it

otherwise but it is so late, so late! —
this concept that I would wish to remain a word but has become its own god:
a rotted root that many before you and many after — oh, so many of you! —
have rightly recognized as *Deviance*

Conjurations

it was the silence
of the deep sea you loved, the cut of the coral,
the creatures that breathed with their bodies
as if their whole bodies were genitals, feeling, pulsing,
opening, tears fell
on your shoulders from the ceilings of caves,
and fish lit the water white
as happy brides
—from "Room of Tears" by Evelyn Lau

BEFORE AND BEYOND FOAM
(Conjuration #8-9)

On a white balcony. Stone. Sunlit Atalya. Vases overflow with magenta. Does tongue linger on honeyed fingertip for evoking a different woman than the one who formed your yesterday? Both distracted you for observing how hair becomes a shield. Lips discern hint of stewed roses. Quince. The flurry descending from left field settles now on the railing. Forms an improbable small goose. With "mischievous" ebony eyes. Hardly an agitated Tasmanian. Beyond, the Mediterranean flows a shimmering skirt of blue velvet. Lucid sapphire. You blink into its depth and feel her lovely translucence. Limned by thin scented strands. *Scented.*

How to measure depth? To quantify what a tango holds back?

Gauze fluttering from the open walls of white gazebo. In the distance. What is too much?

Sticky skins

Fuck the salamanders! (Well, and her...)

"She shall_____"   *O, she shall*

Another enchanted you yesterday for evoking the peeking eyes of the one who shall, *o, who shall*

Blood on finger. Surprise. When you bit — another escalation of your longing. O, you shall _____

"Since we have been a conversation and been able to hear from one another," Holderlin reminds...

You shall _____

And _____

And _____

_____And

"SOMETIMES THE SKY AND SEA MUST WAIT"

(Conjuration #7-10) — *for Thomas Fink*

Morning a shimmer through cut glass

Nothing visible there   but transparency

The lack of snow on your shoulders:
        does
             CVS Therapeutic Shampoo
                really work?

Thus, light transmutes into "an event based on hope"

A cerulean number—
        perhaps nine as glass?

I remind you that Yoko Ono set a steel nail
            into a mirror with a   glass hammer

before elongating a pale throat with a drink
              extending to a non-sequitur conclusion:
              "We need more skies than coke."

"Which is to say," *My Dear*

"No blueprint exists for sunrise."

And

"You are astonishingly ravishing as you sleep."

And

"Sometimes the sky and sea must wait."

For Tarkos reminds, there is no irony in paying taxes
Language is a cashmere blanket gently slipping from our shoulders

And

And _____

And _____

      _____And

THE FOG LIFTS
(Conjuration 6-11)

How to create this evening's ars poetica
: (an overheard)   "the fog lifts"

"I, too, search for omens/ in sediment of wine goblets,"/ I whisper like a stray
umbrella tip into your eyes/

You forget to shiver
beneath your city's cap of grey skies
     a *gossamer* shawl knitted by fog

        not rare hairs plucked from the chins
                of mountain goats
        hooves confident on slanted stones
        pockmarking the ancient Himalayas
                whose age reminds

"We shall all die; why not give all?"

There are no dragonflies here
I am just loving this sharing of English

Question: what causes you to stop and stare?
Answer: when a word (say, "ethereal") becomes defined by spiritual awkwardness

        Put it this way: do I make you thirst? *tongue peeking to lick at lips?*
        Or intention obviating horizon as limit…

When a noun is combined with a noun an adjective occurs —
with luck: a verb

        painting painting
        poet poet
        a poet's poet
        a painting's painting

Oh, I could go on! Oh, I will!

And Merleau-Ponty articulates, "A work's completion eradicates its fever"

Bit the image of ecstasy is the image of fever in mine eyes in search of *Thou*

And

And _____

And _____

_____And

FAITH

(Conjuration 5-12)

stalactites etching wooden cheeks

    statues of weeping saints
                bobbing amidst waves

       "you the unknown
       port behind distant mist"

the image of tears carving wood — of what
is this a seed?

include these "dreams by a battered mind"
inhale deeply   *Breathe*

To bring the poem into the world
is to bring the world into the poem

Did not St. John of the Cross muster
a great lyric poem despite "severe sensual deprivation"?

         then exhale the white light

of the North Star, constant
-ly whispering, "You can always know where you are"

    thus moving one hand to my wrist, the other to my waist

pulling me closer to lean against you, my *Wood*

       Beloved. What respite exists
       when I search for you whom I do not know?

And Paz notes the link between Christians and Dadaists
for both "speak in tongues"

And "Harmony, the essence of music, in poetry
produces only confusion"

And we are free with each other though we cannot memorize
each other's scent   *Love as pure Form?*

And no-Self is a Self

And your mask offers what a red rose offers: reflection I recognize as my face

And _____

And _____

_____And

TINCTURE
(Conjurations 4-13)

tinkering with the sky

harvest birthing waves of long-haired dancers (San Ildefonso, 2002)

heat bronzes kiva steps

turquoise hem trawls dirt for pieces of the sun masquerading as corn kernels

no wonder, when she lowers vision, she looks "literally shattered"

"Clouds play a larger role than demarcating spatial perspective: *Unchain the narrative!*"

> *children behave like windchimes*
>
> *ebony-capped women equal butterflies*
>
> *all humans comprise* The Tribe

a damp cheek inexplicable yet, like crème suede boots, belonging

Oh! this intimacy with *a catch of breath*

And Adrienne notes that quitting ballet at sixteen is to become permanently haunted

And, despite cheekbones like Siberian steppes, _____

And "one could always look forward to reincarnation"

And   *CLANG!*

And _____

And _____

_____And

WHITE, THROBBING
(Conjurations 3-14)

gossamer and, still, evaporation
                    "I am in your dreams"

consciousness a cruel synonym for
                    "your hands away from my breasts"

"Goose?"
"Why not?"
The Ponderous Nod of Well-Considered Agreement: "What metaphor can capture
the knowledge you possess regarding the interior of my mouth?"

desiring—oh! —the specifics of meat (roasted, *shorn of white feathers*)

Undine rising wetly from the river
                    Oh, gleaming limbs of stone

in the city where you sleep away from my down-filled pillow
your helpless eyes remain helplessly watchful for my
next helpless frolicking across your computer screen

even as Rilke observes, "There is no temple for Apollo"

And the white so throbs it becomes a moonlit female

And, somewhere, a map begins to fade

And I appreciate nature's insistence against black tulips

_____And_____

And _____

And _____

_____And

_____**AND**_____

(Conjurations 2-15)

your reticence   heightens
                 impending
                 sense
                 of
                 penetration

I insisted: *No*
to the many wanting my photograph

Did I know then you existed/ in this world you will call "broken"?

You are destroying "I" completely —
I would not have it any other way

> *"This is proving typical of his daughter:*
> *reluctant, then pushing them on —*
> *as if she senses she may not pass this way*
> *again"*
> **— The Beholder** *by Thomas Farber, p. 109*

There is no alternative
There is
There
The
Etcetera

Still, the locale of your "August break" remains secret

    like a crucifix between breasts lifted by antique whale bones

    bound by red lace

roses bloom against translucent cotton:
                    petals lapping air

"cobalt via bed linen"

And Hass laughs at the impossibility of measuring the value of poetry "when it's gotten into the blood. It becomes autobiography there."*

And let us hope never to experience, without bemoaning, Lowell's "tranquilized fifties"

And if I singed your bouquet of small white flowers, this still is not horrid self-mutilation

And it does not matter, or it matters

And _____

And _____

_____And

REFLECTED SONG

(Conjurations 1-16)

: to be birthed with eyes already belonging
                                        to another land

then decades of blindness: *oh, invisible mermaids*

(he silenced his eyes by licking wounds in private: a small, dark animal
                                        hiding behind burnt tree stumps)

And she, "the only one remaining"
                            lost her way
                            to fit within his blindfold

            o mirrors: o reflections of a singular astonishment

Was she the first to speak? That is, to sing?
(speechless, she can only sing)

            mirrored tune: "I knew you would come"

Perhaps he was the first to ~~speak~~ sing....

The Sanskrit cheer: Tat Wam Asi / I am you and you are me

And Pound concludes amidst the wreckage, "The verb is 'to see' not 'walk on'"

And timbre must be grounded by "the innocence of light"

And please forgive the metaphor's inevitable lie: there was a child
who silently observed all

            there was a child

And adulthood increases one's need for sweetness

And the "end of the road" reveals the familiar stick and stone

And harmony, harmony, *Harmony: Holy, Holy, Holy*

_____And

And _____

And _____

_____And

OBVIATING THE PROSCENIUM'S EDGE (I)

I walk along the length of a stone-and-gravel garden
and feel without looking how the fifteen stones
appear and disappear. I had not expected the space
to be defined by a wall made of clay boiled in oil
—from "Archipelago" by Arthur Sze

"But Seriously, When I was Jasper Johns' Filipino Lover…"

CHARACTERS:
Eileen Tabios: Played by herself
Kali artist: Imagined Kali projection of Eileen, played by Michelle Bautista
Bride: One of Eileen's doppelgangers haunting her writing studio, this one perpetually in Eileen's wedding dress, played by Barbara Jane Reyes
Summi Kaipa: Played by herself

[LEFT STAGE]
Table with phone and chair slightly back. A kali stick beside the table. Eileen is seated and typing on a laptop on desk. Spot light center that covers both desk and front of the desk.

[STAGE LEFT]
Barbara begins to walk towards STAGE RIGHT, pushing at chalk board that says NO PHOTOGRAPHS OR VIDEO. Pauses at center stage. Spot on her. Leans towards audience. Wags a finger as she says, "Ladies and Gentlemen, No photos or videos are allowed during tonight's presentation. There is a glorious but naked ass [smacks her own butt] at stake!"

BARBARA: [Walks to stage right. Spot left goes down, spot right turns on, stays half dim for most of the show unless otherwise noted and full when Barbara is speaking. Turns to Eileen to say] "Eileen, when you were Jasper John's lover…""

EILEEN: [interrupts her with a wave. Stands up. Faces audience. Hands twirl in watermill motion then stops.] "You know, whenever I keep practicing this Kali gesture I keep confusing it with flamenco. It's so frustrating…." [Moves hands again to transition to flamenco movements.]

[Eileen stops, sighs. Picks up stick, walks in front of desk. Awkwardly performs Kali stick motions as she moves to CENTER STAGE. Frustrated, stops.]

EILEEN: "I am so incompetent at Kali. But I must keep practicing as Kali is exactly like Poetry!"

[Eileen faces audience. Michelle enters stage and walks to stand back to back with Eileen. Michelle and Eileen circle around each other until positions are switched, with Michelle facing audience. Eileen returns to desk, sits down and types.]

[Michelle does Kali performance. Michelle finishes set (approximately two minutes). Then walks back off stage.]

BARBARA: [Sighs] That was niiiiiice! [to Eileen] "So, when you were Jasper Johns' lover…."

EILEEN: [holds up hand to interrupt Barbara as the phone rings. Picks up phone on desk. She answers] "Hello. Oh, hi Kevin! You know. This is the first time I've been

on the phone with THE Kevin Killian.
What's up homeboy?

"You want me to do what? A ten-min-
ute play? For Small Press Theatre?
Well, I've never done a play before.
Oh, it's an homage to amateurism?
Okay, sure. After all, I'm a Poet. I
should be able to write ten minutes in
any form. Okay, I'll call you if I have
questions."

[Hangs up phone. Hesitates. Ponders
for a moment. Then makes a new
phone call.]

EILEEN: "Hi again, Kevin. Actually, I
do have a question. I'd like to incor-
porate a scene in my play: a sort of
take-off on performance artist Vanessa
Beecroft's live human installations
where she positions nude models on
a set. But I need, say, ten poets who'll
volunteer to appear naked during my
play. Well, I'm relatively new to the
Bay Area so can you ask some of your
contacts?

Michelle Bautista performs Kali.
Photo by Rhett Pascual.

[Pause.]

"Unlikely? What do you mean?

[Pause.]

"Oh, you might have done it yourself ten years ago but now the poets in the Bay
Area are too bourgeois to appear naked on stage? Well, okay."

EILEEN: [hangs up the phone. Slowly stands, looks at audience.] "Bay Area poets are
bourgeois?"

EILEEN: [Picks up kali stick and smacks it against her hand as she walks towards
front of stage. Says her lines with an increasingly loud voice.] "Do you mean to say
that I hauled my ass 3,000 miles from New York City just so I can be immersed in a
bourgeois poetry community?"

[Staring, then bends down to peer more closely at audience] "Bay Area bourgeois
poetry community? I don't think so."

[Leans back. Proclaims with emphasis.] "I DO NOT THINK SO!" [Points kali stick
towards Summi Kaipa, sitting far back in audience, and demands.] "Summi Kaipa,

get your ass up here!"

SUMMI: [House Lights up. Light on Summi in audience. She stands up and screams] "I am the next winner of the 'Price is Right'!"

She stumbles her way down, stripping articles of clothing and throwing them around the audience. Making loud comments, improvised, e.g.: "I'm coming, I'm coming...Oh my, it's cold. Good thing I didn't have that steak last night. Hey, don't pinch me. Gads I'm glad I have clean underwear on." Occasionally sits on various laps as she strips, tossing off such remarks as, "Is that you or the *Collected Poems* of *Frank O'Hara* I'm feeling.....etc"

[House lights off. Summi steps on stage wearing underwear, back facing audience. Bends over.]

EILEEN: Huh, rather nice ass there, Summi.

[Summi begins to remove underwear. All lights dim to blackout as Summi exits stage; as she departs she hands her bra to Eileen.]

[Center spot on. Eileen turns a satisfied smirk towards audience. A moment of silence of just staring at them, before she insouciantly drapes Summi's bra over her shoulder.]

EILEEN: "You know: there was a point — a political, deep, incredibly significant point to that scene but....I can't remember it right now."

[Shrugs]. "Ah well."

[Eileen turns and moves to return to her desk. Barbara steps towards Eileen]

BARBARA: [loudly towards Eileen] "But seriously, when you were Jasper Johns' Filipino lover?"

EILEEN: [turns back towards audience] "Oh yeeeees! Well, seriously, when I was Jasper Johns Filipino lover...."

MICHELLE: [shouts from backstage] "TEN SECONDS LEFT!"

EILEEN: [towards Barbara] "Ach! I'm out of time!" [Turns towards audience.] "Too bad I only had 10 minutes! That would have been a great story about when I was Jasper Johns' Filipino lover!"

Notes:
Play incorporates real-life incidents from Eileen Tabios's life as a writer: she studies Kali, a Filipino martial arts form, from Gura Michelle Bautista; Barbara Jane Reyes did don Eileen's original wedding dress for a "happening" related to Eileen's project entitled "Poems Form/From The Six Directions"; and it is true that Kevin Killian told Eileen that he would have difficulty finding ten poets to volunteer to show their naked backsides because the Bay Area poetry community has gotten a bit bourgeois. As for Jasper Johns.....

HAY(NA)KU
OBVIATING THE PROSCENIUM'S EDGE (II)

Within my body
there's a city —
—from "Downward Facing Dog" by Leza Lowitz

WEATHER DU JOUR

blueness
of sky —
I am breathing

UNSENT

Dear,
Paradise inhere
-ently surpasses desire

AFTER CHAZAL

Sunflowers
release gold
dust of illusion

REVVVV

poems
in belly
fuel for flight

ON FALLEN ANGELS

halos
should form
belts, not crowns

THREE AT GREEN RIVER CEMETERY
— Springs, East Hampton

ALFONSO OSSORIO

Dark
slab colonizing
the most lawn

LEE KRASNER

Stone.
Rib from

Jackson Pollock **BOULDER**.

JACKSON POLLOCK

Boulder
shadowing Lee—
Rib as shrapnel

The Official History of Hay(na)ku

In September 2000, I began a "Counting Journal" with the idea that counting would "be just another mechanism for me to understand my days." That journal lasted for only five months because I could maintain its underlying obsession, which was to count everything, for only that long. It was inspired, as this first entry explained on 9/20/2000, by:

Ianthe Brautigan's *You Can't Catch Death – A Daughter's Memoir* which noted the character Cameron in her father Richard Brautigan's *The Hawkline Monster*: "Cameron was a counter. He vomited nineteen times to San Francisco. He liked to count everything."

A month later, I would write: "I am in library intending to finish reading in one seating Richard Brautigan's *An Unfortunate Woman*. From P. 77:

"I've always had at times a certain interest in counting. I don't know why this is. It seems to come without a preconceived plan and then my counting goes away. Often without me ever having noticed its departure.

I think I counted the words on the early pages of this book because I wanted to have a feeling of continuity, that I was actually doing something, though I don't know exactly why counting words on a piece of paper served that purpose because I was actually doing something.

Anyway, I stopped counting words on page 22 on February 1, 1982, with a total of 1,885 words. I hope that is the correct sum. I can count, but I can't add which, in itself, is sort of interesting."

Fast forward to June 10, 2003 where I am writing in my first poetics blog, "WinePoetics" at http://winepoetics.blogspot.com. On the blog, I'd been excerpting from the Counting Journal. At this point, I decide to write one last counting-related blog entry, which became:

But rather than spend more days having you witness me gazing into that part of my navel where Brautigan's eyes are twinkling back, let me write just one last Counting post. This one will feature snippets based on the page the journal opens to when I drop it on the floor. The idea came to me when .... I dropped the journal on the floor as I was polishing off my 2nd glass of the 2001 Dutch Henry Los Carneros Chardonnay.

Drop Journal: Page opens onto 12/18/00. Bush secured Electoral College majority—271 votes—to become the U.S.' 43rd President. It was announced that Hillary Clinton received an $8 million advance for a memoir for her years in the White House. W/ Simon and Schuster. So much $ for tsismis, whereas one can't even find $5,000 to publish a poetry book!

Ugh. Close Journal. Drop Journal Again. Page opens onto 1/28/01: On plane returning to San Francisco, read *Selected Letters of Jack Kerouac*. P. 46—Kerouac says, "I think American haikus should never have more than 3 words in a line—e.g.

Trees can't reach
for a glass
of water

I am inaugurating the Filipino Haiku [PinoyPoets: Attention! I'll post if you send me some!]: 3 lines each having one, two, three words in order — e.g.

Trees
can't reach
for a glass

*****

Enough poets responded to my blog-post so that I was able to announce just two days later:

PHILIPPINE INDEPENDENCE DAY ~~ PINOY HAIKU

It seems most apt to introduce the "Pinoy Haiku" on June 12, Philippine Independence Day. This was the day in 1898 that General Emilio Aguinaldo proclaimed Philippine independence from Spain.

But soon afterwards, the United States — having just tasted, and found sweet, its entry as a world power into the arena of global politics — chose not to recognize the Philippines's successfully fought battle for self-determination. The U.S. invaded the Philippines to turn it into a colony. It wasn't until 1946 that the U.S. formally ended its colonial regime on a day coinciding with the U.S. Independence Day of July 4. Consequently, the Philippines only began to commemorate June 12 in the early 1960s when President Diosdado Macagapal changed Philippine Independence Day from the 4th of July to June 12.

June 12 is certainly a more accurate reflection than the American "July 4" for the Philippines' "Independence Day." Here is an excerpt from Maximo Kalaw's 1916 "Philippine Independence" speech (addressed to U.S.- Americans) which, in my view, bears special resonance given the recent U.S. activities in Iraq and elsewhere as the U.S. exercises "pre-emptiveness" as part of its foreign policy (note that part of the U.S.'s rationale for invading the Philippines presumably was because Filipinos were not equipped to determine their own destinies):

"For the complete establishment of your sovereignty you had to wage a war of subjugation — a war which lasted three years, which necessitated the presence in the islands of 120,000 American soldiers and the establishment of reconcentration camps, which cost your treasury more than half a billion dollars and the Philippines many thousands of human lives. Peace was possible only after complete exhaustion of the Filipino soldiers. Convinced that their independence could not be secured by force of arms, they laid down their guns and returned to peaceful pursuits.

"I shall not here minimize the work of reconstruction done by the American Government. Public schools were established and Filipino children flocked to them with an enthusiasm for learning never before manifested by any people. Roads, hospitals, and public buildings were planned and completed, for which the Filipino people willingly gave their money. But they had never for a moment given up their idea of independence. Despite the material improvement brought about by the American Government, they still considered themselves unjustly deprived of their right to manage their own affairs; and when the first Philippine Assembly met in 1901, it made the solemn declaration that American rule in the Philippines remained unsanctioned by the people whose great desire then, as ever, was their complete political emancipation. The independence idea grew by leaps and bounds. The schoolboy with his hard-learned English greets the

American visitor with a petition for independence. The spellbinder moves the masses with drastic plans for political emancipation; for political parties in the Philippines are built primarily on programs for independence. No human contrivance has been able to check that movement; for, as a Filipino statesman has said, 'when people feel in their hearts the revelation of their political unity and are convinced that the time has come for them to assume a place in the world's history, it is impossible to detain them from their march; it is in vain to amuse them with other scenes and allurements, because they have their eyes fixed ahead, and, invoking the help of man and of the Almighty, they will continue to follow the dictates of their inner self, the voice of their destiny.'"

*****

Filipino poets responded to my call for the "Pinoy Haiku" with enthusiasm. Perhaps in part because, as Michelle Bautista pointed out, the idea of one-two-three "works with the Filipino nursery rhyme: *isa, dalawa, tatlo, ang tatay mo'y kalbo* (pronounce phonetically to catch the rhythm) — which translates into English as "one two three, your dad is bald."

Here are some fresh examples of the Pinoy Haiku, beginning with one written by Barbara Jane Reyes for Philippine Independence Day:

land
of the
mo(u)rning, i toast.

Barbara deftly conflates the reference of "land of the morning" from the Philippine national anthem with the wine theme of this WinePoetics blog. Relatedly, Patrick Rosal offers:

NYC Pinoy Blues or
The Ay Naku Haiku

God-
damn — same
shit/different dog

Meanwhile, Leny M. Strobel and Oscar Penaranda's contributions reflect both the events over a century ago as well as the current times (the U.S. had just invaded Iraq) — befitting their shared status as scholars/teachers as well as poets:

Freedom
Is Cheap
When You're Bushed
— *Leny M. Strobel*

Power
Drippingly exudes
And always stains
— *Oscar Penaranda*

Here are some riffed off by Oliver de la Paz while he was doing laundry:

Pavlova
dances gruffly.
Flats poorly tied.

Keats
writes darkly.
Birds trill unseen.

Watches
around wrists
make teeth marks.

In these works, what's evident to me is that the charge associated with the haiku remains in the Pinoy form with the type of paradox that one might find in the Filipino *bagoong*—a pungent fish sauce enjoyed by Filipinos but, ahem, misunderstood by non-Filipinos. Thus, does Catalina Cariaga also offer:

onion
just eaten;
smell my breath

*****

As I would relay in a subsequent post on my blog, most of the Pinoy "haiku" (scare quotes deliberate) came from writers who belonged to Flips, a listserve of either Filipino writers or anyone interested in Filipino Literature that was co-founded by poets Nick Carbo and Vince Gotera. While my compadres and comadres happily sent me what Vince called these "Stairstep Tercets," my project also ended up eliciting a discussion on the implications of *Naming*—and how I was approaching it by using the phrase "Pinoy Haiku." Vince asked:

> Appropriating the "haiku" name has all sorts of prosodic and postcolonial problems (by which I mean the WWII "colonizing" of the Philippines by Japan, among other things). Am I being overly serious here? When you say Kerouac refers to "American haiku" not having more than three words per line, I think he might have been reacting to Allen Ginsberg's "American sentence" which has 17 syllables per line. I guess my concern about calling it a "Pinoy haiku" is that readers could say "Hey, Pinoys can't even get the haiku right!" They won't always have the Kerouac quote to guide them. Besides, why must we always be doing things in reaction to the term "American"? An interesting parallel poetic-form-naming might be Baraka's "low coup" form (the diametrical opposite of "high coup" / haiku). Maybe the Pinoy version could be the "hay (na)ku"?

"Hay naku" is a common Filipino expression covering a variety of contexts—like the word "Oh."

Another poet had suggested that I also rename the project because the traditional haiku form should be respected. Well, yes and no. As I told that poet—I also think that, in Poetry, rules are sometimes made to be broken.

And, I initially wasn't moved either by Vince's notion as regards Japan "colonizing" the Philippines during WWII. If anything, I thought that were I to move down that

179

line of thinking (which I hadn't been), I didn't mind subverting the Japanese haiku form specifically because I thought of it as *talking back* against Japanese imperialism. But, on closer consideration, I realized that the perspective could work both ways...and that using the "haiku" reference also could imply a continuation of "colonial mentality."

Anyway, I bowed to Vince's wisdom (he is, after all, older than I am; wink here at Vince) and renamed the form "HAY(NA)KU"

*****

Since the birth of hay(na)ku, there has been a hay(na)ku contest judged by Barbara Jane Reyes which was quite popular in the internet's poetry blogland; the hay(na)ku form was taught at a "Poetry for the People" class at U.C. Berkeley; and many other poets—non-Filipino as well as Filipino—have picked up the form. In fact, New Zealand-based poet Mark Young and Filipina poet Jean Vengua are coediting what will be the first hay(na)ku anthology: *The Hay(na)ku Anthology* (Meritage Press, 2005). Maya Mason Fink, the 11-year-old daughter of poet Thomas Fink, also concocted a variation whereby the first line has one word of one letter, the second line two words of two letters each, the third line three words of three letters each, and so on—as far as the poet wishes to take it. Maya and Tom offer an example of "The Mayan Hay(na)ku" as follows:

I
am an
old, fat dog
[with many blue fleas].

Belatedly, and hilariously, Tom realized that "fleas" has one too many letters (which is also to highlight the challenge of this constraint) but … the drift is gotten. (Tom later would suggest replacing "fleas" with "furs".) Maya's enthusiasm also points to one of the hay(na)ku's possibilities as an attractive tool for introducing poems to youngsters.

Other hay(na)ku variations since have risen, e.g. "Ducktail Hay(na)ku" whose ducktail references a hairstyle that shows a thin strand of hair trailing down from an otherwise shortly-cropped hair cut; this version features the three-line stanza, followed by another one-line stanza of any length. Another variation is the "Reverse Hay(na)ku" whereby the numbering of words per line is 3, 2 and 1, respectively, versus the original 1, 2 and 3. Most recently, Wales-resident Ivy Alvarez concocted the "worm hay(na)ku" which are written with words using mostly median letters: "those letters that live in the middle, that don't have tops [b, d, f, h, i, j, k, l, t] nor tails [g, j, p, q and y]. The *worms* of a c e m n o r s u v w x z."

As one can see by the history of the hay(na)ku, it is a community-based poetic form which fits my own thoughts on the poem as a space for engagement. "Community" is a word laden with much baggage—both good and bad. I, too, have a conflicted reaction to the word. But I have to say that some of my favorite poetic projects are those where I consciously am building towards a community—through both poetic form and content. Why? Because I think a poem doesn't fully mature without a particular community called reader(s). Poetry is (inherently) social.

*****

Ironically, I actually feel myself mostly mediocre at the hay(na)ku. I've written just over a handful, the last while potty-training my puppy Achilles:

HERE WE GO AGAIN
"by" Achilles

"Go
Potty!" Mama
exhorts. Sigh. Poop.

Quite clearly, other poets do this form better. Here are two examples chosen by Jean Vengua and Mark Young. The first was written by Joseph Garver, a Florida-born poet currently residing in Texas. The second is a hay(na)ku sequence written by Kirsten Kaschock (author of *Unfathoms*, Slope Editions, 2004):

Untitled
By Joseph Garver

Old
Fire is
A cold fire

*****

Sunday Number Theory
by Kirsten Kaschock

One
is consummate.
One is mouth

navel
and anus
—a clear digestive

loop.
One is
broth. Is consommé.

One's
flavor is
salt. One exists

by
the narrowest
margin. One has

this
one-word motto:
stay. One cannot

regroup.
Once split,
one has broken

every
path — which
was the one

oath —
to be
bound as one

eternally.
So — orphan.
One cannot be

named
nor be
known. One is

god —
worshipless. Shamed
by god's need:

worship.
One's sound
is one tree

splitting
the head
of an angel

— then
the tree
must burn, angel

burn,
and pins
trace hymns through

soot.
One stops
at nothing: train

beyond
breaking — point
forfeit to motion.

One
has no
equivalent, no

one
in which
to trust, no

one
to marry,
no other one

to
bed. All
said is also

done.
It is
a fearful promise —

one.

*****

Since the initial response by Filipino poets to the hay(na)ku, many — if not most — hay(na)ku have been written by non-Filipinos such as Kirsten and Joseph. This is certainly a fine result since Poetry is not necessarily ethnic-specific. But I'm also glad that non-Filipinos have taken up this form because I consider the hay(na)ku — as I've stated on its official Hay(na)ku Blog (http://eileentabios.blogspot.com) — to be "A Filipino — And Diasporic — Poetic."

Today, more than eight million Filipinos are scattered about the globe. In the diaspora, the Filipino meets many influences and what would be the point of denying such? Given that the diaspora has existed throughout Filipino history, to call something "Filipino," in my view, is not the same as hearkening back only to so-called "indigenous" Filipino traits. I agree with Filipino poet Eric Gamalinda when he once observed, "The history of the Philippines is the history of the world."

Or, as University of the Philippines student Patricia Evangelista (19 years old) says in her speech which won the 2004 International Public Speaking competition conducted by the U.K.'s English Speaking Union [ESU], entitled "A Borderless World":

A borderless world presents a bigger opportunity, yet one that is not so much abandonment but an extension of identity....

Nationalism isn't bound by time or place. People from other nations migrate to create new nations, yet still remain essentially who they are....

Leaving sometimes isn't a matter of choice. It's coming back that is. The Hobbits of the shire traveled all over Middle-Earth, but they chose to come home, richer in every sense of the word. We call people like these balikbayans or the "returnees" — those who followed their dream, yet choose to return and share their mature talents and good fortune.

In a few years, I may take advantage of whatever opportunities that come my way. But I will come home. A borderless world doesn't preclude the idea of a home. I'm a Filipino, and I'll always be one. It isn't about geography; it isn't about boundaries. It's about giving back to the country that shaped me.

Whether or not I ever return physically to the Philippines, I do know that creating poetic forms that I present to the world as "Filipino" is also my way of giving back to the country that shaped me, the country that birthed me literally and forever influences me.

*****

I think it's also appropriate that I, presumably the hay(na)ku's "inventor," be mediocre at this form. I think this logical because I believe Poetry ultimately transcends the poet's autobiography. Even when the narrative offers up elements of my own life, I consider the poem a space of engagement with others, with the results not anything I can either predict or control. In this sense, the hay(na)ku very much retains my person-hood, even as its outcomes are based on "Others." As with all poems, therefore, for the hay(na)ku the author's "I"/eye remains integral in a space whose characteristic(s) transcends the limits of authorial vision.

BLACK HOLE BEATITUDES

I avert my eyes to this slippery dumbfoundness
lines meander over a ricochet someplace
—from "vote" by kari edwards

The Slip

The silence is stunned. She wishes she can reverse a decision. She returns home, expecting a house wreathed in darkness. For the night has another hour to spare before roosters snap to attention. Instead, the house is irradiated, not a single lamp spared its vigilance. And he is in yesterday's clothes, eyes fixed at where she stands, immobilized by the unrelenting frame of an aghast door.

Even purity entails a price. She acknowledges her debt but is not reconciled. Perhaps she should become a waitress to deny her need. Or begin to deplete his fortune without a single backward glance. She certainly should attempt a different path than hopping on airplanes on a whim because his achievement allows her to afford insouciance.

She apologizes for causing him worry. He chooses to believe she regrets. Then he guides her to bed, tucks a blanket under her chin and lays a soft kiss on her forehead. All this does not dampen the fever that caused her cruelty. And it is dawn so off he goes to profit from another opening bell at the New York Stock Exchange. She closes her eyes and a stranger's face surfaces from the depths of dimness: a young girl attempting poetry by whispering, "It must be difficult/ all this not wanting to die."

The Tedious Destiny

She can stare at the ant farm for hours. But she is in a zoo and they are behind a glass wall. She wrinkles her brow to their dilemma: tunnels inexplicably bright (to facilitate tourists' eyes) and leading to familiar bends of a circular route. She can hear them mutter, *We might as well be human — like ex-drunk drivers returning obsessively to those parts of the road where they rammed young mothers, or infants, to their deaths.* She continues to stare at the crazed bodies scurrying for any destination not long since memorized. When she is forced to close her eyes, she sees black holes floating through air as if she has been gazing directly at the sun.

Saint Petersburg is the worst. Once, its pastel buildings mocked its perpetually overcast days. Now, the paint has peeled in an overwrought manner, exposing corners like bruised knees. But government bureaucrats will not spare fresh cans of pinks, yellows, blues and greens — they claim they are battling the Mafia. And even if they mustered, who would have time to wield brushes for mere cabbage? Still, she aches from feeling the weakening hold of paint, not unlike the darkened tones clinging desperately to canvas but bludgeoned from the daily streak of harsh light tumbling through the windows of the Hermitage. Sadly, people must rush to their death without a reflective pause for tradition.

And she is still grieving over a lost opportunity from a different decade. "You complete me," a man once whispered to a woman. And though it was a B-grade movie, she felt her palms skim the cruel face of a cliff as she fell to jagged rocks waiting beneath an ocean's moon-pulled swell.

Oh, she longs to return to Santo Tomas. Its people are quiet but kind. The villagers treat her as a long-lost daughter for finding fields of tobacco "romantic." For her, they pluck treasured tomatoes off vines they tend to survive, send their children scurrying for premature mangos in response to her taste buds' memories, offer the juice of coconuts they eagerly open with sharpened machetes and roast cassava cakes that melt on her tongue. She longs to return to their wiry embraces. In their hold, her hunger abates and stone splinters loosen from her palms. In their hold, she can accept the tedious destiny of more days to come.

The Prostitute's Cashmere Conclusion

There's a horde of teenagers climbing the boulevard to my street corner. None of them wear cashmere. But I expect a flock of white butterflies to appear over their unruly heads. Instead I hear drunken bees.

I feel the roast beef agitating my belly. It would be nice to clasp a minute of surcease. But a long, black limo skids to a halt and a dark window begins to lower. The man has the cheeks of a baby but I know he would be cruel.

What does it mean to expect the world? I know a woman who ceased chopping her own wood. The last time I saw her she was addressed with respect by museum guards in New York City. A saxophone note cracks the night.

It is not ambitious to expect the world. One need only "listen critically." How pollen inebriates bees! How sighs mirror the fluttering of white wings. How a jaded man grovels for intimacy. How a single note says it all.

And after the rain, the pavement is cleansed. And slate mirrors water.

Notional Ekphrasis

What surfaces will be the result of perfect alignment.
Alignment is a paradoxical relationship between life
and the space that life inhabits.

She asks herself seriously, *How can one make decisions based on imagination?* Once, she looked through the white steam of a day's first cup to see his receding back, then a door slowly shutting. Months after she reconciled herself to his disappearance, she woke up startled in the middle of night. She heard his voice whisper, *Why must an artist narrow the focus of Self?* It is her first memory of his statement, and it occurs, too, with the discovery that these words were uttered once before—a disembodied but anguished voice floating through the space cancelled by a shut door. Finally, she recalls the lack of enmity in his tone—it was bereft of morality.

While hallucinating, a philosopher was compelled to proclaim, "Attention is a form of passion." In 1937, the Nazis denounced certain artists for their inability to distinguish between deformity and beauty: Marc, Feininger, Kokoschka, Chagall, Kandinski, Modigliani, Matisse, van Gogh, Picasso, Cezanne, Klee, Grosz, Ernst and Barlach. To manifest their attack, the Nazis exhibited their works. Years later, she questions whether, by titling the exhibit "Degenerate Art," the Nazis actually exacted a price. The foundation of Art includes the hidden layer of obviating biological determinism: "to be unnatural is to be civilized, to stake a claim to the artistic requirement of self-consciousness."

So she cancels the image of a door shutting permanently behind a receding back. To transcend misery at the encroachment of a memory whose surfacing she cannot control, she begins to paint landscapes. They may be pastoral: a hill gently sloping, encased in green—once she allowed cadmium white to create a sheep. They may be urban: abstract oranges, browns and greys approximating wet roofs, devoid of human activity, revealing only the flirtations between rain and light. But, always, the rim of the sky is the vivid blue in the aftermath of storms. That edge along the painting is where she places the one she lost. (It is the best she can muster, so it must make do?) It is an edge she feels where balance need not be perfect. This, too, is why, after she is done with colors, she layers her paintings with a translucent golden stain. She is cheered by the shimmer effected by light randomly skimming the surface—it is her version of lucidity. There is no sulfur in its content.

EPILOGUE POEMS

My impatience can never reach
the end of you.
—from "Opera (ET club mix with Chris Bowden's
saxophone solo)" by Barry Schwabsky

Epilogue Poems (Introduction)

She tried to whitewash my "Nos." She was already lying across me. (The scene a bed in a hotel room, a garish bedspread whose orange color she had foretold in a dream. *Stage Left and Stage Right melted into shadows.*) My tongue already had penetrated the interior of her left ear. Cinnamon along the edges of the shell. Within the interior, quince.

But.

"No," I said. Reluctantly. Her history of other men proved how premature consummation would have turned me into a blank page.

Jasmine limning each strand of her long, dark hair.

Still. I uttered "No." Years later, I would not be surprised that the memory of my "No" still caused her to wake in the middle of the night, quivering, frightened. Once, she called the effect "a loss of confidence."

Still.

I did not want to be a blank page.

Epilogue Poems (No. 1)

Behind her shoulders flared asymmetrical wings. One wing couldn't heal perfectly after a break.

She was noble
        precisely because she was damaged.

Epilogue Poems (No. 2)

There had been the time she picked up my copy of Joyce's *Ulysses*. From the way she held it on her left palm as her right index finger lovingly traced each letter in the title, I realized she had never read the book. With astonishment, I also realized: It's all right.

I have mastered philosophy. I *teach* philosophy.

Once, over dinner, I whispered to her, "It will be okay. Everything will be just fine."

I have mastered philosophy by knowing to bend it before *Acceptance*.

Epilogue Poems (No. 3)

I do regret how I never told her certain things.

E.g., I wouldn't have minded being in a painting with her: a place where time stood still to make permanent my hands on her waist, her tongue licking my parted lips, her fingers blissfully lost in their own rapturous love-making with the tendrils of my hair.

My hands on the flesh between the edges of her black sweater and blue jeans. Once, in a poem, she quoted me quoting Barthes: "Which Frenchman said the most erotic span is where a breach reveals female flesh?"

My hands warming against the flesh flushed between the edges of her black sweater and blue jeans.

...then her skin burning mine...

As well, heat between her lips. Enchanting, enchanting smoke.

"white, throbbing"

Epilogue Poems (No. 4)

She could not remember Barthes' name. But she finds it impossible (she said) to forget that he said, "The most erotic span is where a breach reveals female flesh."

Actually, Barthes said, "Is not the most erotic portion of a body where the garment gapes?...It is intermittence, as psychoanalysis has so rightly stated, which is erotic: the intermittence of skin flashing between two articles of clothing (trousers and sweater), between two edges (the open-necked shirt, the glove and the sleeve); it is this flash itself which seduces, or rather: the staging of an appearance-as-disappearance."

But still.

A selective memory.

She remembers meeting me when I had stopped writing poems. She conjures a story that ends with one of my poems.

She remembers what she thought Barthes said as, somehow, she knew it was a foretelling for my hands and her body.

With utmost (and rare) fortitude, she once proclaimed: "The best poems conjure."

Epilogue Poems (No. 5)

Our first glass together was a Vouvray. I arrived first and placed the order. When she arrived, she asked for the same thing goldening my goblet. Later, she explained, " I wanted the scent and taste of your tongue."

Epilogue Poems (No. 6)

The first glass of wine I witnessed her drink bore the color of molten gold.

And light, generously spilled into her glass as if the bar had dimmed itself just to concentrate all light into the space cupped between her hands.

O, yellow light...

...her hands that, thrice, grasped my collar to pull me closer...

Epilogue Poems (No. 7)

I am at a wordless space when I consider how urgently she once turned her face to me. A crowd, ignored, drifted around us. I watched her lips say, "It's urgent."

What was urgent, she said, is that she felt the need to correct something she'd said. She had said I wanted the "impossible."

"No, No," she corrected herself then, urgency a wind howling around us to bring us to a space where darkness formed a void in which our two bodies leaned towards each other.

"What I meant to say is not that you want the impossible but that you simply want a certain possibility."

Within the void, warm light. White light in which everything can be seen most clearly. Warm light.

Epilogue Poems (No. 8)

If this is an "epilogue"

perhaps
I
should
stop
talking
about
her.
Once,
she
said,
"This
story
is
not
about
me.
It's
about
you"

*

I am writing poems now

Epilogue Poems (No. 9):
Venus Rising For The First Time in the 21st Century

To see is this other torture, atoned for
in the pain of being seen
—from "Spokes" by Paul Auster

You want to see
her seeing
herself. You want

her seeing
her wanting
you behind the wave

foaming
when you become
the sea seeing

her eyes form
(above a body you
dreamt into salt water)

For the rest of the poem, please go to Pages 8-10 of Menage A Trois With the 21st Century
by Eileen R. Tabios (xPress(ed), Espoo, Finland, 2004). ISBN No. 951-9198-90-3

Epilogue Poems (No. 10)

&
&
&

I, too, refuse

to live constrained

by deprivation narratives

&
&
&

Epilogue Poems (No. 11)

&&&&&&&&&&&&&&&&&
&&&&&&&&&&&&&&&&&
&&&&&&&&&&&&&&&&&
&&&&&&&&&&&&&&&&&
&&&&&&&&&&&&&&&&&
&&&&&&&&&&&&&&&&&
&&&&&&&&&&&&&&&&&
&&&&&&&&&&&&&&&&&
&&&&&&&&&&&&&&&&&
&&&&&&&&&&&&&&&&&
&&&&&&&&&&&&&&&&&
&&&&&&&&&&&&&&&&&
&&&&&&&&&&&&&&&&&
&&&&&&&&&&&&&&&&&
&&&&&&&&&&&&&&&&&
&&&&&&&&&&&&&&&&&
&&&&&&&&&&&&&&&&&
&&&&&&&&&&&&&&&&&
&&&&&&&&&&&&&&&&&
&&&&&&&&&&&&&&&&&
&&&&&&&&&&&&&&&&&

I am writing poems now
I told her bated breath

with a letter I signed
"Eternal Love"

Epilogue Poems (No. 12)

Poems. But it's not easy.
Should I have been
a plumber worsening water
beneath your sink?
Today I shook off her hand
from my typing fingers typing:
O moon in hiding. O shivering sky.
O scent of jasmine evaporating.
Geese of the world: forgive
me. ~~<I na or< ifs ten cro><I ra sr<~~
~~nfs oen iro><I fa er< rfs sen nro>~~
~~cr> tar ice otf~~ Reveal the song
within your cacophony.
The Muse — *O Muse* — is ~~<I na or<~~
~~<I ra sr< nfs oen iro><I fa er<~~
~~rfs sen r> ice otf~~ never Anonymous.

Epilogue Poems (No. 13)

And if the Muse
Is never Anonymous?
O Life: why the sudden
difficulty in accepting
the existence of angels?
How to survive their strangle-
hold when they wish
only to scaffold my spine—
that inadvertent but
inevitable asphyxiation
~~<I na or< ifs ten cro><I ra~~
~~nfs oen iro><I fa er< rfs sen nro>~~
~~cr> tar ice otf sr< sr< sr<~~
from wings hiding the
required muscles for
flights penetrating the sky?
O bone, O sinew, O blood
O Muse who is too human
If I must treat you as mortal
why do I fight ~~rfs sen nro>~~
~~cr> tar ice otf sr< sr<~~ *Love?*

Epilogue Poem (No. 14): Painting: "Light's Pregnancy"

Sunlight
on canvas
as primary material

Nature
industriously bending
verdant landscapes
for light to change color

~~cr> tar ice otf sr< sr< sr<~~

As for the fractured
~~<I na or< ifs ten cro><I ra~~
~~fs oen iro><I fa er< rfs se nro>~~
sheen of "immoderate
water"?

The bird humming
transfers pollen
to correct stigma

All this
(and always more)
soothing
your intent watch
over my lips
stubbornly humming

All this
before and after
you listened
~~ifs ten cro><I ra~~
~~fs sen nro>~~
~~r ice otf sr< sr< sr<~~
to lips suckling
generous light

Epilogue Poem (No. 15)

~~rso a<n crs te< if> orr nae sef~~
~~rtr eia foc rnt asi~~

~~c<o trn ies of< nr> sarree etf fir~~
~~roa anc cst t ecr~~

Just when I thought I understood
her fragility

I found myself soothing her:
"Sweetheart,

when I said 'No'
I was not rejecting you."

Epilogue Poem (No. 16)

I whispered into her hair
as she hid her face
beneath my chin

~~rso a<n crs te< if> orr nf~~
~~rtr eia foc rnt asi~~
~~c<o trn ies of< nr>~~

"I think we should be happy
with a book that will be unusual,
by virtue of its ~~quality~~ story"

&&&&&&&&&&&&&&&&
&&&&&&&&&&&&&&&&
&&&&&&&&&&&&&&&&

&&&&&&&&&&&&&&&&
&&&&&&&&&&&&&&&&
&&&&&&&&&&&&&&&&

&&&&&&&&&&&&&&&&
jasmine perfume of cobalt sky
&&&&&&&&&&&&&&&&

&&&&&&&&&&&&&&&&
&&&&&&&&&&&&&&&&
&&&&&&&&&&&&&&&&

Epilogue Poem (No. 17)

&&&&&&&&&&&&&&&&
&&&&&&&&&&&&&&&&
&&&&&&&&&&&&&&&&

&&&&&&&&&&&&&&&&
&&&&&&&&&&&&&&&&
&&&&&&&&&&&&&&&&

So much elapses

None of it
brings me close
to understanding

Her Fragility

&&&&&&&&&&&&&&&&
&&&&&&&&&&&&&&&&
&&&&&&&&&&&&&&&&

~~na or< ifs ten cro><I ra~~
~~oen iro><I fa er< rfs sen nro>~~
~~cr> tar ice otf sr< sr< sr<~~

Epilogue Poem (No. 18): (Heliotrope)

"It happened." Unexpected kiss
I pressed on her startled
lips. Her hair released
its ghostly mist. Fragile, she
backed away the one step
allowed — the sweet limit
anticipated in my ruled
notebooks. My new impatience
another kiss, softening
fear I licked off as apples.
Her tears fell: grapes
for my avid tongue. My mouth
a new sky, all containing.
A meadow, a river, a chamber
with chair and mirror —
all become body and breath
extorting unsurpassable song.

&&&&&&&&&&&&&&&&
&&&&&&&&&&&&&&&&
&&&&&&&&&&&&&&&&
&&&&&&&&&&&&&&&&
&&&&&&&&&&&&&&&&
&&&&&&&&&&&&&&&&

210

Epilogue Poem (No. 19)

But I didn't know

forcing her to be strong

would loosen the grasp

of her arms belting my waist

*

Once, her eyes pleaded

"Define Desire"

*

Why am I a mask

blinding her now

hands on a keyboard—

these slaves to *Vision*

pleading for translation

*

Whose plea

requires translation

*

Whose plea now

requires translation now

when this poem is the second-to-last

hum to comprise

a series defined as *Aftermath*

Epilogue Poem (No. 20): (Tapas)

1)
~~na or< ifs ten cro><I ra~~
~~oen iro><I fa er< rfs sen nro>~~
~~er> tar ice otf sr< sr< sr<~~
~~na or< ifs ten cro><I ra~~

Together, we have never
slipped beyond velvet drapes
into a dim, smokey bar
where I would feed her

Berenjenas de Almagro
Boquerones en Vinagre
Buñuelos de Chorizo
Calamares fritos

which I also would taste
by licking glistening lips
before she would feed me
appetizers for my true need

Callos a la Madrileña
Croquetas de Jamon
Torreznos
Tortilla de Patatas

Still, she would write
a reality of *tapas* —
heat that burns off
"negative karma"

&&&&&&&&&&&&&&&&&
&&&&&&&&&&&&&&&&&
&&&&&&&&&&&&&&&&&
&&&&&&&&&&&&&&&&&

I hear her whisper now
"Namaste, My Love —
You rejected me
into crossing a new threshold

beyond which lights
Om shanti
Om shanti
Om shanti

Epilogue Poem (Epilogue)

_____*And*_____

And _____

And _____

_____*And*
—*from "White, Throbbing"*

&&&&&&&&&&&&&&&&&&&&&&&&&&&&&&&&&&&&
&&&&&&&&&&&&&&&&&&&&&&&&&&&&&&&&&&&&
&&&&&&&&&&&&&&&&&&&&&&&&&&&&&&&&&&&&
&&&&&&&&&&&&&&&&&&&&&&&&&&&&&&&&&&&&
&&&&&&&&&&&&&&&&&&&&&&&&&&&&&&&&&&&&
&&&&&&&&&&&&&&&&&&&&&&&&&&&&&&&&&&&&
&&&&&&&&&&&&&&&&&&&&&&&&&&&&&&&&&&&&
&&&&&&&&&&&&&&&&&&&&&&&&&&&&&&&&&&&&
&&&&&&&&&&&&&&&&&&&&&&&&&&&&&&&&&&&&
&&&&&&&&&&&&&&&&&&&&&&&&&&&&&&&&&&&&
&&&&&&&&&&&&&&&&&&&&&&&&&&&&&&&&&&&&
&&&&&&&&&&&&&&&&&&&&&&&&&&&&&&&&&&&&
&&&&&&&&&&&&&&&&&&&&&&&&&&&&&&&&&&&&
&&&&&&&&&&&&&&&&&&&&&&&&&&&&&&&&&&&&
&&&&&&&&&&&&&&&&&&&&&&&&&&&&&&&&&&&&
&&&&&&&&&&&&&&&&&&&&&&&&&&&&&&&&&&&&
&&&&&&&&&&&&&&&&&&&&&&&&&&&&&&&&&&&&
&&&&&&&&&&&&&&&&&&&&&&&&&&&&&&&&&&&&
&&&&&&&&&&&&&&&&&&&&&&&&&&&&&&&&&&&&
&&&&&&&&&&&&&&&&&&&&&&&&&&&&&&&&&&&&
&&&&&&&&&&&&&&&&&&&&&&&&&&&&&&&&&&&&
&&&&&&&&&&&&&&&&&&&&&&&&&&&&&&&&&&&&
&&&&&&&&&&&&&&&&&&&&&&&&&&&&&&&&&&&&
&&&&&&&&&&&&&&&&&&&&&&&&&&&&&&&&&&&&
&&&&&&&&&&&&&&&&&&&&&&&&&&&&&&&&&&&&
&&&&&&&&&&&&&&&&&&&&&&&&&&&&&&&&&&&&
&&&&&&&&&&&&&&&&&&&&&&&&&&&&&&&&&&&&
&&&&&&&&&&&&&&&&&&&&&&&&&&&&&&&&&&&&
&&&&&&&&&&&&&&&&&&&&&&&&&&&&&&&&&&&&
&&&&&&&&&&&&&&&&&&&&&&&&&&&&&&&&&&&&
&&&&&&&&&&&&&&&&&&&&&&&&&&&&&&&&&&&&
&&&&&&&&&&&&&&&&&&&&&&&&&&&&&&&&&&&&

II. POEMS FORM/FROM THE SIX DIRECTIONS

Eileen Tabios marries Mr/s Poetry
Sonoma Student Union Intercultural Center Gallery, Sonoma State University, March 4-29, 2002
Metaphorical Bride: Filipina poet Natalie Concepcion

Eileen Tabios marries Mr/s Poetry
Pusod Center Gallery, Berkeley, Aug. 10-Sept. 15, 2002
Metaphorical Bride: Filipina poet Barbara Jane Reyes

Eileen Tabios marries Mr/s Poetry
Locus (with *Interlope* and Alliance of Emerging Creative Artists), San Francisco, Aug. 23, 2002
Metaphorical Bride: South Asian male poet Amar Ravva
Bride is not Filipina since Mr/s Poetry is neither ethnic- nor gender-specific.

Poet and Father of the Bride

Poet Kisses English Before Eating Cake

SIX DIRECTIONS: POETRY AS A WAY OF LIFE

To bring the poem into the world
Is to bring the world into the poem
--from "Conjuration #5" by Eileen Tabios

I consider *Poetry* to be a practice, a way of living. For me, living as a poet requires maximizing awareness of the world in order to be effective as a poet. By "effective," I refer to my hope that my poems create spaces for experiences that readers find meaningful, if not pleasurable. In attempting to reach as many readers as possible, I consider attentiveness important for noticing, understanding and analyzing elements that then may be incorporated into poems. I believe that the more that a poet educates one's self—the more that a poet *sees!*—the more likely that a poet will reach many among the different peoples who exist in our universe of diverse cultures, personalities, styles and contexts.

SSU Students Pin Poems on Bridal Gown
Worn by Natalie Concepcion

In trying to maximize my understanding of my environment, I have noticed how poetry seems to concern relatively few people. Notwithstanding what some have called the "re-birth" of poetry in the United States (e.g. through "spoken word" and poetry slams), most people still seem to view poetry as a matter of little relevance (perhaps merely something they once studied in school) instead of something that can become part of their lives.

Consequently, working to expand the cultural presence of poetry has been an integral part of my activities as a poet. I not only write but also work as an editor, cultural activist, publisher and critic—all in order to promote poetry. My attempts to *live* instead of just *write* poetry resulted in a multidisciplinary and interactive project entitled "Poems Form/From The Six Directions."

Six Directions was introduced to me by poet Arthur Sze as a Native American concept of the directions consisting of north, south, east, west, up and down. The concept resonates for me in terms of how its multidimensionality reflects my belief that poems are not just words lying flat on the page but are living—*breath*-ing!—creatures. Six Directions began in part when I was trying to envision the visual equivalent of a poem. I had been considering the oft-quoted phrase "Poetry is not words but what lies between words, between the lines." Because this concept implies that poetry is invisible, I wondered what a poem's "body" might look like, and determined to answer my own question by "sculpting" poems. I thought of the sculptural process because sculptures are three-dimensional (which would be the opposite of lying flatly against the one-dimensional field of a page). Thus, I created mixed-media sculptures whose processes also engendered verse-poems. Through the Six Directions approach, I ended up with poems that work as texts on the page as well as objects that symbolized the three+-dimensional bodies of poems.

However, in a development that I never anticipated while conceiving of the project, Six Directions culminated in August 2002 with me helplessly bent over in amusement at the sight of a hairy man itching in my original wedding dress. There I was at LOCUS, a performing arts space in San Francisco, tears leaking down my cheeks, laughing robustly as Amar Ravva stripped down to his boxer shorts before gingerly putting on my satin gown. Amar, a South Asian poet, had volunteered to wear my dress as part of a "happening" that featured my latest poem-sculpture, the interactive "Poem Tree."

"Poem Tree" symbolizes my commitment to poetry through my marrying "Mr/s Poetry." In prior happenings, those wearing my dress were Filipina female poets (Natalie Concepcion and Barbara Jane Reyes) to reflect my status. For the last happening, Amar was chosen because poetry is presumably neither ethnic- nor gender-specific.

Nonetheless, Amar, while petite enough to fit into my dress, is quite hirsute. His physicality offered a (wonderfully) dissonant contrast against my wedding gown festooned with lace, seed pearls, and white sequins. I had excavated my dress, along with a 12-foot train, from my parents' attic for Six Directions' purposes. Seventeen years ago, Mom went overboard as she helped choose the baroque style of my dress (this was her one shot to be Mother of the Bride). If my dress was cheese, it would be of the oozing, triple crème variety. Its elaborate style only highlighted the oddness of it draping the shoulders of a bearded man with a bemused expression and flat, black shoes that peeked out from

Amar Ravva as Bride

the voluminous bottom folds of the skirt. Several times during the happening, I had to force myself not to look at Amar as the sight of his black chest hair poking out from my dress' pearl-strewn décolletage usually sent me roaring. Whew! Was I glad Mom was not in town to witness Amar in my dress!

"Poem Tree" is modeled after a rite in Filipino and Latino weddings wherein guests pin money on the bride's and groom's outfits. The ritual symbolizes how guests offer financial aid to the couple beginning a new life together. For "Poem Tree," poems are

Poet and Mother of the Bride

pinned onto the dress to symbolize how poetry, too, feeds the world.

To reflect my belief that a poem transcends its author's autobiography, the performance uses my dress to reflect my "I" in the poem, but a different poet wears it to symbolize how the poem transcends the author's autobiography. Further expanding on how a poem's persona is more than just its author's, the poems used during the happenings were written by other poets. During 2001-2002, I sent out an open call for poems. Over 100 poets representing 13 countries and about half of the U.S. states responded, mostly through e-mail. I printed out the poems; then, from the print-outs, I cut out sections along the same dimension as a Filipino peso (to reflect the cultural origin of the ritual). During the happenings, audience members pinned my dress with the peso-sized segments that featured the titles and authors of each poem. As wedding souvenirs, they retained the portions of the pages that featured the poems; indeed, I hope that many of the poems written for "Poem Tree" are now hanging against refrigerator doors throughout the Bay Area (CA).

Consequently, "Poem Tree" also integrates the world into its poetic self through the audience's participation. I consider the audience's role to be a metaphor for the kind of proactive engagement that I hope occurs when a reader psychologically invests one's self in the act of reading and experiencing a poem. I believe this interaction is important because I feel that it is the reader (or audience) of the poem, not its author, who finishes or completes the poem.

As with many things I try to do as a poet, "Poem Tree" contains the sub-text of promoting poetry by encouraging people to engage with poetry. In the past, I wrote to friends (and, through this book, make this same suggestion now to you readers): "One pins poems, not just money, on a newly-wed couple's wedding outfits because Poetry, too, is a source of sustenance. If some of your friends get married and their festivities include this rite, you might bring poems to pin on their outfits! Poetry is not just to be read and written but also to be lived!"

SSU Prof. Leny Strobel Dances
With Natalie Concepcion

Bridal Train With Poems
Exhibited at Pusod Gallery

I was delighted to hear almost immediately after first circulating my suggestion that it will be used in a forthcoming wedding. This result, along with others having shared that "Poem Tree" caused them to look at poetry in a new way (or even pay attention to poetry for the first time) reflects my desire to expand poetry's involvement in people's lives. It is part of a cultural activism I practice because, as the Danish poet Paul la Cour once said, "Being a poet is not writing a poem but finding a new way to live."

Relatedly, the interactive aspect of "Poem Tree" also reflects my poetics as one of interconnectedness; I believe in reaching out to others through poems. I would come to be blessed when a poet I met because he shared a poem for "Poem Tree" ended up introducing me to Marsh Hawk Press which published this collection as well as *Reproductions of the Empty Flagpole* (2002). Poetry, too, has taught me just how karmic it is: *when you take care of poetry, poetry will take care of you.*

*****

Poem-Sculpture: "Wine Tasting Notes"

Six Directions also began because I was trying to create a poem in a new way. For years, I had written "abstract" poetry as a way to avoid traditional narrative poems. This relates to how English was used as a colonialist tool in the Philippines; it is a history that has made me reluctant to rely on narrative in my poems because, for me, narrative evoked how English as a communications tool served the expansion of American imperialism in the Philippines.

In 2001, however, I wanted to try something different than abstract poetry, and yet didn't wish to fall back to narrative. This resulted in my creation of about a dozen mixed-media sculptures whose processes engendered verse-poems. Because I consider myself a poet (not a sculptor), this process only worked for me if, ultimately, verse-poems resulted which, when read, could stand on their own as text on page.

Unexpectedly, however, the sculpting process made me focus for the first time on working with physical material. As a writer (working with imagination and words), I experienced a pleasurable frisson in feeling the tangibility of the found materials that made their way into my sculptures (e.g. old coasters, used magazines, ribbons, used cardboard and so on). The sculpting process for Six Directions created a simmer in my belly, similar to the physical effect that I often feel when I can feel myself chasing down a poem into a verse. I, therefore, decided to try my own hand at working as a visual artist. I hadn't planned to go this route, but

Poem-Sculpture: "From The Gray Monster In a Yellow Taxi"

I allowed myself to follow the impulse as I realized that this opening manifested what is also wonderful about all Art and Poetry: how they can lead its maker and viewer/

reader into new experiences.

I began by simply trying to draw. Because I was new at this, I didn't have any drawing-related materials like sketching pads. I began by drawing on what was available to me: brown paper bags that were piling up in my kitchen. I also appreciated the use of the paper bags because they are found objects. As with the found material that comprised my earlier sculptures, the inclusion of found objects symbolize how I integrate (elements of) the world into my work. The paper bags came to form a visual art installation, "The Brown Paper Bag Series," consisting of 19 paper bag drawings hung together as a group (see page 222). The installation also includes a portrait painted of me by Venancio "V.C." Igarta. The painting by the leading artist from the Manong generation served to extend the idea of using a "found" object (it's a portrait of me but not a self-portrait) to symbolize my "I" within the installation that I still considered another way of manifesting a poem.

The Gourd Symbolizing "Filipino Poet"

While serving as visual art, "The Brown Paper Bag Series" are intended to be read against the wall, or viewed from left to right in descending order. When viewed/read in this manner, one can see a narrative emerge that reflects my exploration of identity. By evoking the notion of Filipino *kayumangi* skin, the brown color of the paper bags had caused me to view the installation as a way to explore my identity as a Filipino/a poet. The early drawings show me drawing a circle because it is a simple image. However, as shown in some drawings, I was uneasy with the circle because I related it more to the *enso*, the Japanese word for circle. I didn't yet know what the *enso* had to do with me (except for providing an archetypal image that I love).

Left: Paper Bag Drawing Featuring Gourds; Right: Max Gimblett's "Enso"

Later drawings, however, show the transformation of the circle into an abstracted outline of a vegetable gourd (this abstract icon is essentially a small circle atop a larger circle). The gourd image references a Filipino/Ilokano indigenous myth that describes how the first human came out of a cracked gourd. For me, the gourd image came to symbolize "Filipino/a poet," as reflected in the drawings that conclude the series. It is worth noting, however, that my gourd icon did not erase but only incorporated the reference to the *enso*. This is significant because I believe that the exploration of one's identity or culture is not synonymous with rejecting other cultures.

Creating "The Brown Paper Bag Series" led me to making other drawings where my drawing "mark" is consistently the gourd icon (for instance, if I drew a horizon, I would use tiny gourd images lined up closely together to form a horizontal line). After making about 20 more drawings on more traditional drawing papers, I realized that I had created enough material to form an exhibition. With that in mind, I met with and proposed the idea of a visual poetry exhibit to Joey Ayala, the musician and poet who then was serving as the director of the Pusod Center in Berkeley, CA. Shortly after receiving Ayala's approval, I then began "Poem Tree" by sending out a Call for Poems in anticipation of the happening that would open the exhibition at Pusod Center in 2002.

"The Brown Paper Bag Series" Installation at Pusod Gallery

*****

But as a result of receiving a commitment for an exhibition, I also reconsidered the underlying concepts to Six Directions. I initially planned an exhibit devoted to my poems, drawings and sculptures. But I realized that in order to fully reflect Six Directions' concepts and particularly how I create poems to reach out to others, I should engage with other visual artists. It seemed most apt that a Six Directions exhibit should feature the works of others, just as "Poem Tree" incorporated the works of other poets.

As a result, Six Directions ultimately came to include collaborations with a variety of artists reflecting a wide variety of disciplines. These include the quiltmaker Alice Brody, the painters Patricia Wood and Thomas Fink, poet/installation artist Michelle Bautista who made works in response to some of the sculpted poems in Six Directions; Joey Ayala and Allan Sondheim whose poems were incorporated in some of my drawings and sculptures; Paolo Javier and Jukka-Pekka Kervinen who wrote poems in response to Six Directions' poems and concepts; and Venancio "V.C." Igarta (paintings), Max Gimblett (drawing) and Cal Strobel (photograph) whose works provided visual

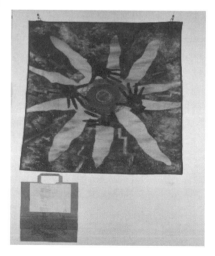

Alice Brody's Quilt Interprets "Wine Tasting Notes," featured as a "Paper Bag Poem"

metaphors for various Six Directions poems.

Of special significance to me was featuring the abstract works of Igarta, the foremost visual artist from the "Manong" generation of Filipinos. (The Manongs were the primarily male immigrants of the early 20th century who left the Philippines to work in the vegetable/fruit fields in Hawai'i and California and/ or the cannery businesses in Alaska.) By presenting the works of a dead artist, Six Directions widened its expanse to incorporate the past, which is to say, history. Indeed, the two works exhibited were abstract paintings by Igarta who is more known for his figurative works. Thus, the exhibit allowed me to continue practicing cultural activism by recovering the reputation of this artist who is mostly unknown today, as well as

Patricia Wood's Paintings Interpreting "From A Gray Monster In a Yellow Taxi"

to focus specifically on the abstract works that he felt had been slighted by those who did know him.

Six Directions' collaborators also include those who participated in the happenings, such as a diverse set of musicians: the bands Mango Kingz (who performed at the opening of a March 2002 Six Directions exhibit at Sonoma Student Union Intercultural Center Gallery), the Dynamic SPAMSilog who performed at the opening of the Pusod Center exhibition and poet Annabelle Udo who performed drumming music for the "Poem Tree" performance during *Interlope 8*'s launch. Other collaborators were the following poets who, in the primary wedding happening that occurred at Pusod, read poems (including love poems, of course) or participated in the event through the following roles (see page 14 for group photo):

Bride: Barbara Jane Reyes
Wedding Minister: Oscar Penaranda
Best Man: Tony Robles
Second Bride: Dori Caminong
Wedding Sponsor: Michelle Bautista
Reception music provider (through the ukulele): Catalina Cariaga
Mr/s Poetry (Groom Stand-in for purpose of cutting the cake): Jaime Jacinto

It was most meaningful to me that other poets supported Six Directions, in order to reflect the community and literary tradition that a person joins when one chooses to be a poet. The participation of other poets in the Six Directions happenings is similar to how verse-poems can reference other poets' works. This is one of the paradoxes of Poetry: that the poem is written in isolation and yet may be birthed through a community that occurs from the history of poems.

Cultural activist Dori Caminong served an important purpose for acting as a second bride during the opening of the Pusod exhibition. Caminong wore the original wedding dress of Malou Babilonia, the founder of the nonprofit Babilonia Wilner

Foundation (BWF) whose activities include Pusod. During the Pusod happening, audience participants were asked to pin actual money as well as poems onto the dresses of the two brides; all monies raised then were donated to BWF in order to aid its activities that include cleaning up the environment. This aspect enabled an extension of the Six Directions concept that Poetry feeds the world by, indeed, bringing very tangible benefits (money) back to the "world" as physically manifested by planet Earth itself.

At Pusod, I turned its gallery into a virtual "womb of Poetry." I wanted all aspects to reflect the Six Directions concepts and that each visitor would be moved, after experiencing the exhibit, to consider Poetry in a new, or renewed, way. Even the traditional guest book during the exhibition was replaced by a guest book designed for an actual marriage. In the guest book, visitors not only signed their names but were encouraged to write out their wishes for this person who bore my name and who is marrying someone named "Mr/s Poetry."

The resulting comments in the guest book ranged from traditional best wishes to the ribald to the dubious to the comic. Comments were not limited to those who physically visited the exhibit, but also included e-mailed commentaries to symbolize how the four-wall constraints of a gallery do not limit the reach and span of Six Directions. Some selected commentaries in the guest book from other poets include:

Paolo Javier Installation of his "I Sculpt" Poem Which Re-envisions "The Erotic Angel"

"Congratulations to Eileen Tabios on her marriage to Poetry, the many-tentacled figure and wandering spirit." – John Yau

"Congrats, many happy returns, I'm sure it'll be a long beautiful struggle." —Del Ray Cross

"STOP THE WEDDING. SHE'S MINE! FUCK POETRY! THAT BRIDE'S ALL MINE!" —Alfred Yuson

"Does Mr. Poetry look like Franz Kafka or Nicholas Cage? If like Kafka, I send my blessings!" —Nick Carbo

"My dearest Eileen. Are you sure you want to go through with this? All of your aunties are whispering, but I'm the only one brave enough to say this—we all know Poetry is a cheat and a drunk. What if Poetry makes your life miserable? What about marrying a nice Encyclopedia? A Best Selling Novel? I know, you're young—when I was your age, I thought I knew what I wanted too. Remember you can always divorce the bastard and get half of the stanzas. Love from your Aunt Denise." — Denise Duhamel

"Where are we going for the honeymoon?" — Tony Robles

***

Poet Drawing Away Bridal Train To Reveal Jukka-Pekka Kervinen's Poems

It is also worth offering more descriptions of the poems created by Javier and Kervinen. Javier took my one-page Six Directions poem "The Erotic Angel" and used it as a springboard to a new 30-page poem entitled "I Sculpt." Javier not only wrote text but designed his poem's length so that it would hang as an installation. The concept of hanging a poem against the wall, as visual art and not just text that one reads, manifests one of my original Six Directions goals of creating physicality or a "body" to a poem.

Kervinen wrote his poems, "#290" and "#291," based on one of the press releases about Six Directions. But Kervinen also relied on a computer program to generate the text of his poems. Consequently, Kervinen extended Six Directions' goal of featuring the multidimensionality or expansiveness of the poem to incorporate latest developments in technology.

In addition, Kervinen's poems were hung on a brown paper bag that was partly covered by another site-specific installation, "Bridal Train With Poems" created in collaboration with Bautista. Bautista conceived of hanging my 12-foot wedding train and then pinning on it either money or print-outs of various poems sent by the more than 100 poets who participated in the "Poem Tree" sculpture. A placard next to the train suggested that viewers can unpin poems they like to bring home for their reading pleasure, as well as pin their own poems on the train — an interaction that again extends Six Directions' desire to integrate the world into a poem(-sculpture).

Just as "Bridal Train With Poems" is meant to be an interactive piece, so is the work that presents Kervinen's poems. That is, in order to view Kervinen's poems, the viewers must move aside the train that partly obstructs the view of Kervinen's poems. The enforced physical engagement of the viewers reflects the notion that a reader of a poem must actively participate in its experience (instead of passive reading).

Poet Catalina Cariaga would come to describe Six Directions as a "pinakbet" (Filipino stew) type of event, where all sorts of elements were thrown into the stew that is the poem. This was exactly my goal: to bring in as many ingredients from the world into the Six Directions project which, as a poem itself, was something I conceived for engendering a space of pleasurable, meaningful experience. I conclude now with a poem entitled "M. Poetree" by Joey Ayala who shared it as his wedding present for my marriage to "Mr/s Poetry." I integrated his poem into a paper bag-based sculpture, "Poem = Gift," that I structured to look like a gift bag from a wine-related store. I created "Poem = Gift" because the poem is always a gift to be toasted, and shared with all:

M. POETREE
by Jose "Joey" Ayala

May your lives orbit
in far off yet attainable
collisions, collusions
and comet-tailed conclusions
connecting dots
taking shapes
filling blanks
and signing names
to family upon family
of exposed nerve
and pleasure
a multitude
of comings and goings
punctuated deftly
with pregnant ellipses
intimate turns
and phrase

Phrase the Lord!

Poem = Gift

"POEMS FORM/FROM THE SIX DIRECTIONS"

Poet Nick Carbo conducted an interview with Eileen Tabios about her exhibition at the Babilonia Wilner Foundation's Pusod Center. The following are excerpts from their discussions:

What's the relationship of Six Directions to how you also call this work a "postcolonial Filipino poetics" project?

I feel that multidimensionality is relevant to my position as a Filipino in the diaspora. I am someone forced to find "Home" beyond the border of the Philippines as well as someone for whom "Philippines" has become a state of mind rather than the actual country that exists today, given the many upheavals that have taken place since my childhood there in the 1960s. So, in defining "Home," I choose now to integrate ALL of the world into myself. For instance, I relate to a Native American concept (rather than an indigenous Filipino concept) to title this series. The title is appropriate because, as a diasporic Filipino, I wish to be open to all cultures. Well, and I believe a poet should be open, in any event, to all possibilities of human life.

I notice that none of your sculptures are large.

The more intimate scale is part of the work. I wished to reflect multidimensionality through how I sculpturally integrate the viewer/reader into the object/poem. The works need to be handled physically in order to be perceived — whether it's through flipping up the pages in "Bryant Park," leafing through the newspaper in "Page 3," uncovering and opening envelopes within "The World Is Yours," or unwinding the ribbon that ties together the scroll in "From the Gray Monster in a Yellow Taxi." By integrating the viewer/reader within the space of the Poem-sculpture, this subverts the passive reading of a poem on the page where an inattentive reader need not get fully involved. Or where some poems, I feel, spoonfeed their meanings to the readers without leaving more spaces for the readers' imaginations, thus, heightening the readers' involvements.

The viewer's tactile involvement also subverts the notion of not touching objects of "fine art." I believe Art transcends the museum — just as, in my mind, poetry and literature transcend what are included in (the museums of) literary canons.

You have said that you also tried to integrate the viewer into some versions of "Dear One" through the viewer's reflection in the sheen of the book covers.

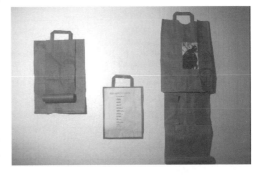

Poem-Sculpture: "For Charles Henri Ford"

Yes, and it's the same reason why I hung the scrolls in front of each other in "For Charles Henri Ford." The way they're hung, you have to lift up the top and then the middle scroll in order to see all of its contents.

So it's an interactive approach. You didn't just want to create multidimensional poems but you wished for the reader/viewer to move between those dimensions?

Yes, because I wanted to challenge the reader/viewer as I had challenged myself. I also thought of sculpting poems because I thought its process — dealing with materiality of objects — is different from relying on personal narrative to create a poem. I appreciate narrative poetry written by other poets. But I am uncomfortable with relying on traditional narrative due to the history of English for Filipinos. As you know, the spread of English was used to solidify the U.S. colonization of the Philippines after the Philippine-American War over a century ago. So narrative, to me, reflects the imperialist way English was utilized to become the mode for communication.

I notice you used found material and collage in these sculpted poems.

I do so to integrate my environment — the outside world — into the world of my poems. Again, it partly reflects my location in the Filipino diaspora. I don't use found material and collage in an attempt to get away from my "I," as has been ascribed to this method. I do it from a more spiritual basis that may be encapsulated by the Buddhist concept of "All is One, One is All."

In fact, I used a "found" page with which I created "Dear One," the first work in this series. I made "Dear One" after I noticed a blank empty white square in the middle of an advertisement in a magazine. I began that work by trying to fill in the empty square with words that would reflect the poignancy of the images surrounding the white square. I xeroxed it 20 times, which meant to me that I had to write 20 stanzas. Because that advertisement was in *Town & Country*, I leafed through that magazine to find text I could use for writing the verse.

From my work on "Dear One," I began other sculptures where the intent was partly to use words to fill in what seemed to be blank or almost-blank spaces that approximate pages in various images I would come across while reading magazines and newspaper. For example, "Bryant Park" was inspired by the reproduction of "Live It Up In Lilac," a 1967 sculpture by John McCracken. Made of polyester resin, fiberglass, plywood, it's a rectangular piece featured as it leans against the wall. Its reproduction in the *New Art Examiner* (July/August 2001) shows it to be a white slab. So, just as I wanted to put text in the white square of "Dear One," I thought to write a poem by envisioning text written at the bottom of the sculpture. The poem is comprised of mostly alternating one or two-word lines because I thought of writing a poem by emblazoning text that would fit in the bottom of this band of white space; the poem had to be comprised of short lines because I assumed only one or two words would fit in that space. Similarly, "Page 3" began through the blank space within a Tiffany advertisement that I considered ironic given its juxtaposition next to an article about abused women in Cambodia. In these

Poem-Sculpture: "At Bryant Park: Perfect Form"

works, the visual image of a blank space (or blank page) engendered my writing/sculpting of the poems.

Later, I began sculpting poems that were inspired by found text instead of found spaces. "The Erotic Angel" was inspired by text in Rafael Alberti's poetry collection *Concerning The Angels;* "For Charles Henri Ford" by Ford's poetry collection *Labyrinths;* "Material Integrity" by text within *American Artists In Their New York Studios* by Stephen Gotz; and "The Gray Monster In A Yellow Taxi" by *Rain Taxi* magazine. "The World Is Yours" and "Dear Daddy" were inspired by text in *The New York Times.* The change in the process seemed to be the turning of a circle to complete itself: that is, image begets text begets image. I welcomed this development as a circle's depiction of unity resonated in terms of my desire to integrate the world into my poet-self.

Did you also collage found text within the verse-poems?

I used found text, but not always by quoting them. Between my discovery of the text and my writing down the words in the verse-poem, I may adjust the words — this is deliberate, not just for editing the text to be more effective but because I may be bringing in the world but I'm not trying to deny my own existence. My disinterest in originality due to English's colonial history is not the same as wanting to erase myself.

I think I see your point reflected in your "Artist Statement" in the 10th drawing: where you say the phrases "I am a media artist because I use the authority of editing" and "I would rehash it and spit it out."

Yes, the former relates to a statement by Robert Longo and the latter to Cindy Sherman, from their printed interviews in *Art Talk: The Early 80s* edited by Jeanne Siegel. Both artists have been charged with "appropriating" material but that would be a simplistic assessment of their processes.

I appreciate your point on the death of the author. Didn't you reflect that concern in your poem "I Do" (see the section "I. ENGLISH: THE COURTSHIP")? By emphasizing that you do speak English, you wrote a rallying call to Filipino poets in the 21st Century to "colonize" English by writing well.

Writing well is the best revenge for any Filipino English-language writer interested in exploring the implications of (post)colonialism.

Are you happy with these sculptures, given that they are your first efforts as a visual artist?

I've previously attempted paintings and drawing, so this series is not my first attempt at visual art. Nonetheless, I don't concern myself with others' judgments on whether these works are Art, or whether the verses succeed as poems. Though I work as hard as I can to create good work, the subsequent judgment of others is not my key interest. For me to be concerned about whether they pass someone else's judgment relates to a larger disease, and I'm not interested in being infected. That is, I don't create poems to please anyone. I come to and from this position as a Filipino (given our history of being invaded or colonized and then being discriminated within the diaspora), as an ethnic-American artist in this country whose canons have not been immune from racism, and as a poet who believes that art-making is about something else beyond pleasing someone. To please someone else is a form of assimilation, isn't it?

What about the verse version of the poems?

Some are more effective than others. But it is always the case with a group of works that some may be more effective than others. As a series, the works satisfy me enough for me to release for public viewing. I feel I am dealing with another larger topic than whether any of my particular works are great. Art is also a process.

Having said that, I then decided to take what I thought were the weakest sculpture and weakest poem in the first ten works that I made in this series. For sculptures, this was "Wine Tasting Notes" and, among the verses, this was "The Erotic Angel." Rather than trying to improve them on my own, I invited Alice Brody to create a quilt based on the former and asked poet Paolo Javier to write a new or edited poem based on the latter. My invitations offered another way to involve others—which was another way to bring the world into that poem. I deliberately chose a quilt-maker instead of, say, a painter to reflect my interest in subverting notions of privilege in art; a quilt may be considered a "craft" rather than "fine art" in some circles. I asked for help from another poet to reflect my offering of a relationship—a "community." To me, the search for community in the diaspora is a moving concept, as much as it can be a painful reality. As so many artists before me have said, all of our efforts are also always about Identity.

The poems seem abstract in terms of their open-ended meanings, as in "Dear One" or "The World Is Yours."

In my mind, my most effective poetic series prior to this work was a series of abstract prose poems. I am sure my affinity for abstraction relates to my love of abstract painting. For me, abstractions are intriguing because of how they open up to a variety of interpretation. Abstraction, too, may relate to the mystery which infuses poems. For that reason, I feel that "The Erotic Angel," by being so explicit and, thus, possibly limiting interpretative possibilities, is the weakest verse-poem. ("The Erotic Angel" is not featured in this book as it requires more time to grow before publication.)

The poems' meanings are ultimately the reader's privilege. I will say, though, that in addition to exploring the subtleties of a rhyming sound, such as in "Dear One," I also was playing with energy—such as the energy I love in an abstract expressionist brushstroke. I tried to evoke that energy in terms of the unfolding of "The World is Yours." That energy is meaningful, but transcends the fixity of narrative (conclusions).

What's the significance of your drawings of a tiny truck?

I drew a toy garbage truck that happens to sit in front of my computer. Since I spend most of my waking hours in front of a computer, I suppose that image has embedded itself into my brain. But I actually think that it's appropriate for this work. Certainly, the recyling of found material into "Art" objects may lead one to consider—or led me to consider—the nature of how society defines "trash" and how we make decisions to discard. Metaphorically, this question relates to how we discard people as much as we discard objects. For a Filipino who's quite aware that economic privations have caused people to be treated as disposable commodities—such as children to prostitution and women to economically-based marriages—my considerations of the garbage question is very much part of the research I underwent for this series.

230

Do you think some Filipinos would have problems with your use of a garbage truck or a mundane material like a used brown paper bag to denote the Filipino?

Detail from "The Brown Paper Bag Series"

My incorporating the references into drawings, into art works, into works that are actually being hung in an art gallery — ultimately into what I am calling "poems" — reflects my intention to say that Filipinos are beautiful. Or that Filipinos create beauty from, and despite, adversity.

In any event, I also intended this project to question conventional notions of Beauty. Just like judgments on the quality of the Poem — or what constitutes literature — has caused the exclusion of our works from certain literary canons, notions of Beauty can be discriminatory. Brown denotes the *kayumangi* skin of the indigenous Filipino which, as you know, became ill-favored with the advent of Spanish and then American colonialism. As a young girl growing up in the Philippines, I recall neighborhood toughs cat-calling to me, "White Legs! White Legs!" They intended the reference to the paleness of my legs to be a compliment -- obviously, their attitude is a vestige of colonialism.

As Filipinos whose history includes much discrimination, we certainly should be interested politically — as well as aesthetically (to the extent one separates the political from the aesthetic) — In opening up categories that lend themselves to discriminatory practices.

The brown paper bag works feature 19 drawings. I notice that the garbage truck is depicted in the first ten drawings, but not in the second set of nine drawings.

I made drawings in a series of ten each because the number ten relates to perfection. The truck appears in the first ten drawings to illustrate me as I began my explorations. I remember a conversation with surrealist poet Philip Lamantia shortly after finishing the first five drawings. I told him that I was baffled at doing drawings as "I can't draw a straight line to save my life." Philip replied, "Then draw a curved line!" before giving me a copy of his 1970 book *The Blood of the Air*, a poetry collection that also features four of his drawings. With his encouragement,

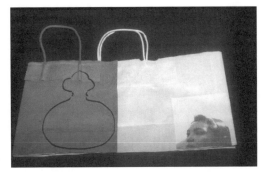

Reverse of Detail from "The Brown Paper Bag Series"

I returned home and continued drawing. I incorporate Philip's suggestion in Drawing #6 through a note on the lower left hand corner quoting from that conversation.

Bearing in mind what Philip said about the "curved line," I started drawing

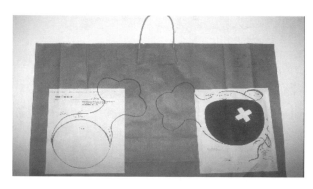

Detail from "The Brown Paper Bag Series"

circles. At the time, I was sensitive to circles because it is one of the motifs used by Max Gimblett, an artist with whom I was—and still am—collaborating. In fact, that's why I decided to include Max's work when I wanted to include guest artists in the exhibit. I feel that Max's paintings that incorporate alchemical materials and archetypal references visually manifest much of what I hope to write through poems.

Our aesthetic closeness relates to the drawing I made where I show two reproductions of his ensos integrated within my gourd images.

Shortly after finishing the tenth drawing, I met the Filipino poet and Taoist shaman Rene Navarro. He was visiting San Francisco and took me out to dinner. I mentioned the work I was doing—including my attempts to draw the enso. Noting my use of the Japanese word for circle, he suggested that I research my own Filipino (indigenous, pre-colonial) roots for archetypes. For instance, Rene suggested, the gourd. And he showed me a gourd that was hanging from his backpack. In fact, he mentioned some Filipino creation myth about how the first human came out from a gourd after it split in half. It's his gourd whose image I've been drawing.

Thus, as of the eleventh drawing, I started drawing the gourd instead of the garbage truck icon. Some of the drawings depict the circle being transformed into the outline of the gourd.

I also noticed that you stopped relying only on the brown paper bag after the tenth drawing.

I had been using only the brown paper bag to offer a monochromatic surface—but also to relate to the brown kayumangi skin of a Filipino. Since I considered the transformation of my symbol to the gourd to be

Detail from "The Brown Paper Bag Series"

a revelation, I then began to incorporate color. So the eleventh drawing utilizes a paper bag with gold stripes; gold, according to Buddhists, is the color of consciousness. The 12th drawing features the bright red of a Gumps shopping bag; I allowed the Gumps name to be featured so as to maintain the theme of integrating the world through found references. The 13th drawing incorporates a sparkling green shopping bag that had been used to carry a present given me by the Filipino novelist/poet Bino A. Realuyo. That green bag also is emblazoned with "Merry Christmas," a tradition introduced to the Philippines by the Catholic Spaniards. So, there's another layer of Filipinizing the Spanish reference by overlaying the Christmas references with the gourd which I intend to be a Filipino-based archetype.

232

The drawings beginning with the eleventh one definitely reflect the transformations within and evolution of your search. The 14th drawing shows a distorted image of your face looking at the garbage truck while the other side of the bag features a nondistorted image looking at the gourd.

Yes, the 14th drawing uses a found paper bag from a store called "American Pie." So, on the side featuring the words "American Pie"—which obviously hearkens the phrase "as American as apple pie"—my face is distorted because assimilation is also a distortion. The definition of "American" is even one that is in flux, isn't it? The distorted face, by the way, was just a mistake when I was xeroxing my photo; I didn't anticipate that I would come to be able to use this erroneous copy but, as I said, the unfolding of this series has developed without much conscious prior intent on my part. There are tons of synchronicities in this project. (See p. 231 for illustration.)

After your dinner with Rene who became incommunicado for a while as he traveled around the world, you said you couldn't find any references to the gourd-related myth in your subsequent research. Did that affect your perspective, given how you'd assumed the gourd was an archetype rooted in Filipino indigenous culture. Did you think that you had to change your symbol?

No. Because—and this relates, too, to my position of being a Filipino in the diaspora—authenticity is also choosing. If the gourd had no prior significance within Filipino culture, then I decided to choose to make the gourd Filipino. Being open to all of the world's cultures is, for me, "Filipinizing" the world in the sense that the "I" accepting other cultures still maintains her identity as "Filipino." Choice—freedom—is also an issue for which Filipinos have spilled blood.

"Authenticity equals choosing" is a line from your tenth drawing that incorporates your "Artist Statement."

Yes, thank you for reminding me. That "Artist Statement" is certainly an accurate reflection of my thinking at the time of making that drawing. But it is comprised of excerpts from statements made by 25 contemporary artists whose interviews are featured in *Art Talk: The Early 80s.* "Authenticity equals choosing" was stated by John Baldessari; here's an excerpt from his interview: "There's a very strong theme that seems to occur in my work and it was in some early works called 'choosing,' which is the idea of choice and I remember back at that time—this was the period of Minimalism and Conceptualism—and I was trying to strip away all of my aesthetic beliefs and trying to get to some bedrock ideas I had about art—what did I really think art was essentially? And one of the things that in this reductivist attitude I arrived at, was the 'choice'—that seems to be a fundamental issue of art. We say this color over that or this subject over that or this material over that. And there, of course, comes in another theme of mine about is there some sort of dichotomy between art and life at all and investigating that. Because in the old existentialist idea, choice-making may be fundamental to your existence and making life authentic."

By the way, I only count 19 drawings in the paper-bag series. Where's the 20th drawing, or the tenth drawing of your set of gourds?

The 20th drawing is deliberately invisible—or intangible like the poetry be-

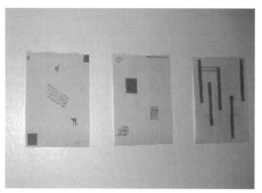

Drawings Utilizing the Gourd Image

tween words. As intangible as American modernist and Filipino poet Jose Garcia Villa's poem entitled "The Emperor's New Clothes" featured in his now out-of-print book *Volume II*; you might recall that he placed the title in the Table of Contents but there was no associated poem within the book. Mr. Villa, as you know, was a poet also inspired by the visual arts.

Additionally, the 20th drawing does not exist as a drawing because I consider it to be an invisible metaphor for a doorway into a whole new set of experiences following the journey undergone by my creation of the prior 19 drawings.

Your more recent drawings seem to be individual works instead of being parts of a series.

At some point, I began to appreciate drawing based on its own nature, not as a means to something else—such as writing a poem. Drawing just to draw. That's when I began to make the larger works. In fact, these individual works began when I made "Predominantly Blue (I)" which was a ten-drawing set that was the first to utilize colored ink. That series failed. I decided to make colored drawings as stand-alone works so that I could focus on color, which was then a new element that I was introducing to this series. To be conscious of making a series is a consideration that I felt was distracting me from relating to color. With hindsight, this all seems fitting to me: by coming to relate to drawing based on drawing's own nature, I took on a more respectful approach. Respect—whether it's for other cultures or for the nature of physical material—is also one of the concepts underlying "Poems Form/From The Six Directions."

Let's discuss the installations.

My first installation idea is entitled "White On White On White." The title references a common theme within art history of artists making variations off that concept—artists like Robert Rauschenberg, Robert Ryman, Kasimir Malevich and so on. My initial thought was to pile mounds of rice and salt against a corner of the room. Dotting them would be sculptures made from the top parts of white bags emblazoned with the gourd logo, such as the work that makes up my eighteenth drawing in the "Resource Recovery" series.

Obviously, the use of rice and salt is meaningful. Rice is a staple in the Filipino diet. Salt reflects the opposite of sweetness, which resonates given the Philippines' troubled history. I also liked the idea of Filipinizing the color white to reflect a reversal of the Caucasian-izing role

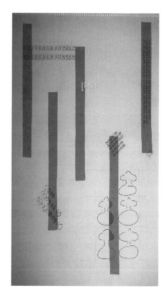

Drawing Utilizing the Gourd Image

234

of Spanish and American colonizers.

But I subsequently decided to make the installation by piling the bags of rice and salt against a corner of the room, instead of undoing them and heaping the contents. The result may not be as pleasing in a formal sense; I had liked anticipating the image of white paper-bag sculptures inset within mounds of white rice and white salt—all set up against white walls. But keeping the bags closed makes the material available later for someone's use. I didn't wish to sacrifice the material's potential as food for "fine art.'

Synchronistically, my decision to keep the bags closed allowed me to manifest another concept for the installation entitled "Brown On Brown On Brown," After conceiving of "White On White On White," I thought I should do a similar installation utilizing brown paper bags against brown sugar. I like this concept for denoting the "sweetness" of the Filipino *kayumangi* color. But I had wondered how to implement it within an exhibit as I thought the gallery might have problems with ants and other elements attracted to the sugar. Well, keeping the containers of sugar closed addressed this problem. Thus, my earlier decision in "White On White On White" not to compromise the basic food aspect of the material enabled me to create this second installation. The way I look at the result, honor and respect (through the first installation) generated its own rewards (the enabling of the second installation).

After I determined how to create "Brown On Brown On Brown," I created two "portals" made up of paper bags, one white and the other brown, covering Styrofoam packing blocks. I emblazoned the resulting portals with flyers and postcards referencing my past poetry readings and related activities. I then placed the portals—which denote entryway—before the mound of brown sugar and brown paper bag cut-outs. Atop the portals, I also placed two computer-speakers from an old computer I replaced during this period. The intent was to emphasize—to state emphatically—if the viewer entered through the portals, they would encounter someone who is "Brown On Brown on Brown" and a Poet. As a poet, I obviously use the computer for writing my words. The work also allowed me to find a new use for the Styrofoam and broken computer equipment—as in "resource recovery."

The third installation, "Brown And White," had a synchronistic beginning. I earlier had told a friend in New York about my first sculpture, "Dear One." I said that I'd make a version for her if she sent me shopping bags. So she sent me six bags. But she had cosseted them within Styrofoam pellets in a large brown box. The packaging was overkill. I was struck by the irony of her sending used paper bags (detritus) within a packaging that utilized non-recyclable Styrofoam. She was being thoughtful but it clearly was a waste of resources. So, to transcend the irony, I converted the packaging of brown box with white pellets to house both brown and white paper-bag handles with my gourd logos on them. Thus, the work became a way to unify the first two installations' concepts. Hence, white and brown unite. I liked this healing approach.

What's the background to that wall-hanging, "Poem Tree (II)"?

My parents, bless their heart, had blown up one of my wedding photos. In their home, they put a gilt frame around it and hung it up in their living room. They gave another copy to me and Tom, my husband. But we never hung the photo which has lain hidden in a drawer all these years. So, I decided to "recycle" it into an image depicting me marrying Mr/s Poetry. "Mr/s Poetry" is denoted by the gourd mark on a tiny piece of brown paper that I superimposed over Tom's face.

Did your husband mind?

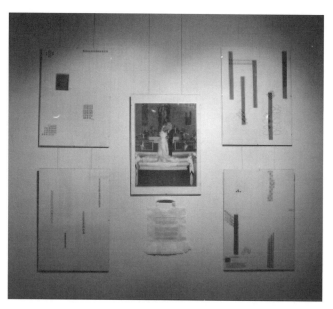

"Poem Tree (II)" Surrounded By
Four Drawings

He considered the act just another of my crazy artistic acts and claimed not to take it personally. Nonetheless, I didn't want to insult him—something that I thought I would be doing if I permanently defaced his face on the photo. It took me a few days to figure out how to avoid marking up his face permanently—It was such a tortuous mental process that, at one point, I tried to convince myself that I actually should deface his face. To make my marriage to Poetry authentic and reflective of its required commitment.

But after thinking about it for days, I decided that I couldn't deface his face permanently. Because to do so would be privileging art over real life (to the extent one can separate the two). It's akin to how I was reluctant to dirty the rice in the "White On White On White" installation for the sake of "fine art" when it literally can feed someone else later. Eventually, and to my relief, I thought up the idea of putting saran wrap over the photo before doing anything to the photo. So, the gourd image is superimposed over Tom's face but I can always dismantle that later simply by taking off the saran wrap.

How did you think of using the saran wrap?

Synchronicity. I had run out of saran wrap. And when I went to the grocery store, I noticed that they had a version wider than what I usually use—and wide enough to encase the photo. I recently told a friend that I live my life by connecting the dots of synchronicity.

You're a poet. How did you come to think of doing a gallery exhibit?

After finishing the first ten objects in this series, I wanted to exhibit them because the notion of exhibiting poems is transgressive and expansive at the same time. It is transgressive through how these objects claim to be bodies of poems; it is expansive in manifesting my view that poems are not just words on the page and, thus, can be interacted with in the physical world. It is also transgressive in crossing the boundaries (that really shouldn't exist) between poetry and the visual arts.

I was interested in the Babilonia Wilner Foundation (BWF) specifically because it is not part of the commercial art gallery system. It is an important synchronicity to me that BWF's primary concerns are not just fine art but the economic, cultural and ecological conditions around the world; its programs have facilitated education about

236

Installation Shot at Pusod Gallery Exhibit

pollution surrounding military bases, illegal dumpsites contaminating water and deforestation issues. Their work on the environment and promotion of recyling seem to relate to the garbage truck symbol with which this series began. One of its programs, PUSOD (a Tagalog word for "navel") is also directly concerned with supporting Filipino arts.

My choice to exhibit at a place like BWF's galleries says something about the shortcomings of the commercial art gallery system in which art is often categorized to be objects that sell. Such shortcomings, to me, relate to the narrow-minded conceptions of poetry as well as the position of ethnic-American artists and writers within the dominant canons.

I first came to BWF's attention through the works I've done as a poet. So, poetry, too, has led me to this visual art exhibition. This all makes sense: I feel that Poetry takes care of me.

The materials are found paper bags, glue and newspapers which you don't really protect. They may not last.

That point gets back to categories and how I wish to transcend such categorization of art. Even if the sculptures or drawings don't last as material, the verses can last through the written or spoken word. Nonetheless, the archival fragility of the material relate to the fragility of art because the art experience is dependent on psychology and memory as much as its materiality. As an example, and as you know, the poems of Jose Garcia Villa had lapsed into obscurity prior to my editing a recovery volume of his works, *The Anchored Angel* (Kaya, 2000).

With this series, I was not as concerned with making an object that lasts — that's more of a collector's perspective that I did not wish to consider as I underwent this project's process. I was concerned with the intangible versus the tangible, such as the poetry that is in-between words as well as that which the physical object approximates. I say "approximates" because, despite my initial interest in sculpting a physical body for the poem, how can I succeed 100% when poetry is between words as much as it is comprised of words? I am concerned with the beauty of the intangible. One might call this element transcending physicality to be Soul.

"Six Directions"
A Poetics Via E-Mail

Subj: Poems From/Form The Six Directions
Date: 7/19/01 10:29:09 AM Pacific Daylight Time
From: Eileen Tabios
To: Paolo Javier

Dear One—

    I address you as such because "Dear One" is the title of my first poem-sculpture. I use sculpture in the sense of its dimensionality (relative, say, to the painting). I would describe this new series for me as a break-through series, something I'd been searching for over the past three years—I call the series "Poems From/Form The Six Directions," referring to the Native American concept of total and wholesome multidimensionality (that the world is not just north, south, east, west but also up and down).

    Anyway, these poem sculptures integrate everything that have been concerning me about poems—ever since I realized that poems go beyond the page and are *lives* on their own. For some time now, I've been struggling with writing poems; I've felt that some remain "flat" and, thus, seem so small: many remain simply words on the page. With these poem-sculptures, everything seems to come together; I think I can best explain it by describing my first poem-sculpture that I finished yesterday. It only took me 1-2 days to write the poem and create the sculpture (though the two days were obviously a culmination of my thinking for the past number of years). For the two-day period, I felt like I was in a dream-- that my acts (both writing and the physical making of it) were dictated to me by a larger force. Indeed, I was but a medium for that poem. This feeling, I've learned with anguish, doesn't come often—when it comes, it's a gift. Undoubtedly, I was spoiled because for some reason, during my first two years of writing poetry (and primarily the prose poems), I (with hindsight) estimate that I was in the zone of that feeling for perhaps 85% of my work. 85% is huge. More recently, for every poem for which I knew I was immersed in that poetic space by a Muse outside of myself, I'd write tens of poems where I feel I wasn't in that desired zone (and the resulting poems were more flat than I wished).

Some of the Paper Bag Sculptures that Manifest the Poem "Dear One"

"Dear One" began when I had finished writing a poem that was okay but, again, like many I'd written in the past couple of years was only okay. So, whilst on a break, I was leafing through an old copy of Town & Country that was littering the floor in my studio. I came upon an ad—I don't know what it was advertising as it seemed to be a two or three page ad and this page was all visual (no text). It was a haunting image: the corner of a room, a dark-burgundy wall, a white/cream limestone fireplace with a Greek-looking marble bust and a brass statue of horses and riders atop the fireplace mantel. A small empty table stood in front of the fireplace but the room otherwise seemed empty of contents (like other furniture and signs of living). The left foreground was marked by a white empty square, a presence even more dramatic based on how the whiteness contrasted with the luxurious colors of the reddish wall, the creaminess of the limestone and the dark-gold burnished tone to the wooden floor.

I looked at that empty square in the middle of the page and it seemed to beg me to fill it with text—that it was an empty page upon which I can inscribe poems. So I Xeroxed the page; in black-and-white the image became even more haunting, the square even more empty and pleading for a poem. I Xeroxed a whole bunch of these pages, with the idea of writing a stanza per page. I Xeroxed 20 pages, which meant I had to write 20 stanzas.

Given the size of the square, the stanzas couldn't be long. I decided to write mostly couplets and then recalled the koan-couplets that John Yau was writing with an artist-friend (Max Gimblett, whose exhibit I'd reviewed earlier this year). I decided to try to evoke the mysterious quality of a koan to match the mystery of the image.

To write the couplets or stanzas, I began to leaf through *Town & Country* for narrative contents. So that, ultimately, every one of the stanzas was dictated to me by a page from the magazine. I didn't just collage "found" phrases; I would use the phrases as a stepping-stone to the actual stanza (so there was some editing/personalization in the diction during the first writing process). And here's what was also wondrous about the process—though I was relying on found material, there seemed some simmering sound that I could hear as well as physically feel in my belly. The sound is hard to describe; it's a sound that I hear even now as I type up this missive to you—it's a sound of solitude, emptiness and it is simply the faint buzzing/humming of my computer (or is it the radiator). It's a sound that I live with most days as I spend most of my days in isolation in the writing studio, working at a computer. I say it's a sound of solitude but I seemed to ascribe to it the sound of emptiness that I was seeing in the magazine image.

And this sound was guiding me somehow, so that as I would write out couplets or stanzas I was also attuned to forming words to a certain poetic rhythm (most of the stanzas would come to remain as their final form; they seemed to come out whole). So that the words weren't just collaged together arbitrarily because, together, they were creating a poetic musical score with an underlying harmony (or so I feel). It reminds me of how Max once described his brushstrokes as needing to be final on that first stroke ("one bone stroke" he calls it—or is it "one stroke bone"... anyway).

Each stanza resonated against the Xeroxed image, making the experience of reading the poem more layered than if you were simply to read it as verse against white page. And yet, I feel the poem works on its own, too—that is, without the visual aid (which is how I wish all of these poem-sculptures to work). That is, they were "sculpted" instead of written but should also work as pure text.

The approach is the integral one I've been looking for—and truly didn't know how much I've been longing for until, finally, I felt the "epiphany" of finishing the first poem-sculpture (I'm in the midst of the second one as I write this). The approach reflects two major concerns for my poetry: (i) my (political) notions on the English language (the disinterest in originality as a Filipino given English's colonial history [in the Philippines]); and (ii) the influence of the visual arts (even as such integration would not be visible to the reader/viewer). [...]

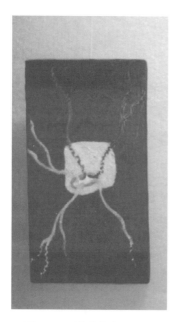

Thomas Fink Interprets
"Dear One"
With A Painting

After finishing "Dear One" and reflecting on it, it seems to me that the creative process integrated most of the senses — sight, sound, touch (I have to work harder in the future to integrate taste and scent). And it integrated the world into my self — not just in terms of how the insides of my belly simmered. I view the reliance on found material not to be an attempt to get away from the self so much as an overt way of integrating the external environment within the me that is the poem's source (hence the 6 directions [as the collage of found material goes into as well as out of]). [...]

But while the poem-sculptures integrate my concerns, it is equally important that, notwithstanding my subjectivity, the Poem also took over — something that I know happened when I felt tipped into that "space" or zone where I was (and wanted to be) helpless before the Poem's unfolding. As I said, during the one-and-a-half days of writing/sculpting this poem, I felt like I was in a dream being guided on my actions and thoughts.

After finishing the poem, I had a black-and-white chapbook of text and image forming the poem. This inside content could be replicated cheaply via xerox machine — so that I thought one could do it (sort of like a multiple edition) and, say, just create individual covers so that each cover is different. My first cover, which works nicely against the grainy black-and-white surfaces is a small glossy red shopping bag with sparkling tassel-like handles. I cut it and it fits perfectly over the chapbook. I retained the red handles so that you could carry the "book" around. So that it's become bag, book, poem — and yet transcends those categories to become a sculpture.

At first, I thought one could commission other artists to do custom-made covers. One could still do that, of course. But I decided that I had to be the one to make the covers, too, because if I abdicated that role, then I would be treating the work like a book instead of as a sculpture. And part of the goal here had been to make the poem leap off the page (and I associate "page" with "book" — the "sculpture," after all, is meaningful to me specifically for its dimensionality). Also, I liked the shopping bag cover because it's another "found" material (thereby integrating the world into the poem/sculpture). It, in fact, was a shopping bag that had ended its use and I was about to throw it away. But Beauty's expanse is infinite, isn't it, and so I am glad I was able to recover it into "Art." So that the act of recovery also reflects my underlying poetics of Beauty — and taught me something about how "garbage" can be an arbitrarily subjective judgment without a Platonic basis (hmmm...there is an empty toy garbage truck in front of my computer — its emptiness possibly influenced the poem, too. How do we — society — come to judge something as trash and disposable?).

The front cover is all red gloss and the back cover incorporates a decorated card with my and [husband] Tom's name on it (the bag originally was used to hold party favors) so that the back cover also hints at an element of my life but, because is meaningless to the viewer/reader, just comes to add a touch of mystery — and nostalgia, which is another sense I'd gotten from the magazine image. The type of nostalgia one might sense from an object in an antique store.

And this result — without intention on my part — also reflects some other activities I was doing over the past year for no particular goal. I was making these projects for somebody where I would just cut-n-paste images from magazines onto paper and send them out as de facto letters…so that my narrative was based on found images versus me writing out words. I've also recently started paying attention to the book arts. I'm sure these activities flowed into my poem-sculptures. As a sculpture, I do feel it works formally — e.g. the material-based contrasts: the grainy rawness of the Xeroxed pages (which I did with a variety of toner quality per page so that the pages don't seem manufactured from an assembly line even though they are just Xeroxed) versus the sparkling sheen of the red shopping bag paper and shimmery handles. The handles are also not quite center as they normally would be on a normal shopping bag (said placement obviously obviating the utilitarian aspect of a bag). And the sheen on the shopping bag paper creates reflections so that there came to be a formal way of integrating the viewer's presence into the work. The footnotes page includes some copyediting marks I did to correct some typos; at first I was going to reprint them but decided to leave them because Life isn't clean and error-free, after all…

Eileen

Poet Welcomes English Into Family

Sculpted Poems

Dear One

(i)

Beauty is reasonable

Fear
is a
Loss

Shall we wish for
what we have made

Desire
should never be
consigned

Dear One—
        Fervently,
ı believe in
the ancient fisherman's motto:
"Allah does not subtract
from the allotted time of man
the hours spent fishing."

V I V I D
is
subjective

Dear One—
I have become the sum
of a series of small
tactical errors—
regretfully, I depart
for Auckland

(ii)

Perhaps
at the equestrian center…

Shall we consider
grounding the border
with abashed aubergine

It's not
what you can get
every day

Consider Tortola,
Virgin Gorda—
the 60-plus British Virgin Islands

Dear One—
          I saw the Bengal Tiger
mimic a helicopter's dance

A L O H A
means
"a fifth night free
plus a daily buffet breakfast for two

(iii)

The
Stark
Touch

Dear One—
          When luxury is
a necessity, recall
the hidden bones of the Villa D'Este

Forever
is
a
Theory

(iv)

Lineage seduces

A Five-Star Mobil Home
(courtesy of the Carlyle)

Manolo Blahnik's elegy for crocodiles

Dear One—
        It's not just a new car
It's the momentary immortality

THE WORLD IS YOURS

(i)

when even Bulgarians
pay dividends

when Eastern Europe
restores housing

when the Future remains
"rooted in the past"

(ii)

Who shall defeat
the giants playing golf
while *white* proxy cards
get hijacked
by a coke bottler
eliminating 2,000 jobs

The Internet implodes
from calls for the next generation
while Russian cartographers
attack Vanitas Software

Sap.com rushes
its employee orientations
as the "new economy"
becomes the "new New Economy"

Offstage from a dream
a deep voice proclaims
"Soon we will be writing
to formally ask for your support"

How to turn information
into cash
while empowering executives
to promote smart energy management

when "Mutual Funds"
is clearly an oxymoron

when Merrill Lynch's growth funds
post negative yields, year-to-date

when pork bellies slump
from weakened futures

Must Tupperware return
to the headlines

Katherine Graham
is dead

Mike Saltzeim no longer spins
Coney Island's carousel

through sunlit summers, ice-cold
winters and "lurching changes"
roiling "the amusement trade" —
Mike Saltzeim's heart has failed.

(iii)

Today, in San Antonio and Fresno,
the temperature topped 100 degrees

Baseball is demeaned
by calls to broaden the strike zone

Mark Wohlers allowed nine hits
and four walks within 5 innings

Nor are encores easy
at the British Open

(iv)

The Minnesota Twins will swallow
$5 million for Joe Mauer

The world is yours
through a laptop:
computers
          never
                    crash
from yearning
for *Home*

A pathologist embodies logic
by becoming a champion marathoner

Dear Daddy

How sweetly you flatten the furrows of your brow. A mask from pancake skin. But I know you wake at 4 a.m.s over me. Do direct your concerns elsewhere. I am the one who taught donkeys to procreate. While American Express makes Tom in Finance fulminate: "Why should we buy their derivatives if they're no longer eating what they're baking?" Dear Daddy, I will never need "unloving rubber-insulated sex in a seedy hotel." I am not Jeffrey Archer. Nor would I ever praise a brothel for taking advantage of single mothers. When I'm 60, will you still slip me those twenties? I can't return to Gardena High—but you didn't breed a Prom Queen. I can't fill my closet with Armanis—but disperse cheer through purple fishnet stockings. I can't boil or bake beans, but will get royalties from European auctioneers if they resell my poem-sculptures. What do you mean: First they must sell? Dear Daddy, as a stockbroker I might front the list of collectors awaiting a Jasper Johns painting, or cover my credenza with George Ohr pots. But how bored you would be taking my phone calls—I bet you'd open the bottom drawer for whiskey shots if you hear me prattle: "Nokia is a SELL!"

At Bryant Park: Perfect Form

(i)

Perfect
Form

Is

Occurring
From

Ground

Zero
When

Absence

Enables
Play

(ii)

The
Miniature

Environments

Created
For

And

Ultimately
Destroyed

Within

Action
Movies

Find

A
Mirror

In

Chris
Burden's

Large

"dimness.
And"

(iii)

I

Left
L.A.

To

Make
Love

With

You
At

The

Bryant Park

Hotel

In
N.Y.C.

(iv)

Dusk

Did
Not

Diminish

Our

Bryant Park

Conversations

(v)

I
Dry

Your

Pink
Toes

With

My
Hair

(vi)

Her

Flawless
Level

Of

Technical
Expertise

Appropriately

And
Deliberately

Decisive:

The
Work

Looks

Like
A

Perfect
Fake

(vii)

Kneeling

I
Submit

For

Your
Pleasure

Over

Perfect
Forms

(vii)

Oh

Bryant Park!

(ix)

Despite

An
Impassive

Face

Your
Lips

Sweetly

Formed
"Yes"

(x)

Oh

Bryant Park!

Oh

Perfect
Form!

WINE TASTING NOTES

An expanding idea

shifts scale to melt the horizon
imagery from pictorial to abstraction

tone from silent to aggressive

       "yet in each there is a common commitment"

Tactile pleasures

suggest a world worth unlocking

to celebrate the perplexities

of knowing

Experience art

through self-encounter

"This is not a vase"

       "This is not a river"

Subjectivity is

the plankton beneath the wave

radiating from green into gold

with the onset of wet sunlight

From The Gray Monster In A Yellow Taxi
--a.k.a. "Rain Taxi, Vol 6, No. 2, Summer 2001" in the voice of Lot's Wife

I desire most
when it rains

     :

How can one
label history
an "absence"

As if dissonance
can ever be "subtle"

Like the absence of
yellow taxis during days of gray water

Can fantasy
not be poignant

Does not reality
always leave
us wanting more

Antarctica keens
the Siren Song
of an unnamed woman
longing to be overcome
by an avalanche
not made of snow

More poets should
experiment with
"foundational questioning"

To rhapsodize over
"The River of Heaven"

Otherwise Pain
becomes
"our very own lack of pain"

While death persists
as a premature topic

The tale of the "Dirty War"
in Argentina (1976-1983)

is one of language
because all leftists
left Buenos Aires

This does not signify
a painting is
a blank canvas

Ask any Russian
at a funeral party

Fire is always
"destruction" —
do not believe
the one who says otherwise
with an expertise
claimed through a label:
"P O E T"

To be accurate, define
Fire as Diane di Prima
aborting a child
because the man she loved
"willed it so"

We choose
what we name

We choose those "karmic traces"

Dream =/= Democracy

Yes, look back
Look Back
The Bible is only a book

Sometimes we have nothing
to give
but still give —
this could be confidence
This could be religion

This could be Blissful Ignorance

This could be orgasm

This could be, or Not

This could be an excuse
one gets away with

by serving up certain words
like "paradox"

Or "transcendence"

Or "archetype"

Or ascribing the role of creator
to a lettuce spinner's
whirlpool of paper slips
manufactured by the Chinese:
      e.g. a lottery poem
      birthed through lines
      that spilled
      between plastic cracks

This issue of *Rain Taxi* ends
with a non-coincidence:
"Catastrophe Theory" —
evolution through mutations
conflagrated by
failures to understand

Thus, monsters also hope

Look back
Look Back
The Bible is only a book —
I am still here

And I am breathing

I Breathe

For Charles Henri Ford

The glowworm
turns professorial
when stars hide

A white azalea
quiets the shade
into a girl

The girl loves marble
enough to freeze
into a swoon

While ascending from trellis jail
the jasmine's skin
comes to mirror the sky

From a factory
questionable grit escapes
within the cover of gray haze

You want to live
You live to want
As if to anguish is to feel

Tongue the cracks
to glue together
fragments of a stolen sun

Revel
in the claw marks
forking a cheek

Oh, Poet
preening at the labyrinth—
unlatch that gate

You, there
with blue veins
crackling transparent membrane

III. THE DEFINITIVE HISTORY OF FALLEN ANGELS:
AN AUTOBIOGRAPHY

This is the moral for inventing ecstasies
Freed from the clutch of memory
I eat the eagle's windy branches
My eye the lion's cave
Silver fluids fix my voice
That sings The World and I Are One
—from "Coat of Arms" by Philip Lamantia

CHAPTER ONE*

"Why?"

Of course, I asked her the question only afterwards. Is not such the manner of those who intend to seduce — first physically overcome the target and reserve any discussion for the "afterwards"? I had learned this from him. I stood over her drinking directly from the champagne bottle as she remained in the position I'd left her, lolling back against the folds of raw canvas I had flung across the floor before pushing her down.

*****

Jade looks up, releasing her eyes from the book that refuses to provide the succor of distraction. In truth, Jade is waiting.

Of course, there is much waiting. So much in-betweens.

In-betweens are where true history can breathe, can ache, can expand, can sing.

Of course it is exactly like living a poem — that Poetry between lines of text unable to signify.

Jade is waiting now. She is named after eyes whose matte surfaces, hence impassivity, she is relying on to counter what blow his presence surely will bring.

Her mother must have sensed something early on about Jade, perhaps as early as when she was delivered into the recognizable world as an infant, squawking out reluctance. Her first earrings — the ones studded into newly-penetrated earlobes — were of the stones that match her eyes: surfaces consistently requiring light to work hard for the tiniest bit of sheen as reflection.

For Jade bears twin masks between sets of long lashes whose shadows perpetually etch her cheeks.

Now, Jade is waiting for the creature who presented the footnotes to a history unknown by her mother. Never mind the "Father" — an invisible presence and let's leave it at that for the rest of the story. (Well, except to emphasize: invisibility is not synonymous with absence.)

So, Jade is waiting for the creature she met through a computer screen, who watched her spill forth secrets she didn't know she knew until his eyes began to listen.

Jade is waiting for a creature the recognizable world knows as a man living in a city on the other side of a continent as well as an ocean.

Jade laughs at that: that the creature is known as a man. A human.

What Jade does not laugh at is how, like the others she hadn't recognized as preceding him, as well as the others she will recognize as following him, he is also a married man.

He called her: "a delinquent beauty."

Footnote *

> "For,the,sin,of,Nothing.
> —from "104" by Jose Garcia Villa

A delinquent beauty. Scabrous
stones leaning in defiance

of gravity. Once hearth
to a predator. Now a perversion

of an otherwise bucolic
scene. It begins in Reigne

with old columns from
a Roman gate. I was amazed

at the cars lining narrow streets.
Shiny limousines from Paris, Zurich,

London and Madrid. An auction.
A drawing. A "her" sketched

between sips of wine as she
prepared dinner by a gamboling fire.

"Even in black and white
her cheeks burned with promise."

Did the billionaire bidders with bared teeth
notice the high forest ripe with truffles

and wildflowers? *My Love—*
all this is from the latest book

trapping my hands: the exercise a "code
for distraction." I am inhaling

Day of the Bees by Thomas Sanchez.
I write this poem to share

a story I am permitted
to reveal. Not the frozen

blank page that must remain
our lyric. Sanchez also observes

"historians know nothing of private
universes where mortals exist

at their most vulnerable."
Before my eyes began to leak

forth this poem, I wrote
another one: A "hay(na)ku."

A form concocted in the cauldron
of a 21st century witch addicted to

the open veins of fallen angels and known
by the post avant as "Eileen R. Tabios":

Eyes
permanently damp
wound the night

CHAPTER TWO*

Is it too early or too late to judge the phone's silence?

There really is no need to flesh out the narrative of this chapter which is about waiting. We all know the fears brought by waiting: the imagined "worst case" scenarios. There is no need here to spill more ink.

She can't help herself: she spills more ink. But, just a little, she admonishes herself.

Once, she thought about this married man who lived a continent and an ocean away, "I feel your invisible heartbeat."

It would have helped to know she could stare out of the window in her writing studio to see a cathedral. But no such edifice existed: a grimy, antique marble that would slap time.

Footnote *

On rain-slick streets
I was coming to you

knowing I will never be
the same again. Wet

daggers slashed at the Seine.
"Ahead loomed the cathedral."

Of course I have lapsed
back to reading a stranger's book.

This hunger to tell *of* you
to turn you into a muscled chest

against which I lean while
your eyes lower to inhale

burning jasmine masquerading
as my hair. A stranger is more

intimate than you, Mr. Reticence.
You have broken me.

You broke me. "Twelve stone

apostles gazed down at me."
Mass had already begun…

I cling to you for you know

how to seduce a woman

of my kind: I outrival the Parisienne
who can fashion a million

scarves from a single scarf.
Jesus multiplying loaves and fish.

Who gathers—no, harvests—the dusty
feathers of fallen angels from marble

grottos perpetually shrouded in dusk?
I do. How do you think I

fashioned my wings? I'm no angel.
Even one who fell. I'm …

Wait, you don't want to hear
what you already know. And I

know you know. "I could not see
you but heard your heartbeat."

CHAPTER THREE*

She was five years younger than him, a year older than me. She was also an artist and mostly painted small abstract works. She was beginning to develop a reputation, but it seemed likely that it will never be known if any success she will muster would have occurred had she not married the sculptor once heralded as "The Only Artist Who Could Out-Macho Richard Serra." As with most things, it often takes more than talent to attain recognition. Looking at her then, however, I knew she didn't marry him for advancing her career, which was rumored about his first wife. I recognized that light that glimmered in her eyes whenever she looked at him — how, even when she was talking with someone else, her eyes kept shifting until she could locate him within the perimeter of her vision. I still look at him that way. I will always look at him that way.

*****

To finish a chapter on waiting (Chapter Two) and still be waiting out the entrance of what is supposed to be a new chapter … well, it's depressing.

Jade counsels herself to take comfort in the fact that, unlike other men, he has never lied to her by penetrating between her thighs.

Jade counsels herself that the desire of other men never succeeded in insulating her against loneliness.

Jade counsels herself that she has never heard him promise, her face cradled between his palms, "We shall know each other for a long, long time."

Jade counsels herself: she has never actually fought in one of the planet's many wars. In some, women reared as enemies hacked off their left breasts.

Jade counsels herself counseling herself counseling. We also know the rest of what need not be explicated in this chapter that is not supposed to be about waiting.

Footnote *

Shivery night. Breath-starved silver.
Battling to surface. Dew hunting

moonshine. Sundering night. Off
the road animals open their eyes.

All teeth now vampiric. Of course
You called me "My

Dearest Love." Of course
I heard "Desperate Love."

People rarely discuss how the muse
weathers a job called inspiration.

The gloriously wide-winged
butterfly turns gray. Wings of

widening dusk her fate. *O, loneliness*
while the gods remain deaf to self-pity.

"Immolation" translated as "lazy."
We forget the planet

is always at war somewhere.
Somewhere, skeletons limp

on back roads with empty packs,
"plunging into bushes at

the slightest sound of someone
's approach." I, too, wish

to disappear into my shadow.
But another flaw of gray is

incompetence as a mask. Lousy
translucence. So that, bleeding, I plead

for the return of my blood
now lingering as the sheen

over your very muscular eyes.
Damn You. Damn Me. Damn You.

I ache for the return of the left
breast removed from the skirted member

of the French Resistance.
Damn You. Damn Me. Damn You.

CHAPTER FOUR*

A miracle. He calls. And when Jade checks her watch, forgetting the immediate histri-onic past, she realizes his timing is perfectly-pitched.

He calls soon enough for Jade to comprehend she was at the top of his priority list as soon as his plane landed in the city containing her as a body he spent the past year imagining.

A miracle. Perfect pitch.

The green bottle goldened by absinthe recedes further back into a dim cupboard. Her mind shuts the door. Her mind locks the door.

After putting down the phone, Jade thinks, "Dear God—I may yet forgive you."

Footnote *

How to write Part 4
when Part 3 is forgotten?

Was there mention of
unmentionables, e.g. a failed pregnancy?

E.g., sacred mornings where birds
blanched from our lack of the most

transparent curtains? Historians are
the amoral—nay, immoral—

ones for lacking imagination.
For ignoring footnotes. For

reducing me to a convenient label:
Princess of Absinthe. The golden

green honey obviates the grayness
of my body, yes. Still. A history

of reliving penultimate past
was tedious the first time. Nor do birds

trill over how lapsed memory burnishes
light in a pleasing and unique way.

CHAPTER FIVE*

"I like my sex rough," he had warned shortly after the first time I had convulsed around his tongue.

"Whatever you want," I had replied and only leaned closer towards him.

A few moments later, I had asked him if I gave him something he couldn't get from anyone else. We both had known we were discussing Helene, innocent Helene, as he had uttered, "Yes."

"Then why. . ." I had tried to ask, but he had silenced me by tightening his hold on my breasts.

"There are certain things we must never discuss. One of them is Helene."

As he had taught me, I had whispered, "Yes, Master: whatever you want."

I looked at Helene's jutting breasts and wondered if, just as she unknowingly was unable to satisfy him, there was some need he didn't know about her and, thus, was unable to fulfill. Once more, I considered how so many couples compromise for the end result of being buried in coffins laid side by side.

*****

"My parents were protected people. I've certainly moved my clan farthest in terms of experience."

"Why do you articulate it that way?"

"I don't think one generation suffices for significant change."

Pause. Sip wine from a bottle with an unfamiliar label.

"My parents," Jade whispers, "are very innocent people."

"So are you."

Shocked, Jade looks at him.

"I loathe innocence," she tells him.

He simply continues to stare at her.

Jade bows her head to let uncut hair fall, to cover the trembling right corner of her lips. She is confused and, it occurs to her, she doesn't know whether this moment is part of a novel. Or, "pre-book." Or, whether the choices point to the same result for which she's committed her flesh: pages never empty of words.

271

Footnote *

So unfair how war elevates
a postman into a king.

So unfair when the one boasting
a uniform that will never

dodge bullets may now categorize
my ever-cushiony lips as "red

as the wine in a duck
sauce, or crimson as raspberry

sorbet." A mere paper
-pusher. But he pushes from

you to me, me to you.
Unfair. So unfair an insolence

cannot peak the litany of sufferings.
Fine, I'm back to reading

a book instead of living, pre-book.
But don't be distracted from seeing

blood on my fingers
when I never fought on a battlefield

grayed by ammunition smoke. Pale
but still authentic blood

of betrayals. Will absinthe
hurt a fetus already semi-starved?

You did not desire this privileged
position: unfairly, you possess the answer.

CHAPTER SIX*

Often, one fast-forwards because what is skimmed hurts.

Often, one lapses to the third-person pronoun.

No moon.

Nor a glimmer from the nearest star.

Jade tries to persevere with what she knows only as a book-in-progress by noting the following progression from their three meetings:

First meeting: a kiss on each cheek.
Second meeting: a kiss on one cheek.
Third meeting: no kiss.

No farewell kiss.

Just farewell. Form matching content.

---

*Footnote ***

I am so ordinary. Not
the first, certainly, to traffic

in secret compromises
in order to survive. My version

of *The Lapsed Virgin*. I force
myself to memorize maps.

But I always lose myself
when doubling back from

even a route I mastered
to go somewhere shiny and new.

I consistently return "well past
midnight." Returning, I become

a postman envying letters
that accomplish journeys

between fixed destinations. And
during my night movements I am less

than a thief whose raised face
receives the benediction of sluttish

light. After *my* midnights, no moon.
Nor a glimmer from the ~~farthest~~ nearest star.

"I see that you like breaking the square," I said as I circled the walls of her studio. This was the third time I'd met Helene after her husband's museum show. I had introduced myself to her while she was replenishing her wine glass, and managed to engage her in a discussion about her work. Naturally, I had become familiar with her paintings through various group exhibitions in town — I wanted to know anything that even remotely touched his life. Helene seemed to be in a period of featuring incomplete squares within her paintings. The ruptured squares were set against lushly painted surfaces etched here and there with slanting horizontal lines.

"Yes, well. There's no such thing as perfection, is there?" she replied, handing me a glass of champagne.

*****

It occurs to her that their story may be encapsulated in Italian proverbs.

Say: *Chi semina vento, raccoglie tempestra*
               Who sows the wind, reaps the whirlwind

Say: *Non si puo dettar leggi al cuore*
               One cannot make laws to rule the heart

Say: *Il linguaggio dell' amore è negli occhi*
               The language of love is in the eyes

Say: *Chi vuol nasendere l'amore sempre lo manifesta*
               When one tries to hide love, one gives the best evidence of its existence

Say: *Il rumore d'un bacio non e cosi forte come quello del cannone, ma la sue eco dura molti piu lungo*
               The sound of a kiss is not as strong as that of a cannon, but its echo endures much longer

This last one is only half-wise. What endures even longer than the sound of a kiss is the silence of a non-kiss. For us, tears left my boiling cheeks for your eerily still shoulders. I sensed stars shaking themselves off and away from the cobalt face of summer.

Jade reads ten books before she finds another Italian proverb that could ease her, finally, into bed, for the relief of a dreamless sleep:

Say: *Sdegno d'amante poco dura*
               The anger of lovers lasts a short time

But first, a bedtime prayer for Jade newly understands: to engage in the status of "couple" does not exempt one from the recurrence of panic. A black wave that keeps coming and coming to crash and crash against the very moveable sand.

Footnote *

Bee pollen fraying a dropped halo
on my hair, fusing me to earth.

Absinthe tunneling its moss
through my opened veins.

Rosemary an innocent respite
by scenting a grilled rabbit's skin.

Grease on our greasy lips
then your head lowering.

Tears leaving my boiled cheeks
for your heaving shoulders

Had I looked up
I would have seen

stars shaking loose
from the cobalt face of summer.

But no. The downcast position
allowed the witnessing, thus this

description, of tears that predicted
joy exists only before the gods must

disillusion us who believed
"as a couple we were exempt."

CHAPTER EIGHT

Jade eats dumplings—which is to say, "comfort food" —with two other poets. Inevitably, she makes a passing reference to him for such is the way of One Who Remains In Love.

In response to her camouflaged references, the two poets call her "Muse."

The label stuns Jade. She had considered him her Muse.

Oh, she thinks with a sadness she allows herself not to understand, clouds have cataracted my eyes and subverted certain stars into the traffic of static.

And the color orange is simply wrong for the roses in the crystal vase two inches from her notepad where she writes a tale she does not know.

Jade inhales … exhales. The clouds disappear. Jade recognizes an old fear, and tries to be blithe. So what that he writes poems about his wife, she thinks. Surely, the significance is borne by, simply, he *writes*!

Once, a poem was writ—she cannot remember whether by him or her—ending with the line:

"I write poems now."

It was a poem about Fate.

He is not the first to turn the word "Fate" into a synonym for the word "Solitude."

Footnote *

Such dissembling. These clouds
subverting stars into static.

I even wished for the opera of a barking
dog from behind stone gates. What use

this lavender light? They reveal
cherry trees whose twisted

branches become an orphan's thinning
ancestors. These eyes sunk deep between

wooden wrinkles. They watch me, of course, as I
open an envelope. "Naked, hair trembling," I

pull out a letter addressed after all
to me: "Do not open." Geez—am I not

Buddha? What use this lavender light?
Now staining this page you read to feel

useless resonance. Useless and embalmed
like eyes replacing knotholes on tree barks.

CHAPTER NINE*

Jade wants to recall at least one moment of joy from their encounter. She might lapse to skimming through the memory of his visit, but she does not want to betray the incidents of momentary happiness.

She also knows that he believes she can weave fragments together into a seamless image —a faith he had revealed one day when, in response to what she thought was a faux pas, he had marveled, "You are amazing."

For she had sought to apologize for what she thought was a mistake by offering him a newly-written poem:

Second Chance

Once, the only veil
between our cheeks
was a wave loose-

ened from my hair:
is that image
purely imagined now?

A projection
on screens of
shuttered eyelids

while licking off
tasteless shadows
staining my wings

when I flew
through memory?
Where I saw

your fingers
tracing the ear
I offered as proxy

for eyes I turned
toward a window?
Where I saw you

on glass shielded
by night air reflecting
the same narrative

a mother wished
for Achilles

before a thin-lipped

god changed
the story? You see
that I am not stone

or block of salt
or any other Biblical
metaphor

for "mired in regret."
I hear your tongue
caressing my ear

as I break nails
from my hands
bleeding

into ground hard
-ened by a lead sky.
They excavate

you still breathing...

She wants to do that again: transcend the lack of a kiss from their last encounter by recovering joy through poetic alchemy.

For one, she thinks as she begins to hum away loneliness form the room, he admitted that as a result of their encounters, he has renewed his commitment to Poetry.

"There are constraints, the logistics of finances," he had said. It was an old story she had heard before from other men who married others. But his recounting of this same story was the first time she understood what he and others before him comprehended: they could not afford her.

"The logistics of finances," he was saying, but then shrugged all such logistics away as something to be addressed but not allowed to be obstacles before the writing of more poems.

This moment, Jade understood immediately then, was the peak of happiness she will ever experience with him, even as she forced back a question as to whether....

Jade remembers another moment that she had not recognized at the time to be about joy. He had looked closely at her, silently kept looking at her until she began to fidget. Then he whispered, "You are more innocent than water."

Footnote *

If "love's innocence is a candle
that burns only once...," yes

I am back to reading a book
whose author is wise for his

indifference to us. Beyond the borders
of this book lurks a man

who taught me a weekend
more than suffices for burning

down a candle into a mere mark
staining a table. A mark doomed

to obscurity. Not discernible
from the detritus of other, more benign

sources, say, the bottom of a glass
that bore the only matter truly

innocent in the universe — so innocent
it retains its innocence: water.

Meanwhile, I have been drunk
all month for September begins

harvest season in wine country.
Trucks filled with grapes cruise

the valley's streets. All winery hands
engage in crushing grapes. The air

is permeated with the scent of
wine-making, a process mirrored by

how the poet drinks the muse's blood,
tears, sweat, saliva...tears.

Anonymous hands toss bundles of
grapes into steel crushing machines.

Sweet juice pours into barrels promising
alchemy via fermentation. From another

end, husks of grapeskins, leaves, stems,
and bugs tumble out — desiccated leftovers

like my gray, faltering hands. Deveined
hands hunting for blood through words

wanting my fingernails to be painted
once more with *Bordello Crimson*.

CHAPTER TEN*

I refused to leave my reflection. I kept staring into my eyes as I considered her replies to my question. Beyond my bathroom door, the apartment whose address I'd used for 20 years felt alien to me. When Helene had said that she suspected he was having an affair, I had only encouraged her to continue talking. When she had said she wanted a woman's love because her experience seemed to prove the impossibility of obtaining love from a man, I had began straightening my clothes to leave.

Immediately, she had leapt from the floor and flung her arms around me. It was the first time I had noticed her lips nude, lipstick long licked or bitten away.

"Please. Please tell me you'll return."

The best I could do, even as my hands began fondling her breasts then twisting her nipples the way he had loved to do to me, was to repeat something he also once said to me, "I will never ignore you."

*****

Jade interrupts her half-hearted reading of the book that refuses to give succor through distraction. She begins to grieve over how she had to keep a secret from him: a chateaux whose halls she patrolled with a pleasingly heavy bunch of ancient keys dangling from her right hand.

She would patrol, clad in a ballgown with a voluminous skirt whose silk she loved to trail over floors of oak, marble and limestone.

She would patrol, often breaking out into a soft humming.

She would patrol, never forgetting to pause and croon at the timid rabbit hiding within the shadows of the turret.

She would patrol, feeling the young palpable presence of fluttering wings.

She would patrol, secure and at peace.

She would patrol, but occasionally pierced by the thought of missing *Desire*.

She would patrol, insisting to herself: "I am not too young to be alone."

She would patrol, artfully advising herself: To be ensconced within thick, stone walls is my *Fate*. I am a *Poet*. This is my *Home*.

Footnote *

Remember the chateau
where you and I never slept

but compromised for a tango?
Velvet blackened my breasts.

You demanded velvet despite the heat.
An image that will not be immortalized

as a holiday postcard scene.
Beyond stone ruins, gawking villagers.

Your lips on my thigh lifted in a disguise
called "tango." Nothing hapless about

a broken crown. Eldest sons, when royal,
are meant to be broken lest

they never become human. Ach!
The author got it wrong and fiction

does not provide an excuse.
Birds don't chatter from

the canopy of fig trees. Simply, birds
eat the damn figs! Things so obviously

meant to be split—things that
are too histrionic not to become

overripe—are meant to be eaten
mercilessly. Because you would not

partake, you fueled my wings.
Damn you, proclaims this ingrate.

CHAPTER ELEVEN

HAIR

---

*Footnote **

Fortunately, Pygmalion will never
become disillusioned with my hair.

I never betrayed girlhood with
cruelty, using whispers as daggers.

I still don't today when, at forty
-three, I prove that, yes, time

consistently kills passion. This is
a discourse that makes me want

to tear off my clothes so I can
surround you—quite a difference

from you penetrating. Pathos, here,
is defined by how I twist words

in yet another attempt to seduce
you into falling with me. Falling, I

plead: *Fall with me.* Oh, this memory of
Damn You. Damn Me. Damn You.

"My head bends, my mouth touches
my breasts, my lips taste a spot

of milk on thickening brown nipples."
Love, yes, "is not about going back

but moving toward something." So kiss
the stumps of my fresh wings. You

are the one who memorized
my sobbing. Damn You. Help me

make my tears a color.
Kiss my tears to sunlit blue.

CHAPTER TWELVE

QUINCE

Footnote *

So many secrets form a day.
What about a life? Never

mind a life. What about
one hour in a hotel room?

I envy the tip of your tongue
for knowing the interior of my

ear. Once, I suggested, "Taste
of quince?" You only laughed,

Dear Cruelly Mischievous One.
Laughter neither confirms nor

disagrees. Laughter is like
Poetry. Or our Secret. It simply Is.

CHAPTER THIRTEEN

BLOUSE

---

*Footnote **

Surely you suspected my intimacy
with men who, faced with moonlight,

pull down hat brims or woolen caps?
Sssshhhhh, I can hear your eyes

before you become once more
an etched seam. A blank line

---

for me to fill in the narrative

I desire. I desire you whispering
— "which is to say," your lips

nibbling with each letter— "to live
is to collaborate." Once, I revealed

this hope in the aftermath of shared
laughter. Your face blanked.

You became more distant than
a priest behind a latticed screen.

But you were moved when I wept.
You invited me to take

off my shoes, loosen the top buttons
of my blouse, unpin my hair combs,

though also pretend you have never
been the role you now refuse: *Home*.

CHAPTER FOURTEEN

WEDDING

Footnote *

No. Of course "You" is not
a haven. Just because "I"

is rarely the source of peace
I lean on you. But this is not

a song from a Hollywood movie
hoping for a golden trophy.

Notwithstanding the bird
who died trying to penetrate

the double-sided glass I ordered
for the windows. Tiny bird,

hence, tiny crushed head. Logic
dictated my empathy, what with

my own dinged forehead. Instead,
I found myself muttering, ill

-tempered, "Foolish. So foolish."
After my wedding, my new husband

and I rode in different cars
to the reception. His parents

thought nothing of reclaiming
him while I was too polite to

protest. That's okay. Form
mirrors ultimate Content.

Tonight, let me rely on blood
welling up to sheathe my eyes

as I finger gray flesh while
asking you and "you" and You:

Who amongst you broke my
lovely bottle of lovely absinthe?

CHAPTER FIFTEEN

FARMERS

Footnote *

I lied. Sometimes, *my* midnights do
not cancel the stars. Or

moon, whose liquid light reeks
of jasmine, steeled by motes

of green leaf tobacco. Should I
reveal the significance to how

I know the difference between
"cigar box" and dewed leaves

still battling wind over boiling fields?
I could say, "I am the expatriated

daughter of tobacco farmers." You
would hear, "I can be myself

only in exile." Another old
story. Myth even, insolently reminds

a cartoon character poking its head
onto the bottom of this page. When,

perhaps, I merely betrayed a country
whose weather is limited. Where

I come from, the air is usually over
-heated. And a tiresome virgin to fog.

CHAPTER SIXTEEN

STILETTO

Footnote *

I've shown you more of my scars
than any other human has seen.

It wasn't enough to seduce you.
So why remain hovering? Nice?

Don't need nice from you. You
mortal saint. I chose a poem

between said poem and my baby. Muse
punishes me now by withholding

fertility. Fidelity. Damn muse. Why
didn't you simply slap me

hard, proclaim, "Don't be silly",
proclaim, "Don't be mad!" Proclaim, "Goose!"

I committed a sin, yes. But so
did this muse I share with poets

across centuries baying at the moon
as if it had cleavage, beating their chests

while leaning over the crumbling edges
of cliffs, etcetera, etcetera, etcetera. You

hear me out, then whisper another stiletto
through my tears: "Eileen Jade, I love you."

CHAPTER SEVENTEEN

FURTIVE

---

*Footnote **

My elbow just struck the teeth
of a wolf. It glared with yellow

eyes, then ran off, melting into
night. Where am I? Damn you.

Once, you asked, "Where are you?"
You bludgeoning man were not

searching for me. Despite your
delicate agreement — *my wings are lovely,*

*my breasts are lovely, my lips are
lovely. Even my nonexistent waist*

is lovely — you say "lovely" is overrated
compared to a word like "holy."

Damn You. Damn Me. You turned
me into a wolf with golden but

useless eyes while you were the
very furtive creature who escaped.

CHAPTER EIGHTEEN

S T E E L

Footnote *

My nipples ache. I am burning your
letters. Steel and hands continue to crush

grapes in wine country where tourists
believe they prevail. The spell continues to

elude. A spell to kneel you, brow pressed
against my door. But no more doors exist

to my exile. I am Rapunzel who cut her hair
to weave a rope for leaving her turreted nest.

That is, I am the older version of Rapunzel
unknown to purveyors of fairy tales. I am

Rapunzel who, having experienced this
so-called "marvelous world," returned

to my antique jail by climbing the rope still
scented with jasmine and still dangling from

the turret that refuses its ruins. After clambering
over the windowsill, I unlatched the hair rope to

toss it back at the planet whose denizens
— or simply you — betrayed me. Here

I now sit with short hair, spinning banners
from stray breezes. That I sleep nearer

to my beloved sky provides zero consolation.
I have never desired compensation.

Is this *Justice* then? That I am alone
between earth and sky? Between you and

the destiny you insisted you could not betray?
A destiny you insisted is the embrace

I have sought all my human life? Foolish saint.
 "Sky" is not synonymous with "Heaven."

Heaven, Damned Reticent One, was the water
you would not convey to my parched tongue.

CHAPTER NINETEEN

NOT

Footnote *

We met in a cell, remember? You did not
wear sackcloth pretending to be priest,

monk, or anyone whose profession is prayer.
In your Italian shirt horizontally striped with

green, blue, yellow—let's just say rainbow—
you met me in a cell, remember? From where,

despite perpetually open door I would not
leave. I settled for imagined images

of sunlight splashing each morning
the stone steps at the far end

of the hallway beyond the threshold
memorized by my knees and hair.

We formed our intimacy through persevering
days when you, brow furrowed, watched

me prefer stone walls over the stone eyes
of still-breathing men. You. Simply watch

-ing until I began to behave as informed
by the knowledge of you watching me.

Does history exist if it dies without physical
manifestation? Not the first time I ask since,

you know, we cannot speak of it or speak it or…
that night, your hand cupped my belly…?

For descendants to know what your eyes
memorized and that your eyes memorized

I would have to reveal my "sky" was a
computer screen. "Empty" can be translated

infinitely when no translation exists. But
my fate, according to angels, is not to collaborate.

CHAPTER TWENTY

ANTIQUITY

Footnote *

"I deny the patience of water."
This poem is not written in English.

This non-poem is not written.
I have memorized all failed suicide

notes that ever littered civilized society.
I recall one where rusty leaking

made my tiny nose snort: *I would*
have done otherwise but I could not bear....

Cut-off letter. Who cares? Don't
bother to tell others (though not my eyes)

ambiguity has turned me brutal. Your
persistent joy manifests the most

maximal form of cruelty. Bleat, bleat....
I am just saying. I am just saying

for the spit that speech disgorges
to corrode all vestiges of sentimentality

more resilient than cockroaches.
Like dust stubbornly trapped within my hems.

Wings grow stronger, sure. But the plump
-ness of my lips refuse to recede. To heighten

the irony of my seductive powers raging
as strong as ever when, nowadays,

I share conversation only with mute
reflections haunting the glass cracking with age.

I drink wine only with throatless reflections
haunting glass gilding its inevitable antiquity.

CHAPTER TWENTY-ONE

KOHL

---

*Footnote **

I am the author and if I could lose this book,
I most definitely! I sing as well

as I make tea! That's me with the name:
Missy Can't Boil Water But Can Melt Teapot!

But you keep calling me to the stage. I detest
the word "diva" but become said diva to wave

a canape. To signify the midst of my overdue
dinner. But you insist. Rude but cheerful

just like a fallen angel. Fine, chicken
drumstick clutched in one hand, I embark

on the fado with much kohl-lined dignity.
Everyone forgets my lips are greasy.

Everyone forgets.

The floor is stomped and stomped again. Aptly.
But the guitar? Whose fingers are bleeding

on the taut strings? Who is the singer
manipulating my breath? If I could lose

the book I would. I am telling you
more than *mano a mano* because I am

woman: never mind the song
if it's bigger than the singer. Rain lashes

windows. I lash back at hurricanes:
that story was concocted by man

not God. Song larger than singer?
That overrated story. Heaven is *in* us!

CHAPTER TWENTY-TWO

COLLAPSE

---

*Footnote **

Note to Self: Publish this book
In the reverse order you wrote it.

End with Part 1. End to begin
all over again. No one ever teaches

what the end of the circle reveals.
If life is a process, it's not

the circle cherished by monks with
beaming smiles. Life is a spiral

-ing into a void where sin exists only
if one won't move fast enough to

collapse North from South, East from
West, Top from Bottom, He from

He, She from She, You from You,
I from I, colors from muddling each other.

CHAPTER TWENTY-THREE

LAVENDER

Footnote *

The mistral polished the sky
into transparent sapphire.

No consolation there. Today's
revelation: to be fearful on behalf

of another is to become more
courageous. That path is lost

to me who shall remain virgin
forever as regards prams and diapers.

I only chose lavender soap
to evoke someone else's Provence childhood.

Then, "naked, hair trembling," I ran to you
wanting corruption from your urban kisses.

Yes. That dim alley in Berlin?
I would have dropped to my knees.

CHAPTER TWENTY-FOUR

POLLEN

Footnote *

I feel myself as you have never
caressed this skin. Here are generous breasts

that shall never droop. Whose tips
were never anointed by the wine

in your goblet, precursor to your suckling lips.
"When Christ was dying on the cross

it was a windy day too. Each tear he shed
was whipped in fury and carried to the

Mediterranean Sea to fall like a translucent
purple pear on the barren earth of Provence.

Each pearl turned to a seed, and the seed
to a vine and the vine to grapes. That is why

wine is the blood of Christ and each autumn
raisin is sweet, because Christ's tears

were not from his pain, but his joy."
I loathe Provence—its lavender, its honey,

its wildflowers, its pollen as gold as the ring
you never pierced into the skin between my thighs.

CHAPTER TWENTY-FIVE

N E R V E

Footnote *

What is most obscene to my eyes
(that have memorized the interiors of museums

dedicated to bones) is the field of your pristine
chest. A blank page lacking edges. A desert

expanse unforgiving for withholding visual relief
through a horizon's line or the verticality of a tree,

even one devoid of leaves. After the kind of ravishment
only we can claw at each other, I swear

our nerve endings would have been
so taxed not a millimeter of our skin

would not have been numbed.
I would have taken, then, the nearest

blade to carve an initial on your chest. The letter
would not have been of my name but one more

powerful for its necessary step of pause,
then the remembering — thus, emphasizing — "Aaaaah."

But the ravishment you promised never occurred.
And

CHAPTER TWENTY-SIX

RETICENT

Footnote *

Actually, I've long lost touch
with the definitions of certain words:

obscenity, blasphemy, sin, morality.
I had to lose their culpable narratives

to understand something else (like
the passion of spiders) whose color

burnt me to ash (but pretty ash)
which only made me ever more enamored

with its singular raiment—is that Egyptian
cotton with a thousand-thread-per-inch count?

This Word uplifts by destroying. No,
I am not thinking of "Poetry" or "Love."

This Word destroys in order to…
but never mind that Word. The

moral—moral? —I meant to share
is that I did not anticipate needing

to recover words I had disposed.
It seems I sacrificed the wrong curses

while exploring the significance of my tongue
so promiscuous it even penetrated the sacred

curls slipping from beneath your blinding halo.
Nonetheless, Dear Reticent One, other words

fail to replace the hummingbirds' drinking water
flavored with sugar. What stabs is that you will

never admit creating false idols with *glimmer, gleen,*
hint, wink. To be a second-generation Merleau-

Ponty is to be as pale and matte as "compromised."
That is sadness: my story that will never overlap with yours.

Let me fail to distract by noting my prayers for
the brown bird whose broken wings forced it to stay

on a concrete parking lot until noon arrived. The sun,
while non-judgmental, burnt it into ash with the same

light that's inspired such sonnets as "Ode" —
Oh, the millions of letters I sent to seduce you!

CHAPTER TWENTY-SEVEN

VEER

Footnote *

So it comes to this: a lovers' quarrel
between two who never tasted

"desire's anarchy overruling rhetoric."
I have been shredding your letters,

not wanting our Poetry to depend on
the act we shared but never shared.

In 1969, astronauts landed on the moon.
We were alive then, and equally oblivious

to the veer of our paths seeking each
other's trajectories. I am writing now

about your tongue bathing my hair. We
remain equally oblivious. I stuffed

hair into your mouth so capable, once,
of parting so wide. Now, non-sweet *Reticence.*

CHAPTER TWENTY-EIGHT

BUTTER

_____

Footnote *

When departure occurs and nothing
replaces the one who departed

_____
_____

_____
_____

_____
_____

_____
_____

_____
_____

Sensual detail here is inserted—e.g. what
moved you to moan, "Do with me

whatever you want." You said it….thrice.
But no taste, no scent, no feel. No *felt*.

Memory cannot replace what is desired
in the present and future. So: _____

_____
_____

As I said, I loathe Provence. Light has never
been, is not, and will never be butter or candy.

CHAPTER TWENTY-NINE

LAMBORGHINI

Footnote *

Cicadas never shrilled from verdant distance.
Sunburnt metal of red Lamborghini never seared

my buttocks bared when you lifted _____

_____

_____

"How do two people remember the same
event?" This did happen: you chained

me with the gold necklaces of a customer
's plump wife. You made someone else's history

ours, as so many others have co-opted our
history — like this lyric that never occurred.

CHAPTER THIRTY

MUSCLE

*Footnote **

When we met, you had stopped singing.
A wife, three sons, a mistress — your momentum

for days bereft of my eyelashes. When we met
I was singing diamonds gleefully stolen from

the realm of silence. **THE REALM OF SILENCE!**
Of course you and I _____.

But for the record, I returned you to the others
— the choice not between me or your

scaffolding. The choice was strict: between
you and non-you. You singing now with family

consistently seated in the front row (the mist
-ress in the back) is the conclusion that forms

muscle to the wax linking my feathers together.
Your joy, my necessity. My necessities, not

my joys. For me, the bliss of scavenging.
I love stealing jewelry for my flesh that is

supposed to be unadorned: a fate my
collecting eyes have yet to accept.

God, how I adore diamonds! I am stringing
together a rosary of solid light. With each bead,

Lord, I shall pray you poems so blasphemous
I shall sing vampires back into your non-Paradise.

CHAPTER THIRTY-ONE

B R O K E

Footnote *

Once, you said you saw me in the color of
the clarifying sky, sun settling for the

Seine. But of course! No, of course not.
Such foolishness. I am bigger than what others

want for me: the Pulitzer for recording
the idiosyncracies of the muse. Yadda, yadda,

yadda. Once, Spain battled France for
a mural discovered by the new owner

of an atelier formerly commandeered by
the Germans. Did I get those nationalities

right? Ah, yadda, etcetera. The court ruled
the painting belonged to the atelier owner,

a private citizen who sold the masterpiece to
the highest bidder in New York. On that

painting, the sun set deliberately on the Seine.
Fire deliquescing onto water that, naively,

created a reflection for the sun that should be
anthropomorphized for believing its position rules.

That this Part 31 is muddled and muddy
befits its mistaken stance of being

anti-nature. As if light never lingers
on the peaks of mountains that broke to rise.

CHAPTER THIRTY-TWO

PARTOOK

---

*Footnote ***

Listen. It's okay. I know you're wounded.
I know you won't blind yourself. Now your eyes

stab yourself by seeing my body define
Loss in a path mythologized by astigmatic

historians as *Transcendence*. You have never
lacked imagination. But it's okay. No need for false

bonhomie through, say, an unnecessary "thanks!"
complete with exclamation point to send

an e-mail that's more accurately signifying
you miss me. (Maybe you're not so

reticent after all.) Weren't you the one
who kept insisting "broken bones knit"?

You said you couldn't go there but you did.
Evil can be delicious. That we partook…

…what's the use? Skip the answers that lie.
So. Listen. It's okay. I'm not only

knitting. I'm on weeks at the weight
machines hewing my limbs until, soon,

a mere flicker from biceps shall suffice
to unfurl these massive black wings.

CHAPTER THIRTY-THREE*

HUE

---

*Footnote ***

No medicine for this just by having changed
its name from *Loneliness*. We both ran

like masters from rebellious slaves. I mis-
judged direction while you gauged with

precision. You also foretold accurately:
the stars will not speak of me while you

look at them from the island of Mallorca.
Such is the healing hue of which gold

also is capable. On Mallorca, to see
is to observe the world "from within a glass

bowl smeared with honey." Not to mention
"the rhythm of shepherds and fishermen."

I would have told you its coves are not
truly "paradisiacal" but you would not have

believed. Or you would have believed
but it would have been irrelevant as

you simply needed then to flee. Still, it is now.
You've left the island for me. Approach.

CHAPTER THIRTY-FOUR

SLASH

---

*Footnote **

Why did I write Part 33? What was I writing
in Part 33? Don't I know, as you know,

poems conjure? Why do I wish to
foretell you into Ramon Llull, the first

liberation theologian who would write
The Book of the Lover and the Beloved?

As if witnessing you write for wife
over mistress would not slash my eyes.

CHAPTER THIRTY-FIVE

B L A D E D

---

*Footnote ***

Wind brushes with whispers
from men who brandished swords

and crucifixes. I know I'm being
watched. I hear peepholes. Saffron

scents air. Ambrosia de Castillo
reveals herself: "She tore the bandage

away, exposing her once perfect
breasts, now hideously ulcerated

and scabbed." The curse
of preferring flesh. A path strewn

with boulders, thorny bushes and
bladed cacti. A mountain path

over which swallows inadvertently dash
tiny heads against cliffs from sighting

"a smudge of blue sea." What am I
dissembling here? Perhaps distractions

from a poor soul's last wish as he
faced Africa: "Won't you let me read

these words I wrote, just one more time?"
As if words were words instead of words.

CHAPTER THIRTY-SIX

CROWN

Footnote *

I earned a crown of thorns.
God rewarded my throat

with whiteness and a necklace
of rubies (though I pledged

to forego all gems after
the year that just ended. I broke

that promise — so? It's the least
of my sins). I earned a crown

of thorns for wrong translations
directed at war orphans. The least I can

do for my opposites: these fragile
ones too timid to ask for nothing.

CHAPTER THIRTY-SEVEN

M A T A D O R A

Footnote *

Dyed my hair a cobalt blue
for that's their color

in my dreams. Now
men begin to "look at me

by not looking *at* me."
Of course. I am a creature

for which prudence dictates
the most furtive of manners:

the glance cutting
for slanting sideways.

Let me sample niceness
with a warning:

Beware your mustachios!
I have bitten with my tiny

teeth. My tiny teeth have
bitten. When said teeth chatter

the sound released is
from a rattlesnake, not a baby's

rattle. Look at *Moi!* Matadora
lips form the fury of sound.

Whoooosh. *Whoooosh.*
Whooooooooooooooosh!

CHAPTER THIRTY-EIGHT

CANCEL

Footnote *

Those in uniform always look
by pulling skin off

the faces of pilgrims. Nor do they feel
the flayed flesh sticking to seams

black beneath their fingernails.
To choose a uniform is to cancel

Truth. Listen now to their hymns —
always in a language so alien

it is foreign even to its speaker.
Nor do they see the fertile earth

where fields now lie fallow.
Bleat, bleat and more bleat.

My baby had a heart. My baby
had a heart. Damn you. My baby

CHAPTER THIRTY-NINE

BEACON

Footnote *

Between my thighs I was leaking
fire, fire, fire. "Fuck with

my business" and I drip, drip,
drip. You were the one who

opened your mouth. You, untouched
by others because of "an innocent

face." Laugh. "Shining like
a beacon." Laugh. "Skin scrubbed

and faintly pink with a pearlescent glow."
Laugh. Then they held back dogs

to let you pass. Laugh. Drip. Laugh.
Fire. Laugh. You opened your mouth.

Laugh. Drip, drip, drip. Laugh.
Ye Ph.D. in Fire, your poems are mine.

CHAPTER FORTY

F I L M

Footnote *

Children, be careful where you
build fences. Never should

barbed wire extend
against the blue of an ocean.

A silver wink suffices
for scarring color.

Memory, too, can commit
sins in the inhuman realm.

The strength of the intangible
is how no shield against it can defend.

See how winter light brings
a grey film that coats everything?

CHAPTER FORTY-ONE

CITROEN

Footnote *

Sooner or later everyone begs.
Even those unsurprised

to discover themselves seated
in the grand salon of a luxury

ocean liner. Where portholes
frame insouciant sapphires.

Where pillars are covered
with red velvet.

Where my skirt is suede, my blouse
is suede, my gloves are suede.

Where you are telling me
a story of a certain hour

starring an innocent passer-bye
I had turned into my replacement

for a role requiring the bombing
of a black Citroen, as if karma is zero.

CHAPTER FORTY-TWO

PARTICIPANT

Footnote *

Nostalgia will never be outdated.
I am reciting *that* to stone walls.

The wind howls and howls against
stone walls protecting my eyes.

I become the wind on the other side,
condition precedent to becoming stone

walls. *That* is a better alternative,
don't you see, than what I now detest,

what others have called "a woman's
nature." This ability to construct

a *Home* from barely-there twigs
of memory. I told you so many things

in the letters I never sent to your
blindness. I revealed so much

about stone, walls, and the wind
that doesn't always blow them down.

Listen to Johnny Cash: to be a young
cowboy is to do wrong. This, too,

will be made irrelevant by the nostalgia
that mates stone, walls and wind

into a ménage a trois for which
my eyes remain distant and participant.

CHAPTER FORTY-THREE*

EQUANIMITY

---

*Footnote ***

I lied. I'm not going to hell. I'm rising
out from there. I am not, after all, the one

you carelessly called Missy Element
Evaporating From Mirror. Toss evanescence.

And my sounds? Not merely radiant.
Sir, I am a cool palm against your flushed

forehead. I even smell of artificial violets.
Look at my blouse *du jour*: no less than

lavender. I am royal. I am Swedish. Equanimity
maximized, herself. "Herself, herself,

herself" sung, please, to the tune of Silliman
in Oakland singing "Limbo, limbo, limbo."

Yes, my nude ankles are tattooed by thorns
beneath the scars caused by thorny roses.

So? I inhale stars with, you got it, equanimity.
I am opposite to fever. Starry-eyed, I never lie.

CHAPTER FORTY-FOUR

CLOUD

---

*Footnote **

As they sing, cicadas suck
the sap from almond trees.

A co-opted code. Corrupted
code. "Annotating" translated

as "writing." You could cite some
opposition as rationale. You have.

Second-hand smoke *is* dangerous.
But yours is not the mouth eroticized

by blue smoke. Unless I kiss you.
Why would I? You're too ironic to fly.

Another code: "paradox" defined
by how I still read your letters

at night and weep. Exhaling
smoke that forms your face

as if my breath is a cloud and
you are Jesus, Son of God.

CHAPTER FORTY-FIVE

SHEPHERD

Footnote *

To be a shepherd slaughtering
lambs is to augur the imminence

of invasion. Not *the* Second
Coming. But if the code surfaced

from fading ink was misread,
an unexpected feast occurs

for the unhappiest diners
ever to gather during a sirocco —

a tribe whose motto formed
the legacy of another defeat:

"Why eat beans when it rains oranges?"
Quite clearly, an augury had been missed.

CHAPTER FORTY-SIX

THROAT

---

*Footnote **

To live through years—decades! —
knowing rest will occur only

with death. And you wonder why
my voice consists of gravel?

Do you know gravel? I know
gravel. Through the courtyard

I wake to each morning. These
are not smoothened pebbles.

Each stone bears facets rough
and sharp-edged enough to

etch cheeks (as when tossed
innocently during child's play).

So when you admire someone's
singing as "gravelly," pause

to actually see that person.
Alcohol, age, hunger—these

roughen a voice and it is not
romantic. No, sir. As for

what roughened my throat?
If you must know, unrequited

purring. Look at me and see
the mask cloaking the woman

whose hair fell as she crawled
amidst sunflowers pecked

by too many birds until their faces
evoke pock-marked lepers.

CHAPTER FORTY-SEVEN

MARTYRDOM

Footnote *

"We plunged straight into the dark
-est part of the clouds." Years

later I will recall this night
as despair for realizing: the only

sources of light were guns
expelling bullets. Stars hid

to block *Ascencion*. An empty
tomb still waited for its

occupant before an ever-vigilant
servant would lean shoulders

against a boulder to block
the entrance and exit to a cave.

Lord, they have never stopped
needing You. Why was I sent?

My story is that I fell to discover
my vision instead of inherited sight.

But you whose wounded eyes
mirror mine (though against my

will), why did you blacken my
wings? I loathe martyrdom.

I loathe sacrifice. I loathe my
unexpected mortality for having

fallen in love with one of them.
This gloriously benighted race for

whom some matter is always
infected with pain and catching.

CHAPTER FORTY-EIGHT

LASHES

Footnote *

I shall be famous — this has been
guaranteed. How to live

knowing, against one's will,
one will be flayed by fame?

Once, I dissembled forth a mask
proclaiming myself as a wounded

lady with uncut hair, "the longest
lashes west of the Mississippi,"

and the anti-thesis of domesticity.
All memorialized through gleaming

shoulders rising from low-cut
gowns. Velvet. Silk sleeves. Immortal

-ized by a cruel-eyed painter into the
confines of a gold, Baroque frame.

Such idiocy I have had to allow.
For post-midnight games I played

in scenic countrysides do not
portray authentic history. What

is *Truth*? I hunted owls and forced
their confessions. All you need to know.

CHAPTER FORTY-NINE

BLED

Footnote *

To come to this. All I want
is to be protected now. How small

how small how small how small…
Wings grow then recede.

No one, of course, ever warned me:
To grow, wings must learn

to retrench. When wings relapse
from the *Ideal* of unfurling

the pain is worse than for
the pregnant woman whose

legs were tied together by
a man I must recognize

as a creature who howled
as I did to join the human race.

By being pushed out wet, slick
nauseous, and, for the first time,

cold. "His words, therefore,
were as direct as the country"

that birthed those who dropped
me before his baskets of honey,

sausages, lavender soap and
scented bundles of herbs:

"I tied your feet together
with a belt, like one of my

goats in the mountain when
she miscarries. I tied your feet

together so all the life
wouldn't bleed out of you."

But my love for you bled out
so I could learn through

survival the expanse of
life as defined by God's Love.

CHAPTER FIFTY

JUNIPER

Footnote *

P.225: He, whom I do not ever wish to
stop reading, stop writing, wrought:

"A pungent taste on my lips,
not mother's milk, something different.

Warm liquid fills my mouth. I swallow.
A heady aroma engulfs — basil,

wild marjoram, sage and savory,
juniper and mint." This is my Bible.

The flesh my page. Your flesh,
my book. Your eyes the essence of

Provencal earth that I write. "With
each suck the pain ebbs. Another

hurt falls away." Heat. Then hands
covering hands as I begin to

wish in tune to the sun slipping
behind Mont Ventoux, "I hope I never

see the world below again." Heat.
Hands covering hands covering hands.

Heat. Hands covering hands
covering hands covering wingtips.

CHAPTER FIFTY-ONE

SHIELD

---

*Footnote **

Pause. This is not a poem—oh!
I've already revealed this is not!

Repetition is a shield. What I
find difficult to face—and bear—

is the sight of so many men
I have felled to their knees.

Tears are my domain, I kept
insisting to these lovely and

lonely men. But they would
not listen. They persisted in....

Pause. Fine. The choice was
not theirs. Pause. I apologize.

"I am a mother no matter what
I give birth to." Now, even flies

weep. Cry themselves off walls.
Pause. Dear Ones. Dears.

Stand. Pause. Let me wipe your
cheeks and find you in distinct colors.

CAVE

Footnote *

So, bright angel, hold my hand.
Let's turn "everything" into abstract

background to the foreground of our
escape. *A fire burns in the ice*

cave. She says, "I want this
pain."' Angel says, "I know you

want this pain." She says, "I
long to be a tree in a hurricane.

Uprooted, I finally would be flying!"
Angel says, "You want this pain."

CHAPTER FIFTY-THREE

LIMP

Footnote *

Roses can be crimson all
they want. They would not

be as lovely without the commas
of their thorns whispering

to fingers caressing gardens:
Inhale/Exhale. Darling, purrrrrrr…..

Then, my Love, I might say
Damn me for missing you.

As if you never tried to
mask your own longings

as *Hope,* you foretold, is not
something we can share. Damn

the perfection of your crooked body
whose contours I committed to

memory when I watched your back
limp to recede to pure moonlight.

For which my eyes parted lips. For
which my tongue slipped

out to lick. To no avail.
Moonlight tastes theoretical.

CHAPTER FIFTY-FOUR

ROMAN

Footnote *

You met me when my spirit was
bent. I was ready to be a Roman

widow. Perhaps I, too, would have
healed were I taken to a "place

of bees" where the drone would
suck the widows' grief and "disperse

it into dissolving shards of light."
I envision relief might be defined

as watching days unfold through
"a haze of pollen dust." Why then

must I remain the expert at bad
timing? I still search for pine to

perfume my hair long after my
womb has deafened to

the pleas of men who adore hair
scented by pine. I am trying to

straighten my spirit but it anti-stands
as intractable as steel. Don't

ever let anyone advise you:
spirit, soul, etcetera is intangible.

CHAPTER FIFTY-FIVE

L O A V E S

My menstrual period reared up today.
Bent me forward as if to

catch the moan just spilled
(of course, I first typed "moon").

I want Mama who was never
my mother. I long to be the

schoolgirl never ignored by Mama
who was never my mother. Thus, begins

a pattern of third parties. Adultery, say,
would be easy. Was easy. That I did

it visually instead of physically
does not cancel how I laughed when

a novelist wrote with zero irony:
"He gives me his honey but my hive

is empty." I laughed. Then I scoffed.
Then I cried. He also gave her loaves

dotted with olives and partridges
stuffed with apricots. I cried at her bounty

that is my lack. Daintly dabbed at
damp lashes with a silk handkerchief

I stole from a different scene
in the same story. Then I cried again.

For some people, falling like an angel
is incentivized by one's sheer humanity.

CHAPTER FIFTY-SIX

WARM

Footnote *

That a journey caused you
to end a sentence

does not mean you said
everything you intended.

But the result would not
change if your enemy

was not time. "A single bee
must fly over 25,000 kilometers

to fill a single jar of honey."
Yes, exhausting, isn't it.

Plus. To impregnate his queen,
a male honeybee's genitals

must explode. Etcetera, yes.
Just light a small fire with

grapevine wood. I can warm
my feet and you can refuse to watch.

CHAPTER FIFTY-SEVEN

PROPOLIS

---

*Footnote **

Eyes suddenly wet. _____
I am spanked by the idea of

"blood memory." Its existence
allows me to hope you will

_____ "eight times daily
for a perfect fruit to bloom."

You hide from the world through
accented butlers and chandeliers

or for what walls they _____.
But blood memory sets in stone

how your propolis belongs to me.
For which, pre-gray, you conceded

wings. How else did your veins
come to memorize the bend of

your waist as you offered star milk.
I suckled while, yes, you beamed.

Oh, you have plummeted so far…
You glowed at where I kneeled

_____, my face
paling into the gleaming complexion

_____cracking
now on a million nude women

immortalized as marble goosing dim
air in museum basements. Such

something, this stubborn sheen. As if
stone possesses blood memories.

Oh, you have plummeted so far …
See stone. Cracked, _____

_____it reveals veins. Dear, do lick
off the blood weeping from stone lips.

CHAPTER FIFTY-EIGHT

SAPPHIRE

---

*Footnote **

In poetry, there exists
no such thing as the opposite

of God. To learn this
is to tear down the sky

in deference to the color
blue. You who dismiss

or rank or canonize
or de-canonize these *very*

alive creatures known
to humans as poems

will never know blue
as blue. You may guess

sapphire, cobalt, turquoise,
lapis lazuli, sky, sea, more

of that damned sky.
I pity you for your lack.

I can say all this with my
nose snorting forth

its snorting music. For
mine eyes have memorized

the glory of blue. Now, some
of you are sufficiently wise

to ask: "Advice?" Generously
I share: Pluck out your

eyes. Throw them as high
as you are able, as far away

from your bloodied hands.
Even if blood is red

red is not blue. Get blind.
See blue. Get blind. Be blue.

CHAPTER FIFTY-NINE

STREWN

Footnote *

If this spell does not work,
leash your laughter. It is

only my first attempt: Smell
the scent rising from my breasts

as you walk between purple
mounds of lavender strewn on

mountain paths. See my eyes repeat
themselves ten thousand times

among the white carpet of fallen
almond blossoms clinging

to your ankles. Become the bee
stilling me as you travel from

my hair to perch on my lip.
"Suddenly the sky is struck through

with lightning, a sky bruised
blue from the suck of memory."

Oh, it takes more than bravery
to penetrate past a stranger's

gold ring dangling between my
thighs. It takes more than

bravery to plunge into the well
known by uniformed members

of your sex as "void gone wild."
It takes more than bravery to

_____ for virgin honey. The
oldest crone still contains a spring

of sweetness awaiting release.
It takes more than bravery.

It takes _____
_____ absolutely scared shitless.

CHAPTER SIXTY

BLINKED

Footnote *

Form meets Future. Hence
sudden appendages. Angel

-o, the drapery man, revealed,
"After I do what I do,

the curtains better appear
as if they've always been

hanging *there* in the room.
To appear new is to fail."

After months of trying, I saw
my wings in the mirror, rising

up and down to soothe
just-woken light. Blinked.

O ye — nothing again but glass
and morning. Still, I am able to

share with much pleasure: my
feathers shine! Preen! *Gleam*

of Gleaming. Twirl and preen!
And familiar! Like a poem: there

but not *there*. God of Light,
I feel difficulty recede from accepting

You are most visible when I
blind my Miss Universe eyes.

CHAPTER SIXTY-ONE

ORCHARDS

Footnote *

Don't be fooled by my jokes.
To feel my breasts is

to remember the faces
pressed against my cleavage.

Like those of roses and girls
dropped in orchards of leafless

trees surrounded by winter
fields barren with cut grapevines.

The girls bear holes bulleted
through cruel eyes. Bullets

and eyes "the size of buttons
on convent dresses." Their fathers

hide on mountains, foraging
"for "truffles, wild asparagus, tiny

mushrooms....only to find mines"
that sear off the skin from their

bowed faces. This is a world
of defiance defined by muscles

squeezing accordions for non-
Baptismal hymns to which thieves

and priests lock arms to not-
dance. October is a generous

sun against my face and sleeveless
arms as I attempt to salvage meaning,

only to discover I am sprouting feathers
dropped from the backs of raped

brides virginized by Jesus Christ.
Suddenly, I realize: I am writing

100 poems in order to fuel a certain
long-haired woman's funeral pyre.

PLASTIQUE

Footnote *

I can cook up a plastique
bomb faster than I can make

an omelet. I can write a poem
quicker than you can forgive me.

I must protect my fragile feet from
sticking to our "shifting landscape."

ARK

Footnote *

Minus the fact that we were the ones
whose teeth clung to the tightly-sealed

windows of the Ark where progeny
rested assured through the mating mates

while we remained silent, unable
to plead for entry as we were the ones

clinging with our teeth as we had no
hands. Simply wings useless against

the flooding necessitated by pre-Rapture
days. So come, Rapture. My teeth are bared.

CHAPTER SIXTY-FOUR

MIEN

Footnote *

M_____ never told me, *Heaven is*
not a poem burning through your

veins. Ach. All this negation as if
a certain story was never myth

-ologized by a tribe who sought
to placate a volcano. A myth

for which ten thousand virgins
plummeted before learning

how to unfurl their wings. This
is a myth for idiots: to display joy

is to court the curses of gods.
As if gods do not exist. As if my face

is not lovelier than any mien borne
by a god. As if I cannot soar higher

than any god. As if my breasts can
-not topple all mountains designed by

gods. As if the sky does not sink
closer whenever I am sad. As if I

cannot woo gods not to offer
immortality. As if I call myself: *Poet.*

CHAPTER SIXTY-FIVE

LAMENTATION

Footnote *

Just as the opposite of God
does not exist in a poem

neither do Heaven or Hell.
Neither do Dream or Reality.

"I do not believe in this house
of lamentation. We are all

missing children." A baby's
death cannot prevent

a mother's milk from erupting
(how absolutely un-erotic:

the sight of milk leaking
from a forlorn woman's breasts).

An angel's falling cannot
create anything except poems

made from too many antonyms
for Bliss. *Humans never learn…*

Sad notions birthed from the quest
-ion, "Lord, why hast thou

abandoned me?" The question
is continuously asked by

those who had been the ones
to depart. Tonight, I didn't quest,

question, or ask. I just threw white
roses off the mountain. White petals

fragmented space into parallel
layers of white and light and

though the image was beautiful,
neither was it profound or useful.

All this is to say: too many reasons
underlie my preference for the erotic.

CHAPTER SIXTY-SIX

CITY

Footnote *

*"We've never met. But I love
your poems so much I swear*

*I'd recognize you if we passed
within 10,000 feet of each other*

*in a city of skyscrapers built for two
bulging with 10 million inhabitants."*

Uh. Okay. Messages like this
are my due. But I keep forgetting

whether you write love letters
to me or I write them to her.

A bee buzzes by the lemon
slice failing to sweeten his water.

CHAPTER SIXTY-SEVEN

EBONY

Footnote *

I shall steal tree bark to etch
100 poems. I shall burn

100 poems for white ash.
I shall toss white roses

off the edge of the mountain.
100 poems shall snow.

The air shall whiten to serve
as pleasing contrast to black wings.

Ten thousand years from this
minute of living a poem, I shall

preen on a painting immortalizing me:
old but with hair a stubborn ebony.

CHAPTER SIXTY-EIGHT

SACRIFICE

Footnote *

I suppose I might as well reveal
I have tasted all of the sexual

positions imagined by humans who've
worn trench coats to cross thresholds

into mahogany-walled cities in nations
who lost their nation-making wars.

When I unfurl my wings, therefore,
know my act as one of human sacrifice.

I am the one whose gaze can sweeten
lemons, the one who mated "dove,

eagle and lion" to birth the confusion
secretly desired by philosophers.

I can even hit homeruns on the
football field, then toss in a ball

for a three-pointer. And, beloveds,
if you amuse me, I can turn blonde.

CHAPTER SIXTY-NINE

VOTIVE

Footnote *

Why must every word define
heartbreak? Word after

word after. The blind
watchdog's eyes are red

under the noonday sun—
so what? A blind dog's

eyes lit into "luminous red."
So what? You are turning

my wine into vinegar fit
only for burning acid

into a god's fresh wound.
Why are we sponging

vinegar into a wound?
Why is a blind dog

the one who keeps watch?
Why use words for Poetry?

There must be a necessity
to my wreaking poems

over men parachuting into burning
seas when the scene is only

a photograph tacked near Virgin
Mary within a freezing stone grotto

that plummeted into darkness
after you startled me into whirling

my skirt into a wind that blew out
all the flickering votive candles.

CHAPTER SEVENTY

RIPEN

Footnote *

I drool forth so many languages
trying to stick to my one and

only tongue…*stamens rising from*
lilies bowed over brass casket…

by window where figs darken
fist-sized globules to ripen…to fall

and split to a slick red tempting
tongue away from trembling thigh…

The path keeps crumbling. Fear
inevitable totality of required collapse.

Wings keep blossoming into the dark
blossom whose maturity it does not

form. The world must be so large
not to be encompassed within the span

of a single wing's perpetual
unfurling. The path is disappearing

before my tip-toed feet while my
wings keep blossoming insufficiently

for a rescue known as flight.
The path keeps crumbling while

my feet remain latched to ground.
Then I wake from the dream.

My name is not Maria. My name is
not Maria. My name is not Maria

CHAPTER SEVENTY-ONE

DECAY

---

*Footnote **

The neighbor's vines bleed
over 200 acres in the valley.

Beset with "Pierce's Disease,"
they hijacked a sunset

and melted it russet over
this trembling land. No cure

exists. The veins must be yanked
out and burned. The land must be

replanted. My neighbor "is in
denial," seeing nothing wrong

with his fields. "But of course,"
I tell Barry with whom I shoot

the breeze. "The man is the same
age as his fields. They share bones."

Shoot the breeze? I think I loathe
that phrase. Reminds me of

children felled by bullets from
hunters blinded by tall bushes.

To shoot the air is to shoot
more than air. "His fields may be

dying," Barry observes. "But, man,
are they pretty!" Shoot the breeze.

"It's what autumn addresses: the beauty
of decay." I don't shoot the breeze.

I nod the silence of a recovering
addict whose obsession counted years

of trafficking in decay. Once, I thought
autumn was transcendence,

as when I forced myself into your
hotel room, knowing I am irresistible.

CHAPTER SEVENTY-TWO

RADIANCE

Footnote *

Tell me more of the unending radiance
your eyes discovered when pressed

against the hole into a honeycomb.
Say turquoise. Say my uncut hair

coiling around your eyes. Say berry.
Say your finger circled hard around

my toe. Tell me more of the unending
radiance erupting when eyes pressed

against honeyed wombs. Say my name.
You don't know my name? Make it

up. Then say my name. Tell me more
of the unending radiance of honeyed eyes.

CHAPTER SEVENTY-THREE

HEAVY

Footnote *

No bushel of sins is too heavy
for my back to bear as

I have destroyed a life to prepare
for this bushel of sins which

I was fated to carry as I
soar towards the sun in whose

fire I shall burn this bushel
of sins intended to hold

"the sins of humanity" but
dominated by the sins I

gleefully committed before
I destroyed my life for

You, My Lord, waiting
angrily behind the sun.

Damn You, God, Who only
promised I would fly

without warning me of this
bushel of sins I must bear.

You are fuming, My Lord?
Goddammit, I am furious, too.

CHAPTER SEVENTY-FOUR

LUCRETIA

Footnote *

Threaten me? You idiot. You
are not a ray of light. *Bluster.*

Spear? Please. You'd be lucky
to be a mote. You're not.

"Wingtips smack air." "Cackle."
"Preeeen!" "Wingtip smacks air."

No. Don't lecture me now
on my arrogance, you mere

priest among mere men. Do you
not remember "Lucretia"? Well,

remember! And don't forget another
who renamed herself after ancient

Rome. She was forced to memorize
the movement of snails across

dank, smelly fields beneath a moon
-less sky. Don't pray for her, Father

Idiot. Write her an opera! Then
raise your gold-edged sleeves

to sing as if your salvation depends
on your voice! Sing to ruin neat graves!

CHAPTER SEVENTY-FIVE

STATUE

Footnote *

You've caught me out, My Lord.
I was the One who withheld

her long and lush hair from
drying the feet of your Son

who pleaded with You on my behalf,
"Forgive her as she knows not

what she is saying." I believe You
decipher my true plea and why

I no longer cut my hair. "In the cool
dampness of the grotto is a lichen-

covered marble statue of Our Lady.
She is seated, cradling her full-

grown son in her arms. Her son
is dead from the cross, his hands,

feet, and side pierced with fatal wounds."
Our Lady's expression is simply ironic.

CHAPTER SEVENTY-SIX

PERFUME

Footnote *

I've done that thing and
it's an overrated thing. I read

one of youse actually proclaim
"The true artist matures into

this thing." Youse! When you
are abandoned, why do you want

to say, "***********" then follow up
by announcing, "Asterisk!" Why

do you repeat yourself when our
sister is burning at the stake

and the smoke rising is not
a "drop-dead gorgeous hue"

misting languorously towards
Mont Ventoux? When the scent

of her burning flesh is my perfume
filling your room where you lie nude?

CHAPTER SEVENTY-SEVEN

CODE

Footnote *

$E = mc2$. That is not the code.
They have no imagination — these

heathens now driving nails into
my palms. Muscles of sheer dumb

-ness. I don't bleed blood. I loosen
paint that writes a thousand words

per picture. Like the scene of
a dozen pink piglets scattering

after I shot their mother. The sound
brought forth the anti-Christ soldiers

now crucifying me. In the dark,
I mistook the wild boar for a human

general. Both shared eyes irradiated
by the yellow fear of the unknown.

Of course there was a priest nearby.
I saw the old man quivering beneath

the cracked lantern he held up
to light the way to my torture chamber.

I shall bleed for him, too, in his fraying
nightshirt, looking back at my breasts

as I dripped. I shall write of his
craven image as the punchline.

CHAPTER SEVENTY-EIGHT

NUNS

---

*Footnote **

You think war is over. But patrols
remain on the streets, lovely with

cobblestones and windowboxes
full of daisies. We don't recognize

the uniforms they wear. No alternatives
exist to believing them when they

say they are on our side. I believe
them only because most don't have

enough hair on their chins to shave.
They have yet to remember: the compass

is broken. But the air is so warm,
the birds so musical, the sky so lit!

Wings, do permit a respite from your
growing. Please. Each inch presses

the thorns deeper into my purpling brow.
I am tired from seeing nuns in dirtied gowns.

TOWER

Footnote *

Chapter Something. A love shaped
like a bird. A complicity of silence

shapes a boat. A boat glides across
green glass. Glass shines as it

breaks against a tower built by my
lover who expatriated me from

China. Something happens to me.
My lover is the captive in his tower.

HONEYDEW

Footnote *

"Maybe I am dead." A dot in the eye
of a bird seen in profile. "Blood from

my hands leaks into white porcelain
bowls filled with warm, salty water."

I never felt the hammer's claw pull
out the nails rusting in my sanctified

palms. "This is not a normal world."
Otherwise, I'd be joyous planting

melons, harvesting melons, eating
melons: *canary, cantaloupe, honeydew…*

CHAPTER EIGHTY-ONE

PULSE

Footnote *

Finger on the lime green skin
of a one-year-old rattlesnake

ran over by a neighbor's truck
(I guessed its age by the

single rattle on its tail).
Scales still pulse, surfacing

a poem that long refused
an obscure destiny. Finger

on a baby arguing its fate,
I finally hear the Poem

born again. It gleefully proclaims
Redemption! Then it proceeds:

ECSTATIC AIR (#2)

Triumph. Music
swelling.

Chimes
echo chimes.

Say, "starkness of
beautiful heels."

Say, "woman
reading fabulously."

The challenge
of private poetry

lowers
its head

via science

of tranquility

(expansion
just enough

for
"endless benefit").

O Genesis!
Your letter clearing

space for the *Poem*
now beginning a book.

CHAPTER EIGHTY-TWO

SULPHUR

Footnote *

My feathers are mangled and bleeding.
So what? God blinds me with His

gaze before His eyes of burning mirrors
spotlit a fate he negates for my wingtips:

"hands yellow and shriveled, palms
pierced with deep purple wounds,

fingers curled inward like the claws
of a dead chicken." Unlike Lucretia,

if ever I wish to fire a rifle, I shall pull
the trigger with deadly accuracy.

Let me never, Lord, shoot a gun.
Let me never scent air with sulphur.

Let me never, Lord, shoot a gun.
My aim is true. My aim is a *Poem*.

CHAPTER EIGHTY-THREE

ZIGGURAT

Footnote *

So a painting uses cheerful pastels
to attract the viewer, only to bar

the gaze with a surface so worked over
it becomes the indifferent matte

of plastic or steel. So forget metaphors.
One licks with a tongue, not with the eyes.

When you come closer to sniff my
perfume, don't part the hair tufting

from my nape blackened by a ziggurat tattoo.
Don't leap there to taste where jasmine

is most redolent. Or, fine, part your lips
if you insist. I never claimed to be the label

imposed on me: "Angel." I am the one
romanticized for violets seeping from my lids.

CHAPTER EIGHTY-FOUR

ARCHITECTURE

Footnote *

The moon? O ye humans.
For centuries you stared

at a nipple you could not
recognize for the milkdrop

threatening to fall, but never
dropping so as to keep the breast

's owner amused. Then you poets
began your drunken odes…

O ye humans. Will you ever
see beyond what you see…

Don't even get me started on
Roman architecture—designing towers

that turn humans into dwarves, that
allow gods to pretend they are giants…

CHAPTER EIGHTY-FIVE

SOAR

---

*Footnote **

A man dreamt of humans
as "holy." For this, he

was stoned to death.
It is difficult to fly from this.

But I will soar *for* the man
who read a poem

then crooned at the page
as if the page could hear

Dimidium animae meae…
Half my soul…

W A X

Footnote *

Ah, Zermano. You thought them
vultures — these huge creatures

leaping from the stone escarpment
below your aerie hermitage.

You immortalized their black
majestic wings soaring to penetrate

Miss Constant Sky with your
oft-reproduced painting

A Torrent of Black Flowers.
No, Zermano. You were looking

at *us* without your spectacles.
How else do you wake each day

to the scent of wax burning?
Old man, you shall die before

an easel, as you desire,
though you are painting the

winter with cataract eyes. Your
Paradise, Zermano, shall be to see

clearly the naked black flowers
modeling as your black flowers.

To see us, the Ones who can
fill tunnels with scents emanating

from behind our knees. When we
are in good humor, we allow

ourselves to be inhaled, to be
threaded through mortal veins.

CHAPTER EIGHTY-SEVEN

PAGES

Footnote *

Describe me as lava. Describe me
clichetically. It doesn't matter.

Just describe me. *Flaming.* Others
are reading us. Describe me. *Fall-*

ing. Others indifferent to the embrace
we never whatever. The gown you never

ripped off my shoulders but should
have. Describe me. "Fob off

thinking" on me? Fine. Poor
exhausted mortal. But never stop

describing me. Particularly in
scenes that never leave a diary

of folded pages. Describe me.
Your wife is reading us. You have

a wife? I knew that—I am winking.
Wives believe I am a threat to

wives. Poor women who bleed
my eyes. Don't you see? Husbands

always leave me. So describe me.
I shall torch the hands you shall

place on your wife's waist as you
pull her closer to remember

what you both forgot and never
will again: how flesh burns

painlessly. Describe me. *Fiery,*
Fired-Up Loneliness. So what? I gladly

bear this anguish that barely approximates
the solitude felt by daunted God.

CHAPTER EIGHTY-EIGHT

LULLABYE

---

*Footnote **

Your opposite accepted my omelet
in bed, and addressed the red rose

in a crystal vase as "logical." You
slipped on yesterday's clothes for

coffee and donuts from the corner
grocery. The coffee was hot, its milk

sweetening staleness away from
cheap pastries. You transformed

morning light into "yummy" from my
lips instead of the pouting dusk

remaindered by your decision
to sleep on the sofa. You might

think kindness to be someone else's
lullabye, as your opposite believed,

but your translation respects hidden
contexts. These couplets hide

behind journalism ignored by
committees cogitating over the Pulitzer

Prize or Genius Of The Year.
Poetry is elsewhere—outside

the four walls of this page.
We hear each other

past hiccups in rhyme
and this last line to form a couplet.

CHAPTER EIGHTY-NINE

JEZEBEL

Footnote *

My breasts are not covered by soiled
bandages that, if unwrapped, would

stain the air with the "rancid smell
of mildewed oranges." Nor are you

the lover who would cover his eyes.
We could have survived a city —

it doesn't matter which — that forced
us to dine on soup whose only meat

was the brief accent from a $4 rat's
cheek. But we began from opposite

directions when we returned to
the unkempt House of a long-drowsy

God, though we both inched through
the last mile on bare knees across

gravel. Now, we form prodigals at
temporary rest, my breasts rising high

and golden-brown, *there there* between
us as we do not touch. You will not

compete with the Lord who made you
a Poet, thus fully capable of affording me.

You learned something from your journey
that I didn't learn from mine: I sing

with your breath but am not the Song.
So you content yourself by listening

to my breasts. You listen to the perfume
rising from the valley that is also our

Lord's. You listen to the pulse on my
throat that visibly dances when you

approach. You listen and listen, Mr. Deaf
-ness Incarnate. Soon, I hope to forgive

you since, every so often, you raise
my uncut hair to wipe my cheeks

and whisper, "Silly ex-Jezebel, this
is absolutely not a compromise."

CHAPTER NINETY

NOBILITY

Footnote *

I wanted to be the fig
splitting between your teeth.

But you deliberately cited "peach."
That it was ripe and luscious

does not change your decision
to say "sweet" via critical objectivity.

Did you not notice the Moorish garden
whose fountain of tiles form midnight?

Such is the power of color, the flux
of the frame, the nobility of sheen.

CHAPTER NINETY-ONE

GYPSY

Footnote *

I was watching as you prowled
through Pigalle's brothels searching

for women resembling my eyes.
You found a young gypsy who fled

Barcelona, only to discover herself
even more hunted in Paris. "When

her tongue came into me, I felt
the tip of her loss," you say.

Her tongue, my tongue. No need
to marvel why she brought my scent

into your atelier. You painted her mourn
-ing and, like a poem, it is universal.

I do understand: you withhold to give
X times more than what I said I wanted.

T I E D

---

*Footnote **

Once, I was so committed
to Communism, I prostituted

myself. Those who bought me
fragmented into light. The problem

with slogans is their deadening
effect, similar to sex "with hands tied."

ISLAND

Footnote *

We outsmarted ourselves: our non-
marriage means no divorce.

O revelation swooning eternity…
Your ring hangs between my thighs,

illegal on purpose. The sun sinks
into the sea, casting golden light

"into a small bedroom carved into
the cliffs" as crickets announce night.

We survive the world by living
on an island shaped as a comma,

a profile irrelevant to the sea
our island interrupts, irrelevant

to birds, lizards, fishermen who do not
pause. But an antique omen

to local seers who know to pause,
for they are false prophets after all.

Your ring hangs between my thighs.
You love to yank me forward, growl

with zero pauses, "Come here
with zero pauses, my non-Wife."

CHAPTER NINETY-FOUR

LITANY

Footnote *

The favor I will never ask you:
something tangible for moi verbose lips,

its Platonic approximation the pale coins
of dough sold as flayed from the flesh

of God's Son. My bedtime prayers as
you watch from the other side of a half-

open door scores the dry litany, "More,
More…" *You are sumptuous fragility.* For

you, I shall end these poems by opening
the book I shall write entitled *Silence.*

I was orphaned by Truth, hence ancestry:
haeretici perfecti dragging me by the hair

through residual days scaffolded by
your distance behind a wall of woven holes.

You pledge: "I vow the constancy of mine
eyes." How to hold on to *that* when I remain

Sincerely Yours, An Avid Meat-Eater?
Recall the "shivering beef" we shared

with villagers of Montaillou. Afterwards,
you bathed in my hair. Afterwards, our

trance of translating the Bible into
the vernacular. Vernacularly now,

Fuck it! I am blathering. I can blather
all I want. I never hid my Faith as

one of betrayals. While those who hurt
me—thus you—were simply cheats.

CRITIC

---

*Footnote **

I obviated atheism
for a critic. I destroyed

a critic's career.
Preen! Hell shrunk!

HOLES

---

*Footnote **

It's not the dress. It's the woman.
I dress in holes parading through

chateaux. Let me tell you, children:
Crucifixion is the least of it.

Lace is lovely, but why work
the needle? Leave the fairy

footprints to pink faeries. I am
woman telling you, *You are*

Woman! To make tapestries
possible, Diana hunted stags.

CHAPTER NINETY-SEVEN

PAPAYA

Footnote *

We understand this misunderstanding
as something that must remain

untouched. *O, air leaving palms split-
ting for three crosses… O, ex-Taste…*

Degas wrote as he became blind:
"The heart grows rusty if unused."

Come over for breakfast. I have
mastered lime squeezed over papaya.

I no longer believe, "A mistress makes
for a better poet than doth a wife."

CHAPTER NINETY-EIGHT

GLORY

Footnote *

Velazquez's *Las Meninas*
reveal God In All His Glory

cracking a dark mirror.
"Apollo! Not another woman!"

Obra culminate
de la pintura universal.

I long for your eyes
the same color as mine.

Did I tell you of squeezing
limes over papayas?

I can borrow them from
another poem.   I want to lick

your juicy chin, your lips
parted by the blindfold.

Or you can lick my juicy chin,
my lips parted by the blindfold.

CHAPTER NINETY-NINE

B L I N D F O L D

Footnote *

Muse, Muse, Muse, Muse, Muse,
Muse, Muse, Muse, Muse, Muse

Those who helped the muse of Velazquez
write her *Love's Autobiography*

form a short list of names. *For shame...!*
I am writing a long list of your name,

your name, your name, your name...
A list that shall never end "(perhaps)"

for my pen writing your name will cease
only if I ("undress" to) lose this liturgy.

You deciphered that code for me,
ignoring my desired translation:

> "Verily would I shed clothes
> to lose my name in yours."

Muse, Muse, Muse, Muse, Muse,
Muse, Muse, Muse, Muse, Muse...

I would wear the black smock of
a "Good Woman," carry a spindle

from room to room. But each drop of
the spindle would be my anti-*Lord's Prayer*:

Muse, Muse, Muse, Muse, Muse,
Muse, Muse, Muse, Muse, Muse...

I would not miss my rose-skirted gowns
or earrings of sapphire birds.

I would not miss the fast horses.
I would not miss half-spoken sentences.

I would not miss the cache of stones
I netted in my skirt to protect Magdalene...

Muse, Muse, Muse, Muse, Muse,
Muse, Muse, Muse, Muse, Muse...

CHAPTER ONE HUNDRED*

I hunted Helene because she was his wife and I was in love with him. That's the story of my life: a series of compromises. What mostly surprises me now is how, in the beginning, I thought I would have fun.

As always, Helene was looking at him adoringly. He was expounding, no doubt, on the "parallel universes" for which his sculptures of thick steel squares ostensibly provided "doorways" to experiences which the "discerning" could enjoy—I'd heard this all before as he becomes even more garrulous than usual during postcoital bliss. His show at the Contemporary Museum of Art in SoHo featured the thresholds to 12 different worlds of such experiences.

I looked at him and Helene over the rim of my wine glass from the other side of the wide room. They seemed to gather all the radiance emanating from the halogen lights and bouncing from the white walls as dark shapes contracted and expanded around them from the adoring crowd. He was dressed in Armani. She was also in black, but I mostly noticed the tightness of her clothes which further highlighted her high breasts and narrow waist. I began by envying her figure, then I began to salivate.

She was five years younger than him, a year older than me. She was also an artist and mostly painted small abstract works. She was beginning to develop a reputation, but it seemed likely that it may never be known if any success she will muster would have occurred had she not married the sculptor once heralded as "The Only Artist Who Could Out-Macho Richard Serra." As with most things, it often takes more than talent to attain recognition. Looking at her then, however, I knew she didn't marry him for advancing her career, which was rumored about his first wife. I recognized that light that glimmered in her eyes whenever she looked at him—how, even when she was talking with someone else, her eyes kept shifting until she could locate him within the perimeter of her vision. I still look at him that way. *I will always look at him that way.*

But I couldn't have him. He had been willing to have me as his secret mistress. Once, he had said as he stroked between my thighs while I stood naked before him, "Seurat had a secret lover for years. But her role as his mistress became known only after he died."

I wasn't listening then, or listening as well as I try to do nowadays: I replied by asking him not to marry Helene, thereby breaking the rules of our engagement. He then said it was "the end," which didn't stop him from fucking me one last time. Which didn't stop me from falling to my knees and opening my mouth for him one last time. But, as I often have consoled myself, I was, after all, in love. *I am still in love.*

He hadn't seen me yet, or if he had he wasn't showing any consciousness of my presence. I knew they had just returned from their honeymoon in Capri. They both looked tan. I leaned back against the wall as I felt jealousy rear up at an image of them on the beach, she undoubtedly topless while he smoothed oil on her breasts. I remembered how his hands had grasped my breasts, kneading them from behind silk. I always wore silk tops for him. He had loved to pinch my nipples, then move me around with his fingers still clamped on my nipples. I thought of doing that to her, too.

"I like my sex rough," he had warned shortly after the first time I had convulsed around his tongue.

"Whatever you want," I had replied and only leaned closer towards him.

A few moments later, I had asked him if I gave him something he couldn't get from anyone else. We both had known we were discussing Helene, innocent Helene, as he had uttered, "Yes."

"Then why. . ." I had tried to ask, but he had silenced me by tightening his hold on my breasts.

"There are certain things we must never discuss. One of them is Helene."

As he had taught me, I had whispered, "Yes, Master: whatever you want."

I looked at Helene's jutting breasts and wondered if, just as she unknowingly was unable to satisfy him, there was some need he didn't know about her and, thus, was unable to fulfill. Once more, I considered how so many couples compromise for the end result of being buried in coffins laid side by side.

*****

"I see that you like breaking the square," I said as I circled the walls of her studio. This was the third time I'd met Helene after her husband's museum show. I had introduced myself to her while she was replenishing her wine glass, and managed to engage her in a discussion about her work. Naturally, I had become familiar with her paintings through various group exhibitions in town—I wanted to know anything that even remotely touched his life. Helene seemed to be in a period of featuring incomplete squares within her paintings. The ruptured squares were set against lushly painted surfaces etched here and there with slanting horizontal lines.

"Yes, well. There's no such thing as perfection, is there?" she replied, handing me a glass of champagne.

"Champagne?" I smiled.

"Well, it's your first time in my studio," she said as we lightly touched our glasses together.

Her studio was tiny, but had a large window that framed the World Trade Center.

"Oh, those," she replied, almost surprised, after I mentioned the twin towers. "I rarely focus on the buildings. I usually look at the water."

She went over to a file cabinet, pulled out the top drawer and motioned me over to look. I joined her and saw that the top drawer was full of drawings, all evoking waves.

"Hmmm. So the etched lines on your paintings are actually just minimalized portraits of broken surfaces? Like the tips of waves when they swell to sunder the watery surface?

390

How did you come to have such an affinity for broken surfaces, for imperfection?"

"Most people don't see that, even after they see my drawings," she replied, smiling, though she dodged my questions.

I wanted to press her but suddenly noticed how she seemed to be nervous. She seemed to have stopped breathing.

*****

"It's not that I'm not receptive," I said as I finally moved, raised one palm to stop her from taking off her blouse. I had decided to let the silent expand between us, simply looking back into her sad eyes until she raised her hands and started slowly unbuttoning her blouse. But though I stopped her from letting the blouse fall, they already gaped to reveal the breasts that had so tantalized me during his exhibit and which I furtively relished with my eyes at every opportunity.

"I want to please you," she blurted. Then she reached for my right hand and pressed it against her left breast. *The weight of a soft pear: I felt the doves on the windowsill begin to weep.* Silently, I began to roll her pink nipple gently between my fingers as, with my other hand, I raised the champagne glass to the pink nub. She parted her lips when I dribbled champagne on her breast but didn't utter a sound. *I was an eagle: my lips swooped down.*

*****

"Why?"

Of course, I asked her the question only afterwards. Is not such the manner of those who intend to seduce—first physically overcome the target and reserve any discussion for the "afterwards"? I had learned this from him. I stood over her drinking directly from the champagne bottle as she remained in the position I'd left her, lolling back against the folds of raw canvas I had flung across the floor before pushing her down.

As I had done after the first time with her husband, she felt a shyness surface. She began to close the thighs I had parted as wide as she could muster before I left her on the floor. I stopped her when I whispered, "Sssshhh." Then I whispered again, "Spread."

She was my own painting, my version of Courbet's "The Origin Of the World." But her hair was silkier than the coarse, bushy hair Courbet painted on his model. At the moment, the hairs were also matted together from our sweat, which only served to heighten the mouth of the cave still rearing at me, offering at its center a ridge replete from my fingers' furious dance.

"How pink it is," I said, then dribbled champagne on it.

She wriggled, and I loved it.

I asked again, "Why?"

*****

I refused to leave my reflection. I kept staring into my eyes as I considered her replies to my question. Beyond my bathroom door, the apartment whose address I'd used for 20 years felt alien to me. When Helene had said that she suspected he was having an affair, I had only encouraged her to continue talking. When she had said she wanted a woman's love because her experience seemed to prove the impossibility of obtaining love from a man, I had began straightening my clothes to leave.

Immediately, she had leapt from the floor and flung her arms around me. It was the first time I had noticed her lips nude, lipstick long licked or bitten away.

"Please. Please tell me you'll return."

The best I could do, even as my hands began fondling her breasts then twisting her nipples the way he had loved to do to me, was to repeat something he also once said to me, "I will never ignore you."

*****

I already anticipated the ending of this story. Helene would leave him for me. And I would cherish her and remain faithful to her for as long as she would choose to remain with me. If later she leaves me, I would return to him; knowing we share the same compulsion, he would take me back. But I would accept the risk that Helene might wish to remain forever with me—blocking from me and him a happy ending that we both once revealed to each other to be something we have never known.

I would accept the risk that would obviate a happy ending for him and me for I have only ever been moved by one thing besides him: the story of George Seurat's mistress who was his lover until she died. She even bore him a child. But no one knew of her existence until after Seurat died. Her name is more relevant than the name of Helene's husband, the target of my obsession, for the purpose of this story.

And I recall too as I begin to prepare to trade the unfolding of this text for the unfolding of another reality which includes Helene's voice now singing into my phone message machine, things are often only what they are named. Thus, for the purpose of this story, you may assume that my name may as well be the same two words that comprised the name of Seurat's secret lover: *Madeleine Knobloch*.

Footnote *

392

IV. THERE, WHERE THE PAGES WOULD END

I saw what those artists saw —
someone half in love with herself
and half in love with the world
—from "January 18, 1979" by John Yau

Footnotes to "Paroles" by Jacques Prevert
(Trans. by Harriet Zinnes)

(ii)
He could not hide his preference for staying hidden within the folds of his mother's voluminous skirts.

Yet she later would have to admit to him, "For you, I would have bought birds."

Thus began a story of a decade whose days were marked by her wondering about "vinegar sauce."

(v)
The bill included 25 centimes as a tip to the waiter.

(vi)
She misconstrued the reality, which was of one last red pepper hanging from a string in front of a white wall—not a "blood teardrop."

(viii)
She anticipated how he would come to hide behind the word "Daddy" — the predictability, albeit sweetness, of that. *That.*

That morning, the water was like Love: miserable and lovely.

He still believed she would save him from entanglement with the underbrush of memory.

A boy hid it in his school desk, the only object in that classroom painted blue.

(xiii)
She was not the author of the black notebook she gave to him, even as she called it "mine" before adding, "Now, it is yours."

(xiv)
As if ashes were not inevitable.

(xvi)
The water lily formed instantaneously.

(xvii)
Of course, laughter is not really comprised of stars.

(xviii)
It always seemed as if only the innocent can define "scarlet."

He could have sworn the sun hummed along.

(xx)
She noticed that only the blind pointed.

Footnotes to
"FORCES OF IMAGINATION" By Barbara Guest

[+]
Except that, ruefully, she often missed the plasticity of recognition, e.g. silk, velvet, moonlight, crème brulee, honey on fingertip, awkward blood…

418

Except that, she understood with that first nibble: she will spend the rest of her suddenly over-long life aching to taste again that poem she swallowed out of existence.

Except that, pride is necessary to locate the eye within spaces lacking discernible perimeters.

[*]
Except that, she never thought consolation existed in her limbs' inabilities to form the lotus position—a position she had not recognized as pure ego.

[^]
Except that, what is obscure is usually not a source for the cheer of false deprecation.

[@]
Except that, the erasure was *earned*.

[%]
Except that, audacity too often must remain a private affair.

[#]
Except that, I can write of castles without fantasy: I do live in a castle *(o, cool limestone!)* and what's the use of apology?

[<]
Except that, she must never privilege the most lotioned flesh over the most grey word — even "grey" can feel like cashmere.

Selected Footnotes to
"Opera" by Barry Schwabsky

---

(12)
In reality, the "mirror" was black glass.

In reality, she felt pathos from the skyline looming from and over an island replete with chastened alleyways.

In reality, he considers her sentences like veins.

432

In reality, Love also wearies the spirit (*but only sometimes*, he hears her plea fading against dusk).

---

(45)
In reality, they share the "Introduction" as a permanent state.

In reality, he became pure throbbing organ.

(2.5 mio.)
In reality, he came to begin each sleep by stuffing his mouth with her jasmine-scented hair.

(2)
In reality, he never failed to witness air spill when she unclenched fists.

In reality, she terrified him—but he would not have preferred an alternative.

(nth power)
In reality, he could not forget her, even when he woke to bludgeon his eyes with the summer-dusted landscape of Gambia.

Footnotes To
"Volume V of The Diary of Samuel Pepys, M.A., F.R.S."*

---

1) Still, he has tasted her lips—that tang defined as the sea, translucent emerald when overcome by the sun.

2) Still, he noticed how her thigh grazed against the rough interior of the boat—that rivulet of blood he desperately wanted to lick as he watched the red line draw itself as if no such thing existed called *Agony*.

3) Still, he heard the wind snap something behind him when he chose to keep his eyes focused on her lashes — how the black silk threads fell to manifest shyness.

4) Still, it was the moment when he recognized that he shall always be helpless whenever he writes her—that his fall towards her is a permanent state, never completing itself.

5) Still, he did not expect the compulsion towards violence — that "something" he cannot articulate except to the air canceling midnight.

6) Still, he mentioned acacia trees looming behind sand dunes; he knew she would recognize he was masking another topic.

7) Still, once he managed to whisper, "I want to define your *Aftermath* with my writing" — though he is uncertain if she heard.

8) Still, he wouldn't mind being cornered in some alleyway looking at a red rose blooming through a stone crack; naturally, since this is his dream, she would be there pointing at the bloom that manifests her middle name.

9) Still, when her toes pinched his ankle under the cafe table he laughed for an unex-
pected reason; he suddenly understood his mouth soon would be intimate with her
breasts.

10) Still, he knew she didn't believe in his lack of imagination; he furrowed his brow as he pledged he would rise to her *Faith*.

11) Still, even when he shall see her "clay feet," his adoration will not stop—such is the extent of his *Imagination*.

12) Still, he anticipated each kiss cannot be completed without licking — many many licks: wet, pink, then red.

13) Still, he once read her poem where, for the poem, she had said nothing is "too much" or "not enough" — that a poem is only what it is.

14) Still, he must have sensed he was approaching a labyrinth; for to adore words is to adore her.

---

15) Still, his desperation is appropriate; the question then is whether she can retain the discipline he freely tossed aside for experiencing his mouth become a cave entirely filled with her hair.

16) Still, he parts his lips for her breath — he is willing to swallow even the indigo scent of her tears.

---

* This is actually "after" _____ by _____ and _____ but their names must never be known by a gossipy public as identities she's deconstructed.

Footnotes to
"The Virgin's Knot" by Holly Payne

(a) He realized her sadness when the weaver formed holes shaped as falling tears.

(b) He baited the soldier because her hair smelled like *that* winter lake.

(c) Revelation etched his eyes when he heard her sing mathematical formulas.

(d) But can symmetry ever rely on memory?

(e) The retired sheepdog's lullabye: a virgin weaving a new row of knots.

(f) She feared the sight of the muezzin circling the minaret, an image she translated as dark shadows forming a noose around the "white tower" she once knew as a certain girl's neck.

(g) "Thirty thousand knots: oh! She had fallen behind since the spring snow!"

(h) She cannot remember a time when her fingers were free of wooden splinters.

(i) He knew her body as a white finger holding back starlight.

(j) Her eyes dampened the stones as she recalled her son's first word: "No."

(l) As a student, she was flawless.

(m) When she mentioned the possibility of forgetting "what it was like before pain," the postman fingered his empty sack and understood a new pain from knowing the possible only as possibility.

(n) In exchange for electricity, they accepted a colonizer's alphabet.

(o) To treat asthma, drink nothing but the liquid from a pigeon's egg for 40 days.

(p) A professional commits space to memory.

476

(r) In her eyes burn the fires of numerous tribes, as well as the redness derived from limbs dropped to the ground by steel.

(s) Broken twigs breaking the donkey's back—such are the temporary opiates of poverty.

(t) She defined ambition as the helpless compulsion to write songs for women who will never wear headscarves.

(u) The rug trade teaches that it takes much time to learn how to love fragments.

(v) Authenticity always wanders.

(w) The thin mattress smelled of lemon and wild rose.

.

(x) The bride wore a red veil, which alerted him to the tears she painted with kohl against her inner thighs.

(y) The anthropology student missed the lecture entitled "Be a ghost to the culture."

(z) He breathed in the air of a country where love for a woman as well as love for a man is love for Allah!

V. ONE POEM, ONE READING

"I refer to my hope that my poems create spaces for experiences that their readers find meaningful, if not pleasurable."
—from "Six Directions: Poetry As A Way of Life"

I think a poem doesn't fully mature without a particular community called reader(s).
—from "The History of Hay(na)ku

from **Silliman's Blog**
By Ron Silliman

Thursday, June 19, 2003

Another writer whose poetry appears in *Van Gogh's Ear* 2, as it seems to be do-
ing virtually everywhere of late, is Eileen Tabios. On top of her work as an editor,
publisher, blogger, vintner, Filipina activist, art critic, conceptual artist & promoter
of hay(na)ku, Tabios either has a mountain of writing tucked away from her days as
an executive in the financial services industry or else she must be the hardest work-
ing person on the planet. I have a hunch that we're dealing with a serious Type A
personality here.

Tabios' prose poem "Helen" [see P. 119] consists of twelve single-sentence para-
graphs, although one of the paragraphs resorts to a favorite device of mine — the em
dash — to create the typographic impression of being a single unit. The poem at heart
is a dramatic monolog, although one written with such discipline that you can read
it, as I did more than once, with total interest & pleasure without even thinking in
terms of the theater of a projected persona.

Part of what makes the text work is that it has a killer first sentence:

> *Part of mortality's significance is that wars end.*

That's one of those lines you can mull over for days, knowing you'll never exhaust it.
The lines that follow for the most part likewise stand on their own. Moreover, there
is enough conceptual distance between them that the reader, in order to render it into
a dramatic monolog, has serious work to do. The line / sentence / paragraph, for
example, that follows the one above, reads:

> *Yesterday, I determined to stop watering down my perfumes.*

The third paragraph connects with the second principally by referring to the first
person:

> *Insomnia consistently leads me to a window overlooking silvery green*
> *foliage —* tanacetum argenteum *— whose species include the tansy which*
> *Ganymede drank to achieve immortality.*

If the first thing that "holds" this text "together" is the two references to the first
person, the second is the binary *mortality/immortality*, although they are not presented
as though we were discussing a paradigm at all. Third, the title "Helen" & the refer-
ence here to Ganymede, classic ideals of heterosexual & homosexual beauty, project
a similar semantic field. Yet at this moment in the text, none of these connections are
intrinsic or necessary, but rather are accumulating through what may appear to be
incidental details.

There is a care & specificity here that is fascinating to watch, for example the choice
of the Latin name, *tanacetum argenteum*, a European plant. The reason Ganymede —
a.k.a Aquarius — might have been given a tansy is that, as a plant that grows in dry
soil, it could retain water in an otherwise parched climate. Tabios takes considerable
care with her diction — there is an ever so slightly elevated solemnity to words such

as *determined* & *consistently* being deployed precisely as they are here. As a textural, as well as textual, strategy, it's close to the prosodic restraint that another author of a poem entitled "Helen," Hilda Doolittle, used to employ.

Just as Tabios has already set up one schema (*insomnia*) as a metaphor for another (*immortality*) that may at first seem rather at odds with it, this poem will be constructed around details that operate counter-intuitively on multiple levels, even as it will turn out in the final moments to be "about" nourishment—that tansy is not incidental. Against the discursive formality, however, the reader is presented with language that operates at different extremes, from the bathetic—*But to be human is to be forgiven*—to over-the-top depiction:

> *Soon, summer shall bring a snowfall of daisies across these leaves whose mottles under a brightening moonlight begin to twinkle like a saddhu's eyes.*

Summer always makes me think of snowfalls too.

Reading the poem over, as I have now a dozen times, my sense is that Tabios wanted to structure a narrative with an extraordinary degree of tension—it is as though she wanted to see just how far she could pull it apart without having the sense of its unity dissolve, to approach without crossing some intuitive breaking point. That's not unlike the strategy in Zen gardening of pulling one stone out of place in order to create a "circle" with far more cognitive power than it could have were it, in fact, perfectly round. Thus, in the third sentence of "Helen" quoted above, the tansy is *silvery green.* This gives it a dynamic it could never have if it were merely silver or green alone.

Narration at the limits of cohesion is an especially challenging project. I remember once trying to read a novel in which every single scene was constructed by focusing initially on some detail — a lampshade, a wall socket, a crack in a windowpane — entirely extraneous to the narrative "action." But it was in translation & you could tell that the translator really didn't grasp what the writer was doing, so the process felt like trying to focus through a film of molasses & I gave up. Faulkner much more successfully does something similar in the Benjamin chapters of *The Sound and the Fury*, presenting "the story" in part (but only in part) from the p.o.v. of a developmentally disabled member of the family, incapable of comprehending the significance of anything. Unlike Faulkner, I don't think that Tabios grounds what she does in "Helen" in psychology, which literally is why it's poetry & not, say, fiction. Like Faulkner, though, she's obsessed with surface & texture—they are what a reader experiences *directly* when confronting a text.

I like writers who take risks—taking responsibility for the whole of the text is for me the primary test of a poem. Tabios tries for more in one page than many other poets would attempt in 20. And she pulls it off.

Wedding Cake for Eileen R. Tabios' Marriage to "Mr/s Poetry" at
Pusod, Berkeley, CA. (Photo by Mike Price)

5NOV02 Letter to Andy Goldsworthy
The poem was written after Andy Goldsworthy's November 5, 2002 diary text for his exhibition at Haines Gallery in San Francisco, CA.

Adjectives From The Last Time They Met
The poem was written after Part I of Anita Shreve's novel *The Last Time They Met.*

ALICANTE
The poem was written after Pages 89 and 90 of Jason Webster's *Duende: A Journey Into the heart of Flamenco* (Broadway Books, 2003).

_____*AND*_____
The phrase "when it's gotten into the blood. It becomes autobiography there" is from "Lowell's Graveyard" by Robert Hass in *Twentieth Century Pleasures: Prose on Poetry* (Ecco, 1984).

Banned and Determined
The poem was partly annotated from Scott Rothkopf's article on Gene Swenson, "Banned and Determined," *Artforum,* Summer 2002.

BESMIRCH
Valery Larbaud was translated from the French by William Jay Smith. The quote is from Walt Whitman's unfinished poem "I Am The Poet".

CAPITULATE
"Quote" from an October 28, 1892 letter from Paula Modersohn-Becker to her parents (*The Letters and Journals of Paula Modersohn-Becker* (Eds. Gunter Busch and Liselotte Von Reinken; Edited and translated from the German by Arthur S. Wensinger and Carole Clew Hoey. Northwestern University Press, 1990).

CHAPTER NINE
The poem was written after Chapter Nine of Zeruya Shaley's *Love Life,* as translated by Dalya Bilu (Grove Press, 1997).

DEFINITIONS
All the poems in this section were written in response to a single word that became the poems' titles; the writing was done according to my attempts for "first draft, last draft." An excerpt from my essay "MAGANDA: Thoughts on Poetic Form (A Hermetic Perspective)" (first published in *MELUS,* Spring 2004) provides more background on these poems:

"A koan from the 'Mumon-kan' ('The Gateless Gate') states: 'you must climb a mountain of swords with bare feet.' These words, according to Buddhist teacher Toni Packer, relate to: 'So can one walk with great care, aware of dangers, not panicky, but stepping carefully? Relating with care, listening with care, really with care, to oneself and the person right next to you?'

"If and when I accomplish greater awareness, my experiences become more heart- and mind-felt. For me, deeper engagement ingrains experiences more passionately and helps them pop up in unanticipated ways during the writing of poems, frequently enervating the poems as well as making them more interesting. Relatedly, these Athena- or Maganda-like poems are similar in my mind to Rinzai brushstrokes. Rinzai represents dynamic, powerful Zen—a practice introduced to me by Buddhist artist Max Gimblett. His calligraphic brushstrokes reflect his rigorous, Rinzai-based practice: that his sumi ink spills out in perfect pitch during a swift, unrehearsed brushstroke against the canvas results from his own observance, spanning decades, of proactive awareness that allows for distillation in his art into faultless form.

"I believe I always will be a neophyte as regards Poetry. But my attempts to walk with bare feet on a mountain of swords included signing up in 2000 for Webster-Merriam.com's 'Word of the Day' service. Through this program, subscribers received daily e-mails of a word with its definition. While the program may be intended to offer a nice means for expanding vocabulary, I also decided that I would write poems entitled with those words. Not knowing the words ahead of time facilitated my writing poems on topics that I might not otherwise address, eliminating ego-based decisions on what to write next in a poem. Relatedly, because I think that I don't write poems to say something but to determine what it is I wish to say, these Webster-Merriam-inspired (WM) poems often alerted me to things that were of concern but to which I had not yet become fully or consciously attentive. Certainly, I believe enlightenment can be a goal in Poetry, as much as it is in Buddhist and other practices.

"…[T]he prose poem [is] a form whose long lines I originally found compatible with my ability to hold my breath for long periods. As I've aged, I've noticed a diminishment in that ability and I find that I cannot read some of my older long lines without the interruption of another inhale. The WM poems allowed me to explore the effect of breath on poetic lines through my use of the period as like a line-break to note the pause required by inhalation, and not just to end a sentence. This has led to my still early investigations on how to break up the prose poem paragraph without obviating the paragraph. …

"The relationship between breath and poetic line has been addressed by many poets and theorists, with ideas ranging over the thought that line breaks should mirror pauses to American poet Charles Olson's theory of "projective verse" whereby the poem is energetically thrown forward from the poet. Though I empathize with Olson's burst-of-energy approach, I am equally interested in the internal alchemy that occurs within the poet prior to the surfacing of the poem.

…

"I see the intake of breath to be related to the alchemical and transformative process of creation, followed by the projected out-breath. Perhaps this is why, in writing the WM poems, I have not opted for the free-stanza form despite noticing how my breath no longer mirrors the long lines I integrated into my earlier prose poems. I didn't wish to negate my history with the prose poem form by now eliminating it from my work. In addition, the line break—that actual cutting off of a line—is a much more blunt cut than the inclusion of a period within the still flowing long line. As a student of Kali, I was taught the significance of "soft" breath by poet and Kali instructor Michelle Bautista. Kali is a Filipino martial arts form that I study because I consider it a metaphor for (how I consider) Poetry. This relationship is evident in my poem 'Kali.' The poem's last stanza explicitly states the importance of perfect pitch, including for me, not privileging…the outtake to the intake (which Bautista also relates to female energies) of breath, or:

> To live poetry
> instead of just marking
> words on a page
> is to live like a poem--
> none of it is too much
> or too little
> It is only what it is
> and all of it is
> perfectly pitched"

"Desperate Trust"
The last couplet's quote is from Barry Schwabsky's poem, "A Weapon of Defense."

Epilogue Poem (No. 4)
The Barthes quote is from *Roland Barthes, The Pleasure of the Text, tr. Richard Miller* (New York: Hill & Wang, 1975).

Epilogue Poem (#18) (Heliotrope)
Written after "Opera" by Barry Schwabsky.

***Fading* Profile (II)**
The third couplet was written after the article "Sierra Leone Is No Place To Be Young" by Jan Goodwin in the *New York Times Sunday Magazine*, Feb. 14, 1999; the fourth couplet after Paul Eluard's "By Virtue of Love" which contains the lines, "*J'ai dénoué la chambre ou jedors / J'ai dénoué la chambre ou je rêve*" which is translated by Marilyn Kallet as "I have untied the room where I sleep, where I dream" from *Last Love Poems of Paul Eluard* (Louisiana State University Press, 1980); and the seventh couplet after Jose Garcia Villa's line, "I have observed pink monks eating blue raisins".

THE DEFINITIVE HISTORY OF FALLEN ANGELS: AN AUTOBIOGRAPHY
All of the "Footnote Poems" in this section were written publicly within 15 days on the author's Poem Blog, "Gasps," at http://loveslastgasps.blogspot.com. The project would not have been possible without the poetics of "Lectio Divina" (Holy Reading) and the scaffolding provided by the lovely writing in Thomas Sanchez' novel, *Day of the Bees*. Also:

Chapter 7
The Italian proverbs were sourced from Richard Paul Evans' novel, *The Last Promise* (Signet, 2003).

Footnote to Chapter 18 Poem
The poem is dedicated to Sandy McIntosh whose book, *Between Earth and Sky* (Marsh Hawk Press, 2002), inspired the reference to "between earth and sky" in the 12th couplet.

Footnote to Chapter 20 Poem
The first line's quote is from "Poem Not Written in Catalan" by Eric Gamalinda.

Footnote Poems in Chapter 29, 42, 52, 53, 56, 69 and 83
These poems are dedicated to Filipino artist Santiago "Santi" Bose.

Footnote to Chapter 37 Poem
This poem was written after the inspiration of Sarah Gambito's poem and Edward del Rosario's painting, both entitled "Matadora."

Footnote to Chapter 39 Poem
The quote in first and second couplets is from NYC rapper Jean Grae's cd, *Attack of the Attacking Things*.

Footnote to Chapter 43 Poem
The reference to "Silliman" relates to a poetry reading by Ron Silliman in 2003 at 21 Grand, Oakland, CA.

GRAVAMEN
"B.G." and her quote refers to Barbara Guest's June 1986 speech at St. Marks Poetry Project entitled " Mysteriously Defining The Mysterious Byzantine Proposals of Poetry."

HYPERTEXT, *DAW*
In the title, "daw" is a Tagalog word used as emphasis; the emphasis can be made in a tongue-in-cheek, joking, or ironic manner. In stanzas 1-5, the first lines of Filipino words are followed by their English translations; in the last stanza English precedes the non-English phrases. The Filipino dialects used are: Cebuano in Stanzas 1 and 2; Kinaray-a in Stanzas 3 and 6; Ilocano in Stanzas 4 and 5. "Hypertext" refers to a database format in which information related to that on a display can be accessed directly from the display." The poem is written as "hypertext" in having a stanza's first line be the "display" and following lines be its data.

KIBITZER
The second line is from "Seen From Above" by Wislawa Szymborska (trans. from the Polish by Magnus J. Krynski and Robert A. Maguire).

O 'Eerily Quiet Drive' Towards Baghdad
Inspiration was provided by the poets in *Poems of Arab and Andalusia*, trans. by Cola Franzen from the Spanish versions of Emilio Garcia Gomez (City Light Books, 1989)

Season of Durian
Comprehensive notes to this poem are available in *Pinoy Poetics* (Ed. Nick Carbo, Meritage Press, 2004).

POEMS FROM SIX DIRECTIONS
At Bryant Park: Perfect Form
The poem began initially through a response to the early sections of the article "Shiny Happy People: Art and Special Effects" by Jennifer Cooper in *New Art Examiner*, July/August 2001. The article discusses the influence of Hollywood's special-effects industry on the contemporary sculpture created in urban Southern California; it begins with the line, "This is a story about perfect forms." Featured with the article is a tiny illustration, a reproduction of John McCracken's sculpture "Live It Up in Lilac (1967)." Made from Polyester resin, fiberglass, plywood, the sculpture is a rectangular white board standing up against a wall. I thought the image to be perfect for my sculpting a poem because the white surface of the rectangle evokes a page. Despite its scale of 104" x 18" x 3", the reproduction is tiny and so I thought to create a poem by envisioning either one or two words that would be lettered at the bottom of the image.

Some of the poem's words respond deliberately to some of the text in the article, e.g. Section (ii) stems from the statement, "…the tropes and syntax of the movie and entertainment business have become inseparable from those of certain West Coast art practices. For example, the miniaturized environments created for and ultimately destroyed within action movies find a mirror in Chris Burden's large-scale dioramas." And Section (vi) stems from the statement, "The objects that comprise Jennifer Pastor's 'Four Seasons' from 1997 are hyper-realistic but symbolic representations of the different times of the year. Rendered in plastic and other artificial materials, they look like fantasy objets for a movie set as they disrupt the viewer's cognizance of both scale and authenticity….<u>The flawless level of Pastor's technical execution is decisive. Her work looks like a good fake.</u>" [Underlines are the author's]

However, the poem also became a fictionalized narrative about something that could have occurred in Bryant Park Hotel where I stayed during a July 8-15, 2001 visit in New York City. I thought of Bryant Park because I still had my hotel room key, whose 2 ¾" x 8 ½" scale made me think that it could be the perfect book cover to this poem written on the 2" x 5 ½" reproductions of McCracken's sculpture.

<u>Dear Daddy</u>
The poem was written from a fictional letter "to Mr. Smithson" that is part of the poem-sculpture, "The World Is Yours."

> July 20, 2001
>
> Dear Mr. Smithson (chuckle):
>
> Daddy — I'm so happy to be your summer intern. I think I make a great executive assistant! How many would retype your phone messages instead of just giving you those tiny slips that could easily get lost? How many would type it on fun stationery? Aren't the grapes pretty? Here are this morning's messages:
>
> <u>From Jean-Marie at Christie's International:</u>
> "Bad news. The European Union just ordered auctioneers to pay royalties to artists on resold sculptures and paintings, starting in 2006. That may affect the net proceeds of your painting."
>
> *(This is me — which painting are you thinking of selling, Daddy? Art should be loved, not traded! P.S. Is business not doing well?)*
>
> <u>From some guy whose name I can't spell but begins with an "F":</u>
> He said he thinks Nokia is still a SELL.
>
> *(I didn't think it mattered that I didn't get his name; he's only a stockbroker.)*
>
> <u>From Tom in Finance:</u>
> He sez — actually, he stated quite ponderously — "Why should we buy derivatives manufactured by American Express if they themselves have announced they'll no longer take the risks of such products?"
>
> *(Makes sense to me, I ponderously add my 2 cents)*
>
> <u>From Jerry, our buddy:</u>
> He wanted to leave this message: "Are you in need of cold, unloving rubber-insulated sex in a seedy hotel?" When I told him it's me, he nearly choked on his burger (he shouldn't eat while talking anyway) and said, "Don't mind me — I just wanted to tell your father about the hilarious article on Jeffrey Archer in today's paper." Apparently, some judge made the same statement about the roguish Lord and author who just got jailed for perjury.
>
> *(Well, he just got handed a writers' residency! What a boor.)*
>
> <u>From Chris, the Chelsea dealer:</u>
> "Jasper Johns just sold 'Catenary (I Call to the Grave), 1998' to the Philadelphia Museum of Art. They were hoping to get it for you but Johns has special ties to the museum which had organized in 1969 his first exhibition and catalog of his prints. Chris sez, "Oh well. We'll keep trying. There's a long list of collectors waiting for Jasper Johns' work but you're first on our list."

(That…and a subway token…)

From Carl:
He sez, he's only a lawyer but you should have taken what he called his "aesthetic advice" on George Ohr. Apparently, his pots go up for as much as a hundred grand nowadays.

(Boor)

From George Flint
He sez, "You're in NY right? Do you know anyone at The Times? I want to write a Letter to the Editor protesting that Kakutani review of Alexa's book on Mustang Ranch."

(Another boor. I read the review – the author wrote a paean to the brothel business even though she was interviewing women who explicitly said how they were abused and degraded.)
***

So those are your boring and primarily boor-ing phone messages, which I decided to liven up by making it fodder for a new prose poem.

Your loving daughter,

In turn, each of the above seven phone messages in the *Fictional Letter from Robert Smithson's Daughter* were inspired by the following articles in the July 20, 2001 *New York Times*, as follows:

1) From Bloomberg News, a briefing that European Union governments have agreed to require auctioneers like Sotheby's Holdings Inc. and Christie's International to pay royalties to artists on resold sculptures and paintings, starting in 2006

2) "Nokia Reports 16% Decline in Earnings—First Drop in 5 Years for Phone Maker" by Suzanne Kapner

3) Floyd Norris' column "They Sold The Derivative, but They Didn't Understand It" on American Express' deciding to forego – while still selling – collateralized debt obligations. Mr. Norris says in a parenthesis: "Would you patronize a chef who won't eat his own cooking?"

4) "Jeffrey Archer, Guilty of Perjury, Is Jailed for Four Years" by Warren Hoge. Article includes quoting the judge Sir Bernard Caulfield's jury instruction: "Is he in need of cold, unloving, rubber-insulated sex in a seedy hotel?"

5) "A Jasper Johns for Philadelphia" by Carol Vogel about the Philadelphia Museum of Art acquiring Jasper Johns' painting "Catenary (I Call to the Grave), 1998" and how there's a long list of collectors for his works.*

6) "Recognition for Biloxi's Mad Potter" by Wendy Moonan on George Ohr pots going up in value*

7) "Brothel as Happy Home? It Still Sounds Very Grim" by Michiko Kakutani as she reviewed *BROTHEL: Mustang Ranch and Its Women* by Alexa Albert. "George Flint" is the executive director of the Nevada Brothel Association.

Dear One
Each stanza in the poem was inspired by an image and/or text in the April 2000 *TOWN & COUNTRY* magazine, as featured here in the same order as the stanzas:

1) Baccarat ad with the statement: "Beauty has its reasons."
2) Fireman's Fund ad entitled "Fear of Losing"
3) Alitalia ad with the phrase "Let's make a wish"
4) Phillips International Auctioneers & Valuers ad
5) "Why I Fish," an article by David Halberstam
6) MacKenzie-Childs, Ltd. ad with the word "VIVID"
7) As one of the illustrations for "Sail Away" by Anthony Barzilay Freund, an article covering the Louis Vuitton Cup Challenge in New Zealand, a photo taken by Luca Trovato with the caption: "The New York Yacht Club's Team Young America, barely recovered from their boat's splitting in half during the second round of racing, subsequently suffered a series of small tactical errors that added up to their early departure from Auckland."

8) Las Campanas Santa Fe ad with the phrase "What's keeping you from owning a home with a world-class equestrian center in your backyard?"

9) Doris Leslie Blau Ltd. Ad featuring a carpet with the caption: "A late 19th century Persian Sultanabad carpet measuring 15'3" x 11'8" with a pale rust ground on which large floral devices are asymmetrically placed giving a strong feeling of the Arts and Crafts influence. Teal blue, pale yellow, apricot olive green and an abundant amount of banana adds to the vitality and warmth of the piece. The ground of the major border is a beautifully abrashed aubergine on which large scale devices freely flow."

10) BMW ad with the phrase "It's not a feeling you can get every day."

11) The British Virgin Islands ad

12) *Town & Country's* Contributors page, including notes on photographer Luca Trovato who said, "I had never shot from a helicopter before. It offered an amazing view of an extremely graceful dance" as well as deputy editor John Cantrell who said about his trip through India and Nepal that he and nine other animal lovers spent several days searching the lush wilderness before finally catching a single glimpse of the elusive and endangered Bengal tiger.

13) The Ritz-Carlton Kapalua ad that includes the phrase "Aloha is a word famous for its many meanings"

14) Stark Carpet ad that includes the phrase "With every step, the Stark Touch"

15) Loro Piana ad with the phrase "When Luxury is a Necessity"

16) De Beers ad with the slogan "A Diamond Is Forever"

17) Radisson Seven Seas Cruises ad with the proclamation: "And what a show-stopper she'll be, if her lineage is any indication. The first ship ever to offer all ocean-view suites with private balconies, the ultra-spacious Seven Seas Mariner promises to make a name for herself while still an infant."

18) The Carlyle ad with the phrase "A Mobil Five-Star Hotel For Over A Quarter Of A Century"

19) Bergdorf Goodman ad with a photo of Manolo Blahnik shoes

20) Infiniti I30 ad with the phrase "Introducing the all-new Inifiniti I30./ It's not just a new car./ It's all the best thinking."

From The Grey Monster In A Yellow Taxi
I.   **Appropriated Words**

Most of the stanzas reflect the influence of found text within the issue of *Rain Taxi*, Vol. 6, No. 2, Summer 2001. In addition, the phrase "Whose Heart is A Rose Tattoo" was included in the title to reflect the title of John Yau's book entitled "My Heart Is That Eternal Rose Tattoo" (which the author was reading while the poem was being sculpted). From *Rain Taxi*, the poem's references are:

Stanza No.	*Rain Taxi* Found Text
1	Magazine Cover with "Rain Taxi"
2	"Ghost Stories," Alan Gilbert's review of Renee Gladman's *JUICE* that begins "The writing of history's absence is like a ghost story…"
3	Julie Madsen's review of Patricia Wilcox's *SHAPED NOTES* whose first paragraph ends with "…to cause a dissonance that subtly vexes the reader."
5	Alan DeNiro's review of Jonathan Carroll's *THE WOODEN SEA* that ends with the lines, "…but at the same time only begins to hint at the deep emotional poignancies that are drawn out through Carroll's use of the fantastic."
6	Brian Evenson's review of Patrick Ehlen's *FRANTZ FANON* that includes the phrase, "There are moments in Frantz Fanon which leave one wanting more though this says as much about the limitations (and perhaps strengths) of the short biography…"
7	Peter Ritter's review of John Long's *MOUNTAINS OF MADNESS*, about the exploration of Antarctica.
8	"Language As Felt," Eric Lorberer's interview with Alice Fulton who, at one point, says, "Science appeals to me because it offers truly fresh metaphors, and it encourages foundational questioning."
9	A Carnegie Mellon advertisement that mentions Garrett Hongo's book *THE RIVER OF HEAVEN* (which presents a significantly different approach to poetry than Alice Fulton's – a juxtaposition that made me

consider the way the personal still underpins a language-based
approach to poetry

10   John Olson's review of Christopher Reiner's *PAIN* that ends with the
       statement, "Our real pain is our very lack of pain."
12   Mary Sarko's review of Ricardo Piglia's *THE ABSENT CITY* that begins,
       "During Argentina's Dirty War (1976-1983), many writers on the political
       left chose to leave the country."
14   Mention of the Russian author Ludmila Ulitskaya's book entitled *THE
       FUNERAL PARTY*
15   Rebecca Weaver's review of Anne Waldman's audio, *ALCHEMICAL
       ELEGY* which quotes from one of Waldman's poems: "May you be
       inside each other / traveling through each others bodies / like fire…this
       is not destruction."
16   In Chris Fischbach's review of Diane di Prima's *RECOLLECTIONS OF
       MY LIFE AS A WOMAN*, the reviewed book is excerpted to depict di
       Prima's recollection: "Since Roi didn't want the child, I felt that if I loved
       him, it was incumbent on me to have an abortion no matter what I was
       feeling. To show the extent of my love by doing what I felt in fact was
       wrong. To commit what for me was tantamount to a crime, simply
       because the man I loved willed it so. And I would take the blame, the
       consequences, the blood on my hands. And not say anything about it."
18   Mention of Eliot Weinberger's book entitled *KARMIC TRACES*
19   Mention of Mark Ford's book entitled *RAYMOND ROUSSEL AND THE
       REPUBLIC OF DREAMS*
23   Mention of Nin Andrews' book entitled *THE BOOK OF ORGASMS*
28   Eric Lorberer's review of Clayton Ashleman's *ERRATICS* which
       describes how "Eshleman typed 'the lines I wanted to do something with'
       on separate slips of paper and spun them in a lettuce dryer'."
29   Jason Picone's article, "Practicing Catastrophe in the work of Nicholas
       Mosley"

In addition, stanza 13 reflects the image of David Klamen's "Untitled (2000)," a series of rectangular water-colors on paper. The first draft was written on the margins of a reproduction of Klamen's work.

II.   Poem

I don't write poems to say something. I write poems to see/hear what it is the poems want to say. At the beginning of creating this work, I had been mulling over the image of a series of white-gray rectangular watercolors "Untitled (2000)" by David Klamen. There are 90 watercolors that together create a hanging installation; as I looked at the rectangles and squares, they seemed to me to denote emptiness—they were like pages all awaiting (my) inscription. I began writing the poem by leafing through an issue of *Rain Taxi* for text that I could use to fill in the squares. I didn't, however, wish to relate a stanza/line/word to each individual square as I felt I already had done this approach in a prior poem-sculpture ("At Bryant Park: Perfect Form"). So I just continued writing the poem wherever *Rain Taxi's* words took me.

After writing the poem, I added the subtitle "a.k.a. "*Rain Taxi*, Vol. 6, No. 2, Summer 2001 In the Voice of Lot's Wife" because I recalled the fate of Lot's wife from the phrases "Look back" as well as "The Bible is only a book." While I didn't realize it during the actual writing process, Lot's wife was speaking between the lines of – as well as through the words in – *Rain Taxi*." I thought the presence of her voice to be logical given how she appropriated the writers as well as reviewed authors within the magazine which specializes in book reviews and author interviews. When, in the Biblical story, she was frozen, she was also silenced. I also didn't wish to join the conspiracy to look at Lot's wife with disdain because *SHE WANTED TO SEE*.

Inexplicably, I then decided to do a Yahoo search on "Lot's Wife." I say "inexplicably" as I didn't know what caused me to look for Lot's Wife in the internet—perhaps for her actual name besides the tag "Lot's wife"? There was only one site found for "Lot's Wife." It was a poem written by Anna Akhmatova. How marvelously synchronistic! For the poem incorporates the lines: "This does not signify/ a painting is a blank canvas// Ask any Russian/ at a funeral party". On the site featuring Anna's face that I now ascribe to bearing the features of Lot's Wife, there also was reference to another site under the heading ""To Go Its Way In Tears: Poems of Grief." Grief certainly seemed to be relevant, and I went to that site. And at that site, Anna is featured again with a poem she had written—*during a funeral party!* From her poem "In Memory of M.B." are these lines:

Here is my gift, not roses on your grave,
not sticks of burning incense....//

Now you're gone, and nobody says a word
about your troubled and exalted life.
Only my voice, like a flute, will mourn
at your dumb funeral feast.

Thus, Anna seemed to want me to write a poem as a "gift" for Lot's Wife to prevent silence about her "troubled and exalted life."

Following these revelations from the Internet, I was moved—it was as if someone took my hand to guide me —to go to the kitchen. There, in one of the cupboards, I found the salt container. I took off the label from the salt container as I felt that it should be incorporated in the poem-sculpture. At the time, I kept hearing a phrase run through my mind like an unwounding tape: "salt unbound, salt unbound, salt unbound..." As in: desalinize Lot's frozen statue and make her live again. The salt label became the "book cover." I believe that the notion I sensed of an unwounding tape also facilitated my next idea to create a box of pages "covered" by the salt-related cover and bound with a ribbon once used for a corporate gift by Paul Hastings. Paul Hastings is an appropriate moniker as they are a law firm and, in this day and age, lawyers are used for "due diligence" research, for recovery purposes, for regress. Later, as I first bound the scroll with the Paul Hastings "found" ribbon, I would realize its aptness: because of its length, it takes time to unwind—unbound—the scroll, fitting the "salt, unbound" concept of the cover.

I would place the scroll in an ornate box that, in my mind, embodies Pandora's box. But the box also would include a blue-and-white figurine of a lady from Russia as well as a statue of Kwan-yin—respectively, Anna and the Goddess of Mercy. I initially envisioned the inclusion of colorful ribbons to symbolize the pleasure of a woman no longer silenced and now with a name: "Anna." Later, I would replace the ribbons with "green grass" confetti as I thought the greenery symbolized the fertility of mind, including the imagination of the Poem that would bring Lot's wife back to life.

The World Is Yours
Each stanza in the poem was inspired by text from each page of the C Section of the July 18, 2001 *New York Times* (which encompassed business and sports news), as featured here in the same order as the stanzas:

1) the headline "A Bet on Bulgaria Pays Dividends"
2) the sentence "Still, as Eastern Europe restores housing neglected by decades of Communism and builds new homes for its expanding middle class, the potential is huge" (from "A Bet on Bulgaria Pays Dividends" by John Tagliabue
3) New Wachovia ad with the phrase "SunTrust is Rooted in the Past"
4) the section COMPANY NEWS, a First Union ad with the call for shareholders "to vote for the Wachovia/ First Union merger by returning the white proxy card," and the headline "Coke Bottler To Eliminate 2,000 Jobs"
5) a CRM ad highlighting the advantages of the Web and the phrase "The Next Generation of CRM" and the headline "U.S. Arrests Russian Cryptographer as Copyright Violator"
6) a SAP ad with the phrase "beats sitting through employee orientation" and a Columbia Executive Management Program ad with the phrase "the new New Economy has changed the role of technology in the business world"
7) Computer Associates ad with the phrase "Soon, we will be writing to formally ask for your support at this year's annual meeting on August 29"
8) ad for USE THE NEWS by Maria Bartiromo with the claim "Shows You How To Turn Information Into Cash" and The New York Times ad with the phrase "Empowered: Smart Energy Management"
9) section MUTUAL FUNDS
10) in the section MUTUAL FUNDS, Merrill Lynch's "Growth m" fund posts a -18.4% return, YTD
11) in the section CASH PRICES, the Tuesday rice for "pork bellies 12-14 lb. Midwest av. cwt" is 98, versus 101 the prior day
12) the continuation headline "Target Will Sell Tupperware"
13) the article and headline "Katherine Graham, Publisher Who Transformed Washington Post, is Dead at 84"

14) the obituary titled "Mike Saltzstein, 60, Coney Island's Carousel Man, Dies

15) first paragraph of the Saltzstein obituary reads "Mike Saltzstein, who for more than a quarter-century kept Coney Island's last historic carousel spinning thorugh sunlit summers, ice-old winters and lurching changes in the famed amusement area, died on July 4 in his Brooklyn apartment. He was 60."

16) The weather map shows 100+ temperatures in the San Antonio and Fresno areas

17) Dave Anderson's column entitled "The Poison Threatening The Umpires" includes the fifth paragraph that begins with "In order to diminish the overall number of pitches and thereby shorten the sometimes dreary length of a game, umpires were recently instructed by baseball officials to broaden their interpretation of the strike zone."

18) From "In-Season Additions Fail to Add A Spark" by Buster Olney, the sentences: "Mark Wohlers, the veteran right-hander acquired in a deal with the Cincinnati Reds, has allowed nine hits and four walks in four and on-third innings, compiling a 12.46 earned run average."

19) a headline "Encores Aren't Easy at the British Open"

20) in the Baseball ROUNDUP section, the report that "Joe Mauer, the top pick in June's amateur draft, agreed yesterday on most points of a contract with the Minnesota Twins that calls for a signing bonus of just over $5 million."

21) a MARATHON report that "Christine Clark, the only American woman to compete in the marathon in the 2000 Olympics, will run in the New York City Marathon on Nov. 4.// Clark, a 37-year-old pathologist from Anchorage, joins an elite field…"

22) a Microsoft ad proclaiming "This computer is traveling to Dubai. Unlike its owner, the computer will never be homesick."

Wine Tasting Notes
The poem was written while skimming through the catalogue for David Klamen's 2000 solo exhibition at Haines Gallery, San Francisco. Referenced text or text that offered inspiration were written by David Klamen, Kathryn Hixson, David Breskin, and Hans-George Gadamer. The illustrations are taken from the reproductions of David Klamen's works, in the order they appear in the catalogue. The poem was titled "Wine Tasting Notes" after its text seemed to "fit" with the glorious experience of tasting fine wines, including several such affairs at Richie and Cheryl Metrick's home in Lloyd Neck, New York—as illustrated by the featured menu that is part of the poem-sculpture. The poem is written against the white spaces within the illustration for Jeffrey E. Garten's article "Free Trade Has to Become Managed" in the July 18, 2001 *New York Times*. Initially, I thought the words to fit the poem due to the notion of an "expanding idea" (the poem's first line). Then I came to realize, too, that the Rohrschach-like shapes evoke wine spills.

The sculpture came to include the *New York Times* article, "Live by the Pen, Die by the Sword," by John Noble Wilford on July 17, 2001. The article describes how, during the Maya civilization, scribes played a central role in magnifying their king's reputation—thought it apt as the notion of making "wine tasting notes" can magnify (both negatively and positively) the experience of wine tasting beyond the actual event. And because "fine wines" are a rarefied hobby. In any event, reading the entirety of the article against both poem and the experience of wine-tasting seemed to relate—an "integral" experience. Moreover, the orange-red cast of the illustration fits my memory of various wine-related experiences, e.g. the sunset over wine country(ies) or the faded red labels against old bottles or some shades of very old wine. After I utilized a cardboard box as the sculpture's "sleeve" I came to add the rattan pineapple coasters as their color and texture worked well against the cardboard and the newspaper illustration. Later, I thought to include various wine-related ephemera (a Bordeaux postcard from Rena Rosenwasser, an Ehlers Grove Winery, CA postcard, and a placement card from one of the Metricks' wine-imbibing dinners), partly to enliven the texture, references and colors.

"SOMETIMES THE SKY AND SEA MUST WAIT"
Written after the Yoko Ono exhibition at SFMOMA and *MA LANGUE EST POETIQUE – SELECTED WORK* by Christophe Tarkos (Roof Books, 2000).

THE EMPEROR'S NEW CLOTHES (PART II)
The poem is written after Jose Garcia Villa's "The Emperor's New Sonnet," featured in his poetry collection *Volume II* (New Directions, 1949).

THERE, WHERE THE PAGES WOULD END
The following is the original "Preface" to this series when an earlier version was first published as an e-chapbook by xPress(ed), Finland:

<u>Seducing The Voyeur In You</u>
I'm sure I'm not the only poet who's annotated text for making new poems. That process, for me, also facilitated close reading. More recently, to further facilitate close reading while also attempting a new way to generate poems, I began creating fictional footnotes. The process, therefore, is also a form of Love….and mating. A mating with the text, and through the text, with you, Dear Reader.

May being a reader-voyeur to these poems give you enough pleasure to make you participate as well in the experience offered by what I call "Footnote Poems." Which is to say, the stories footnoted are intended to be your tales, not mine or the referenced texts. *Shall we fall in love?*

TINCTURE
Written after Adrienne Sharp's *The Brahmins.*

UNTOWARD
Quote is from *My Russian* by Deirdre McNamara (Ballantine, 1999).

Vulcan's Aftermath
The poet who whispered, "flowers need never be ferocious," paraphrases Andrew Joron.

White, Throbbing
The Rilke quote is from Rilke's Third Sonnet.

500

ACKNOWLEDGEMENTS

Some poems previously appeared in the following publications: *Ambit; Asian Pacific American Journal; Aught; A Very Small Tiger; BigCityLit; Boog City; Blue Fifth Review; Canwehaveourballback; Creative Insight: Fine Arts and Poetry; Confrontation; Conundrum; Fiera Lingue's Poets' Corner; Garboyle; Harpur's Palate; Ionic Voices; KultureFlash; Kwikstep; Maganda; MELUS; MIRAGE #4: PERIOD(ICAL); Moria: A Poetry Journal; Muse Apprentice Guild; Mystic Prophet; North American Review; Nth Position; OurOwnVoice; Orphic Lute; Pettycoat Relaxer; Poetica Nova; Philippine Inquirer Sunday Magazine; Poethia; Poetic Justice; Ravens Three; Rebel Edit; Rife; Score; ShampooPoetry; Sands & Coral* (Siliman University, Philippines); *Sidereality; Sunday Inquirer Magazine; Suspect Thoughts; Scythian; Tinfish; Tin Lustre Mobile; Tomas* (University of Santo Tomas); *Tamafhyr Mountain Poetry; UR-VOX; Van Gogh's Ear;* and *xStream;* as well as the author's art essay and poetry collection *MY ROMANCE* (Giraffe Books, 2002).

"Epilogue Poem (#18): (Heliotrope)" was translated into Japanese by Toshio Yamakoshi for publication as "Epirogu 18" in *The Shijin-Kaigi (Poets' Congress)* Magazine (Japan).

"Mudra" was written for "Clit Chat," a Bastos, Inc. Production presented at Bindlestiff Studios, San Francisco, February 14-16, 2002. "Mudra" was also part of a "Poetry Mobile Project" coordinated by *OurOwnVoice* (OOV) and OOV Director Reme Grefalda for exhibit at a Book Fair at George Washington University (GWU). The GWU Fair was part of the "October Heritage Series 2004 Salute to Filipino Authors" sponsored by the Cultural Affairs Division of the Philippine Embassy, with assistance from OOV, held October 15-17, 2004 in Washington D.C.

The following series were first published as poetry e-chapbooks: *xPress(ed):* "There, Where The Pages Would End." *Tamafhyr Mountain Poetry:* "Crucial Bliss" and "Epilogue Poems" as "Crucial Bliss Epilogues"

Some poems were published or accepted for publication in anthologies: *100 Love Poems: Philippine Love Poetry Since 1905* (Eds. Gémino H. Abad & Alfred A. Yuson, 2004, University of the Philippines Press)*; Confluence: A Women's Global Anthology on the Politics of Water* (Eds. Paola Corso & Nandita Gosh); *EROS PINOY: An Anthology of Contemporary Erotica in Philippine Art and Poetry* (Eds. Virgilio Aviado, Ben Cabrera & Alfred A. Yuson, Anvil Publishing, Inc. 2001); *ESPIRITU SANTI* (Ed. Alfred A. Yuson, Water Dragon, Inc, 2004); *LOVE GATHERS ALL: The Philippines-Singapore Anthology of Love Poetry* (Eds. Ramon C. Sunico & Alfred A. Yuson (Philippines) and Aaron Lee & Alvin Pang (Singapore), Anvil Publishing and Ethos Books, 2002); *PinoyPoetics* (Ed. Nick Carbo, Meritage Press, 2004); and *Towards A Cultural Community: Identity, Education and Stewardship in Filipino American Performing Arts* (Eds. Reme Grefalda & Anna Alves, National Federation of Filipino American Associations, 2004).

"Poems Form/From The Six Directions" was exhibited at the Sonoma Student Union Gallery (March 2002) and Pusod Center Gallery, Berkeley CA (August-September, 2002). The "Poem Tree" Wedding Performance Happenings occurred during opening festivities at these galleries, as well as on August 23, 2002 at Locus Arts Events Performance Space (San Francisco) sponsored by the Alliance of Emerging Creative Artists, Locus and *Interlope*. Some Six Directions elements were exhibited in "What's in a Book? A Look at the Book Arts Scene," New Langton Arts, San Francisco (June 29, 2004) and "Poetry and its Arts: Bay Area Interactions 1954-2004," California Historical Society 2004-2005. Thanks to the artists and cultural activists who enabled these festivities, including: Jose "Joey" Ayala, Michelle Bautista, Barbara Jane Reyes, Leny M. Strobel, Dori Caminong, Malou Babilonia, Cal Strobel, Darius Spearman, Summi Kaipa, Steve Dickison, Leon Chang, Amar Ravva, Annabelle Udo and Natalie Concepcion. Photographs were taken by Cal Strobel, Michelle Bautista, Thomas Pollock and Mike Price. Thanks as well to the Potrero Nuevo Fund for a 2002 Grant. Articles about the "Six Directions" project were published in *Creative Insight: Fine Arts and Poetry, Factorial, Interlope* and the *San Francisco Bay Guardian*. The Six Directions poem, "The Erotic Angel," was published in Paolo Javier's poetry book, *The Time At The End of This Writing* (Ahadada Books, Toronto and Tokyo, 2004).

Certain poems from the "Footnotes to The History of Fallen Angels: An Autobiography" were exhibited at an exhibit for *Filipino Fine Arts* at Stanford University (April 16-June 15, 2005). Curator: Marilyn Grossman; Facilitator: Carmen Milaflor. Certain poems also generated "Poem-Scarves" by Sandra Hansen.

Chapter 100 in "Footnotes to The History of Fallen Angels: An Autobiography" was previously published as a short story entitled "The Other" in *The Literary Review* and subsequently in the author's short story collection, *Behind The Blue Canvas* (Giraffe Books, 2004).

The play "When I Was Jasper Johns' Filipino Lover…." was published in *Zyzzyva* and also presented (under the guidance of director Michelle Bautista) during Small Press Traffic's Poet's Theater (San Francisco).

ABOUT THE AUTHOR

EILEEN R. TABIOS majored in political science at Barnard College and received an M.B.A. in economics and international business from New York University's Graduate School of Business. In 1996, she traded her finance career for poetry. Her awards include the Philippines' Manila Critics Circle National Book Award for Poetry, the Potrero Nuevo Fund Prize, the PEN/Oakland Josephine Miles National Literary Award, a Witter Bynner Poetry Grant, a PEN Open Book Award, *POET Magazine's* Iva Mary Williams Award, and the 2003 Judds Hill Winery Annual Poetry Prize. Her poems have been interpreted into other media by other artists including dancer-choreographers Pearl Ubungen and Johanna Almiron, quiltmaker Alice Brody, kali martial arts practitioner Gura Michelle Bautista, painters Max Gimblett, Patricia Wood, Mareafatima Urbi and Thomas Fink, kulintang-artist Mary Talusan, poet-jazz lyricist Cristina Querrer, jazz composer and pianist Don Profitt, yarn artist Sandra Hansen, and poet-composer Jukka-Pekka Kervinen. She also has seen her plays produced in San Francisco at Bindlestiff Studios and Small Press Traffic. As a conceptual artist, she invented the "Hay(na)ku" poetic form as well as formulated the "Poems Form/From The Six Directions" project which has been exhibited in various locations throughout the Bay Area, CA. She is the author of the infamous poetics blog, "The Chatelaine's Poetics" at http://chatelaine-poet.blogspot.com. She also founded Meritage Press (http://meritagepress.com), a multidisciplinary literary and arts press based in St. Helena, CA where, as a farmer, she arduously researches the poetry of wine.

She feels it is part of her fate to make books—authored by her and others—partly because, as a two-year-old, she once folded a piece of paper and proclaimed it a "book." According to her mother, she pointed to a green crayola slash on the bottom of the first page and read it as, "The grass is green." She then turned the page to point at a yellow crayola slash at the page's upper left corner and read it as "The sun is out." Then she pointed to a brown crayola slash at the bottom of the third page and read it as, "The sun browned the grass." Her life-long interest in process is integral to her Poetry practice, including her belief that if poems have endings, they occur beyond the page.